HAZARDS AND THE COMMUNICATION OF RISK

Hazards and the Communication of Risk

Edited by
John Handmer

Centre for Resource and Environmental Studies
Australian National University
and
Edmund Penning-Rowsell

Middlesex Polytechnic

Gower Technical

Published by

Gower Technical

Gower Publishing Company Limited,
Gower House, Croft Road, Aldershot,
Hants. GU11 3HR, England

Gower Publishing Company,
Old Post Road, Brookfield, Vermont 05036
USA

British Library Cataloguing in Publication Data
Hazards and the communication of risk
  1. Disasters. Communication
  I. Handmer, John 1950-   II. Penning-Rowsell, Edmund C.
  (Edmund Charles) 1946-
  363.34014

ISBN 0 566 02784 4

Printed in Great Britain by Galliard (Printers) Ltd, Great Yarmouth

Contents

Preface

A widely held view is that our world is becoming a more hazardous place in which to live. Whether this is correct or not, there is certainly a perception that action needs to be taken to reduce at least some kinds of hazard. Thus, the United Nations has designated the 1990s as the International Decade for Natural Disaster Reduction, and some member states have already established national committees to consider how best to proceed with the Decade. At different levels, many governments, commercial and voluntary organisations and members of the public are becoming increasingly concerned about the risks that they face.

One important result is a growing emphasis on communicating information on the risks to those assumed to be bearing them. This process may take a variety of forms from *raising awareness* among the public and officials, *persuading* people to take *action to protect themselves,* to the rather different aim of *persuading people to accept* levels and types of risk that they would rather do without. The bulk of the "risk communication" literature concentrates on the last form. In contrast this volume, and much of our risk related research at the Centre for Resource and Environmental Studies and the Flood Hazard Research Centre, concerns the first two forms: raising awareness and persuading people to take protective action. Special attention is also paid to the question of the evaluation of such risk communication activities.

This volume is the result of a small international workshop held at the Flood Hazard Research Centre, Middlesex Polytechnic, London. The workshop took place in October 1987, one week after the "great storm" which did extensive damage to south east England. That storm resulted in the largest ever insurance payout for a single event in Britain, and raised questions about warning procedures. Since then Britain has suffered a range of emergencies, with diverse implications for risk communication.

Many people contributed to the production of this book, and its timely publication at the beginning of the United Nations International Decade. Sonia Royds assisted with the transcription of workshop presentations. Michele Smith and Jan Cuadra, at the Flood Hazard Research Centre, and Wendy Chan at the Centre for Resources and Environmental Studies handled the wordprocessing. The diagrams were expertly drawn by Steve Chilton and his colleagues at Middlesex Polytechnic, and by Kevin Cowan at the Australian National University. The index was prepared painstakingly by Margaret Penning-Rowsell. Sue Armstrong, Ruth Birgin and Dingle Smith undertook the proof reading.

To these individuals, the authors whose work appears in the volume and many others at both Middlesex Polytechnic and the Australian National University we express our gratitude. However, the responsibility for any errors and omissions remains with us.

We hope that the volume will both inform people about the research that we are doing and form a significant contribution to the field of risk communication.

Edmund C. Penning-Rowsell
Flood Hazard Research Centre
Middlesex Polytechnic
London

John W. Handmer
Centre for Resource Environmental
Studies
Australian National
University, Canberra

List of Contributors

John ADAMS
Department of Geography
University College
London

F. Yasemin AYSAN
Department of Architecture
Oxford Polytechnic
Oxford

Jennifer BROWN
Department of Psychology
University of Surrey
Guildford

Lynne FILDERMAN
Hazard Education Consultant
Washington D.C.

John GARDINER
Rivers Division
Thames Water

Colin GREEN
Flood Hazard Research Centre
Middlesex Polytechnic
Enfield

Eve GRUNTFEST
Department of Geography
University of Colorado
Colorado Springs

John HANDMER
Centre for Resource and Environmental Studies
Australian National University
Canberra

David MARKS
School of Psychology
Middlesex Polytechnic

Jeremy NEAL
Flood Hazard Research Centre
Middlesex Polytechnic

Tim O'RIORDAN
University of East Anglia
Norwich

Dennis PARKER
Flood Hazard Research Centre
Middlesex Polytechnic

Philip PATTERSON
Communication and Fine Arts
Oklahoma Christian College
Oklahoma City

Edmund PENNING-ROWSELL
Flood Hazard Research Centre
Middlesex Polytechnic

Thomas SAARINEN
Department of Geography
University of Arizona
Tucson

Joseph SCANLON
Emergency Communications Research Unit
Carleton University
Ottawa

Roger TYRRELL
AIDS Unit
Department of Health and Social Security
London

Lee WILKINS
School of Journalism and Mass Communication
University of Colorado
Boulder

Colin WILSON
Australian Counter Disaster College
Mt Macedon
Victoria

Peter WINCHESTER
Disaster Management Unit
Oxford Polytechnic
and
Flood Hazard Research Centre
Middlesex Polytechnic

SECTION I
INTRODUCTION

1 The Changing Context of Risk Communication

Edmund Penning-Rowsell and John Handmer

Introduction: risks and obligations

Risks and hazards arise inevitably from human interaction with our natural and social environments and from our technology. These risks occur whether that technology is a stone axe or nuclear power. Such interactions and technology generally bring us benefits or opportunities, but also costs. In many instances, perhaps the vast majority, the potential damage from these risks is unrecognised or is considered "acceptable". Identifying new risks, deciding what is acceptable and minimising the impact of "unacceptable" risks, requires the communication of risk information between those responsible for risk management, the risk bearers and the wider community.

This volume considers the communication of many different types of risk, from the natural hazards of floods, tornadoes, earthquakes, landslips, cyclones, and volcanic eruptions, through to the technological and "lifestyle" risks from smoking, road traffic accidents, chemical spills, and nuclear power. AIDS and HIV infection are also considered. However, we are fundamentally concerned not with these risks per se, but with the processes and difficulties inherent in communicating information on these risks - which have very different characteristics - to those who may be at risk and other relevant groups.

Our focus reflects a belief that obligations exist for individuals, organisations and society as a whole to communicate the available information on the risks that people face. In a practical sense individuals and policy makers need this information in order to evaluate the risks faced, and to decide what action is necessary. Communities, with a longer time horizon, need to educate their populations about the hazards that they may face both now and at sometime in the future.

Governments also have both moral and statutory obligations to communicate information on risks to their populations and electorates. Democratic decision making requires an educated public, and information and decisions on risk-related issues require that the public is well informed. If people are to understand their government's policies and procedures - including those required during emergencies - they need information and education. Freedom of information legislation, and "open government", require that governments and their agencies communicate the risks on which they have information to those who might suffer the consequences. Of course, this is a two-way process: the risk bearers and other relevant groups should be influencing government policy and administrative practice.

Legal and moral or ethical obligations, as well as international policies and directives, require that risks should be communicated by a wide range of public and private agencies so that the public, whoever they may be, is informed and ready to respond should it be necessary. Professional codes of conduct may require disclosure of all information about events and phenomena that might harm individuals or identifiable groups. International trends are towards the opening up of all information sources to members of the public so that they are in a position to make informed decisions on the acceptability of risks and on management alternatives. Current radical improvements in communication technologies could greatly assist this process provided people see the information as having value.

However, these obligations bring immense conceptual and operational problems concerning the very definition of risk, the technology for risk communication and its vulnerability to failure, and the changing societal context of hazards, risks, response, and communication itself. This chapter outlines these facets of risk communication and response, to provide a context for the contributions that follow.

Risk communication and technological and social change

There are several trends which are now creating more opportunities - and need - to help the processes of risk communication and discussion between all interested parties. The trends include: the growth of the information society; a greater reliance on centralised infrastructure and modern technology and information systems; and an increasing concern for health and safety. These trends provide clues on how to design and implement hazard information programmes.

New information technologies are creating a revolutionary expansion of avenues for receiving and sending all types of information. Each brings with it new possibilities for risk communication, as well as a set of new problems. Tailoring information to fill identified information needs is part of this movement. For example, in the United States there is now a commercially successful 24-hour cable television station, "The Weather Channel". The channel provides continuous weather-related news reports, including short and long-term national, regional and local forecasts and warnings. In a recent experiment during the peak of the hurricane season, a programme on hurricanes attracted a large number of telephone calls from all over the country. This suggests that people seek hazard information when they feel they need it, and that this information needs to be able to compete with the existing wide range of multi-media entertainment and advertising material.

Hazard education can use the same techniques and principles underlying the information society: tailoring information to meet specific individual, community and organisational needs in ways that can compete for our attention with the mass of other information we receive.

We have an increasing *reliance on centralised infrastructure and modern technology*, covering all aspects of our lives from communications, energy, raw materials, industry, health and transportation to entertainment, sports and weather. We are learning more about the world, but at the same time becoming more dependent on the technology that gives us this knowledge.

Significant problems remain and these new technologies create additional difficulties. For example, new technologies often create the need for communicating risk information to those who may feel threatened by the location of industrial, waste disposal, energy or research facilities. Simply having more information available is no guarantee that people will receive it, want it, understand it or act on it. As we become more dependent on highly centralised complex infrastructure, so we become more vulnerable should system failure occur (Timmerman 1980). Also we are vulnerable to the loss of the source of natural hazards information due to technological failure, especially in a critical situation. Not only may we lose the source for "reading" the environment, we may not even get critical warnings and information from the media and other technologies upon which we have come to rely. This is not to suggest that modern technology is unreliable. However, technical failures occur, the systems still depend on human operators, and our knowledge of natural forces and of our own technology is far from perfect. Even if our knowledge was perfect and we could eliminate human failure, economics would almost certainly dictate that we could not build systems to be infallible.

The growing concern for health maintenance is part of a more general trend to greater *consumer and occupational health and safety*, illustrated by the widespread growth of health and safety legislation and litigation, the fitness and leisure industry, the expansion of the health food industry, and the rise of alternative medicines. Some aspects of these trends are global, but it is basically a feature of western industrialised nations. While much of the world suffers from food shortages and inadequate diets, our affluence has brought other dietary problems discussed in Eckholm and Record's *The two faces of malnutrition* (1976).

Concern over environmental and societal risk resulted in the establishment of the British Department of the Environment in 1970, the Environment Protection Agency in the USA in 1969, and many similar national and international agencies. Laws designed to prevent continuous degradation of our environment have proliferated. Dealing with toxic and nuclear waste is one of the major dilemmas of the industrialised world. Here, much of the critical question of acceptable levels of risk is an ethical issue concerning future generations.

Problematic definitions

Risk and hazard

Definitions of "risk" generally fall into three groups:

(i)   those concerned solely with the occurrence probability of the damaging event, a statistical concept;
(ii)   those embracing both event probability and the degree and type of damage or potential damage, here risk is seen as the product of event probability and the severity of impact;
(iii)   and those where the emphasis is on the distribution of power within society, and on the distribution of costs and benefits. In other words, who bears and who imposes the risk?

English language dictionaries equate "risk" with "hazard". *The Oxford English Dictionary*, for example, defines "risk" as "Hazard, danger; exposure to mischance or loss ..." However, many writers in the field distinguish between these words. Hohenemser et al (1983) see risks as probabilistic but hazards as more general, as "threats to humans and what they value". Mary Douglas (1985, p27) defines hazard as an "inability to cope". Similarly, Suter et al (1987) emphasise the "impacts" in defining danger, not just its probability. The Royal Society has defined risk as "the probability that a particular adverse event occurs during a stated period of time" and "adverse event" as "an occurrence that produces harm". "Hazard" is seen as a "situation that in particular circumstances could lead to harm" (Royal Society 1983, p22).

There is a professional/lay dimension here. What sort of impacts are considered, and how they are considered, are central to the way most non-specialists think about risk. These groups, which include politicians and other decision-makers, may consider aspects covered by the third definition of risk above, such as the potential for catastrophe, controlability, fairness, and familiarity (Sandman et al 1987). Risk, in this view, is culturally defined; there is no real attempt to separate "facts" from "values", a task that in any case is often seen as inappropriate or impossible (Fischhoff et al 1981, Douglas 1985, Smithson 1989).

In contrast, risk specialists tend to emphasise probabilities and numerical data such as mortality rates or the number of events of similar magnitude. They attempt to treat questions of values and ethics separately, or not at all, leading to inappropriate comparisons of different risks. Often, the function of risk communication will be seen as being to "calm people down", to persuade those bearing the risks that it is not too serious as the likelihood of a damaging event is remote (Covello et al 1988).

Uncertainty, vagueness and ambiguity

Risk is about uncertainty, as well as power. However, there are several types of uncertainty of which probability is only one (Smithson 1989). Yet, apart from those concerned solely with the distribution of power, the majority of definitions of risk use probability as the sole measure of uncertainty. Perhaps this illustrates the bias of most risk specialists, who prefer to deal with numbers - probabilities lend themselves to this readily - as opposed to lay people who usually prefer to express uncertainty in words indicating degrees of ignorance, vagueness, ambiguity, and the problems of conflicting evidence. Risk communications may be *vague*, but they should not be *ambiguous* as they would then convey more than one distinct meaning.

Most people will be familiar with quantitative probabilistic statements in certain limited contexts, such as betting odds. Probability is a statistical concept, a mathematical measure of an event's likelihood based on the ratio of number of times it occurs to the number of trials that take place. It is the measure of likelihood or chance that is most common in risk statements. Probability is the standard measure of risk in many professions, including engineering, and may also be more readily accepted as expert evidence by the courts.

However, quantitative probability concepts are difficult for many people, including some risk specialists, to grasp. One major problem has been the use of misleading terminology. A typical example is provided by the term "the 100 year flood". This is correctly described as the "flood with 1 chance in 100 of being equalled or exceeded *every year*". But there is widespread and incorrect attribution of cyclic behaviour to natural phenomena like flooding, so that one such flood is thought to occur exactly *every 100 years*.

7

Therefore, randomness is an important element of risk probability, although it appears that there may now be no general agreement on what is random (Crutchfield et al 1986). Another problem is that statements concerning occurrence probability make no mention of the seriousness, or distribution, of the impacts.

In the (typical) absence of explicit information on the variance and degree of confidence in the available risk data, numerical probability expressions indicate a precision which is often completely unwarranted given the quality of the data and knowledge of the system being described (Smithson 1989). This is especially the case with infrequent events. Douglas observes (1985, p23):

> That quantified methods of risk assessment are highly manipulated is so well understood that they do not carry the authority and objective weight that their users intend. So OSHA [US Occupational Safety and Health Administration] took a hard and fast line against risk quantification ...

Psychologists and others have long been examining how people express uncertainty, both as a research question and a methodological problem. Smithson (1987, 1989) summarises the work. He points out that uncertainty can be expressed linguistically as vagueness or "fuzzyness", and ambiguity. There is also the problem of conflicting evidence. The concept of "fuzzyness" is by no means limited to the social sciences. Most taxonomies exhibit certain degrees of vagueness; colours provide a good example. Most of this research into linguistic expressions of uncertainty has not been concerned directly with risk management. Nevertheless, it contains some important concepts. The term "acceptable risk" is a political concept. In a technical sense it is extremely vague, yet it is generally far more important in risk management than a numerical determination.

There are profound implications here for risk communication. Different viewpoints clash at the very heart of the subject: in its definition. People will be talking in different languages: the numerate and those preferring linguistic variables; thinking about different types of uncertainty; or emphasising event probability versus those who concentrate on questions of equity and fairness. Opportunities abound for communication error or breakdown. The definition of risk therefore, affects the purpose and the nature of risk communication. Is this communication merely to inform, or is it to persuade people to accept the risk or to take protective action?

Risk communication

Definitions and alternatives

To communicate is to impart information or make known through a one way process, or through a two way process where messages are exchanged. Communication about risk occurs at every level of social interaction from impersonal health messages on cigarette packets through to personal experience with, for example, a hurricane. However, messages or data by themselves may not constitute "information": the target audience may not notice or understand them; or the messages may not inform, they may merely confuse. Even worse, risk communication messages may *encourage* risk taking where this is not intended.

A clear idea of what risk communication is trying to achieve is important, and a prerequisite for assessing performance, but views on this vary greatly. Covello et al (1986, p172) define risk communication as:

> any purposeful exchange of information between interested parties about (a) levels of health or environmental risks, (b) the significance or meaning of health or environmental risks, or (c) decisions, actions, or policies aimed at managing or controlling health or environmental risks.

A goal-oriented approach is preferred by Sandman et al (1987, p94), who suggest that risk communication should persuade people to take action: "To mobilize people" out of their apathy, but not so that there is panic or anger. They also discuss an alternative view, which is that risk communication should provide the relevant information as clearly as possible and measure success by what facts the receivers learn. This approach implies that information can be presented in a value free way.

But many risk communication messages attempt both to convey information and to persuade - the boundary between the two approaches is poorly defined (Tompkins 1987). A rather different approach focuses on the way risk communication affects the distribution of power within the community (Arnstein 1969). This links directly with our third definition of risk.

In this volume our primary emphasis is on two of the three purposes typically served by risk communication. They are: organised programmes designed to raise hazard awareness; and, warnings of an immediate threat which are intended to elicit protective action. The third purpose is to persuade people to accept risk or at least to persuade them that their concerns are exaggerated. This is considered by one contributor who examines a programme designed to reassure people about nuclear energy. Our definition of risk includes the gauging of impacts, and we see risk communication as designed to lead eventually to action, rather than merely to inform. Those responsible for the three types of programmes considered in this volume hope to achieve certain results in terms of appropriate action. Risk information is therefore not value-free, but culturally defined; it occurs within a social and political context. The information is also a tool in the hands of those with power, and can affect political processes and economic outcomes. On the whole our

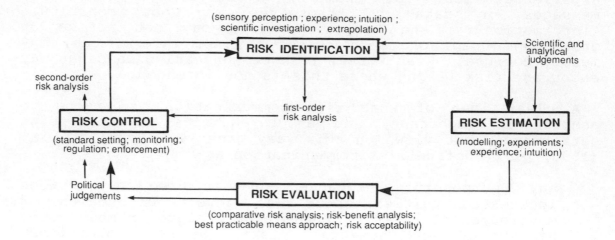

Figure 1.1:   Functions in environmental risk management.
(From O'Riordan 1981).

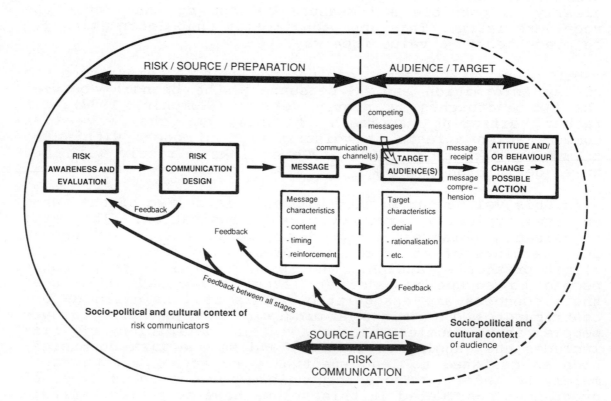

Figure 1.2:   The process of risk communication.

contributors share these views, although there will be differences in interpretation between them, and these differences will have affected both their research and their conclusions.

Conceptualisation

O'Riordan's (1981) simple conceptualisation of risk management (Figure 1.1) involves risk identification, estimation and evaluation. Thereafter comes communication, involving political judgements, as part of risk control or management.

Risk communication is the passing of risk information from those who have that information to those who are presumed to be without it (Figure 1.2). In many cases this involves communicating risk information from an agency, or from government, because government and those agencies tend to have a monopoly of systematic and accurate risk information - and even of unsystematic and inaccurate risk information. Governments and large corporations have a virtual monopoly on technical information because such information is expensive to collect. However, they do not have such a monopoly on the political, ethical and other issues surrounding risk acceptability; and therefore may, and should, seek public opinion to assist with management. The information flow then becomes two-way.

As with O'Riordan's analysis of risk management, risk communication cannot start without risk *awareness* and *evaluation*: only risks that are evaluated as being of significance are usually communicated in official programmes. Agencies and individuals then implicitly or explicitly *design* a risk communication system. This system could be quite simple - such as a single telephone call or personal communication - or very complex, such as a radar-based analysis and communication systems to track cyclones or tornadoes and relay predictive information to those potentially in their path. It could be a huge government advertising programme, such as that mounted to counter AIDS in Britain, or a community group concerned about the location of a toxic waste dump.

This design process - implicit or explicit - involves choosing a communication *medium* and a mode of information *delivery*. It involves choices about what information is disseminated and what action is or is not advised. Judgements of an ethical, legal, political and economic nature are involved, not just the mechanistic application of rules, although those may also be important. A target *audience* has to be defined, and the message or messages tailored to their needs. The audiences may consist of risk bearers, those responsible for risk management, or others who have some stake in the process.

These systems attempt to get the *messages* or some other communication to the target audience. There are then simple or complex processes of message *receipt, comprehension,* and *filtering,* before *action* is contemplated or possible.

The message recipient, however, may find the communication incomprehensible or react negatively to the message, using psychological processes such as denial, to avoid message receipt, comprehension, or action. These processes in turn may involve individuals, groups or agencies, or even governments themselves. At each stage there is the potential for error and misunderstanding, and also the potential for communication improvement and better *feedback*.

The political and cultural context: differing philosophies of risk communication

Inseparable from the whole risk communication process is the *socio-political and cultural context* (Figure 1.2). This will affect the perception of risk, the design of the communication system, the communicators, and what is communicated. It will also affect the receipt and comprehension of risk information, and what action will result. To ignore this context is to ignore the political and economic reality of the world in which we live, where power and influence is unevenly distributed and where cultural values affect, and in many cases determine, interpersonal and inter-agency actions and reaction.

Different countries have different philosophies of risk communication, related to cultural and political values. This affects the approach taken by government, and the processes of risk communication and response (Wassersug 1989).

We can illustrate - and caricature - this situation with two extremes: the "welfare state" philosophy and the "enterprise state" society. (We could have chosen a theocracy. a religious state, as another extreme case.) Under a welfare state philosophy there is a strong and central role for government and all government agencies. They are the prime source of risk information, and their "mission" is to protect individuals and society from the risks that they face. Society as a whole is the locus of action.

In the "enterprise state" the key difference is this locus of action and responsibility. The individual is the focus for risk communication: the role of the state and government is to provide information on which that individual makes choices, just as they might choose one brand of soap powder in preference to another. Equity is less important than the efficiency of communication processes.

These different philosophies arise from different cultural and political values, but there are contradictions. In Britain the dominant political philosophy has appeared to focus on a welfare state approach to collective societal enhancement. Yet very little relief is given by the government at times of major disasters; this is left to voluntary agencies and local appeals. In the United States, where one might expect the domination of an enterprise philosophy, the state has a major role in declaring national disasters and in providing substantial relief. Many of the world's poorer countries with a socialist political ideology – such as India – have not the resources for a universal welfare approach, and therefore individuals are in reality left to their own devices to cope with the risks that they face.

What, then, are the implications of these differences? Fundamentally, we cannot separate the policies and practices of risk communication and response from the dominant political economy of the country concerned. The role of government, government agencies and private enterprise will be different in each case. Who takes responsibility for risk communication is crucial, and this will vary according to political systems and cultural values.

The expectations of the public will vary accordingly. The lack of risk communication information may contravene rights established, either formally or informally, in an enterprise society and this will affect a government's aims and objectives. These rights over information may mean that risk communication takes place not simply so that those to be warned can respond, but merely because otherwise the government and its agencies will be held liable for negligence. The process of risk communication itself becomes a political gesture, rather than a protective device.

Organisation

The following chapters should be seen in the light of the conceptual framework discussed above, and encapsulated in Figure 1.2. Not all the authors will be working with the same mental map of the risk communication process, but there are many similarities. To help integrate the volume an attempt is made, at the end of each section, to synthesize the main points arising from the chapters and related discussion during the workshop.

Following this introduction, Section II of the volume examines the links between persuasion, information and response, at the level of the individual. These links should be seen in terms of contextual factors including the role and orientation of the media, and the local political economy, as explored in Section III. A key theme throughout the volume is the assessment of risk communication success, since a prerequisite for continued progress in the field is rigorous programme evaluation. Evaluation is both relatively unexplored in research terms and highly problematic. The examination of this area in Section IV highlights the importance of definitions.

In Section V the final group of contributors consider how risk communication systems might be better designed. We conclude by commenting on the question: can risk communication success be achieved?

Note

The authors are indebted to Lynne Filderman for much of the material in the section "Risk communication and technological and social change".

References

Arnstein, S.R. (1969) Ladder of citizen participation. Journal of the American Institute of Planing. Vol 35, No 4, pp 216.

Covello, V., Winterfeldt, von D., and Slovic, P. (1986) Risk communication: a review of the literature. Risk Abstracts. Vol 3, pp 171-182.

Covello, V., Sandman, P.M. and Slovic, P. (1988) Risk Communication, Plant Statistics, and Risk Comparisons: A Manual for Plant Managers. Chemical Manufacturers Association: Washington D.C.

Crutchfield, J.P., Farmer, J.D., Packard, N.H. and Shaw, R.S. (1986) Chaos. Scientific American. (Dec) pp 38-49.

Douglas, M. (1985) Risk Acceptability According to the Social Sciences. Routledge and Kegan Paul: London.

Eckholm, E. and Record, F. (1976) The Two Faces of Malnutrition. Worldwatch Institute: Washington DC. (Worldwatch Paper No 9).

Fischhoff, B., Lichtenstein, S., Slovic, P., Derby, S.L. and Keeney, R.L. (1981) Acceptable Risk. Cambridge University Press: New York.

Hohenemser, C., Kates, R.W. and Slovic, P. (1983) The nature of technological hazards. Science. Vol 220 (April 22), pp 378-384.

O'Riordan, T. (1981) Environmentalism. Pion (2nd Edition): London.

Royal Society (1983) Risk Assessment: Report of a Royal Society Study Group. Royal Society: London.

Sandman, P.M., Weinstein, N.D. and Klatz, M.L. (1987) Public response to the risk from geological radon. Journal of Communication. Vol 37, No 3, pp 93-108.

Smithson, M. (1987) Fuzzy Set Analysis for Behavioral and Social Sciences. Springer Verlag: New York.

Smithson, M. (1989) The changing nature of ignorance. Presented at workshop on Risk Perception and Response in Australia. Australian Counter Disaster College and Centre for Resource and Environmental Studies, Australian National University: Canberra.

Suter, G.W., Barnhouse, L.W. and O'Neill, R.V. (1987) Treatment of risk in EIA. Environmental Management. Vol 11, No 3, pp 295-303.

Timmerman, P. (1980) Vulnerability, Resilience and the Collapse of Society. Institute of Environmental Studies, University of Toronto: Toronto.

Tompkins, R.K. (1987) On risk communication as inter-organisational control: the case of the aviation safety reporting system. *Colloquy on Natural and Technological Hazards*. University of Colorado: Boulder.

Wassersug, S.R. (1989) The role of risk assessment on developing environmental policy. *International Environment Reporter*. (January), pp 33-43.

SECTION II
PERSUADING INDIVIDUALS

2 Imagery, Information and Risk
David Marks

Abstract

The psychology of risk communication can be approached at a number of levels: the cognitive, the motivational, and the emotional. Imagery, mental models of reality from different points of view, is an important process in communicating information such that it relates directly and simply to desired behaviours. Major barriers to successful communication in the receivers of risk communications are ideas of personal invulnerability, denial, and dissociation. The message will be more successful in changing behaviour if it is simple, positive, concrete, and encourages active social responses. Some of these principles are illustrated by reference to storm warnings provided by the electronic media and an anti-smoking programme.

Introduction

The psychology of risk communication is an important area at the interface between pure and applied psychology. Many of the fundamental mechanisms of human information processing studied in the laboratory can be seen in action when real-world risk communication takes place. In this chapter some of these fundamental psychological processes will be outlined, and their application to two specific examples of risk communication will be considered. The first example is the English storm of 16 October 1987, still very fresh in our memories during the Workshop. The second is the familiar problem of the risks from cigarette smoking.

19

Of key importance in any analysis of risk communication are three sets of variables pertaining to the communication "system": the sender; the communication; and the receiver. The "system" carries overall responsibility for the assessment of risk, the planning of the various actions, and the preparation and delivery of appropriate communications. This paper is intended to facilitate the preparation and delivery of risk communications from the viewpoint of human psychology. Therefore we shall not discuss total "systems" per se, but look at the operating characteristics of the human receiver and also at the essential characteristics of messages designed to communicate risk.

Psychological defences against threat

It is impossible to consider risk perception in isolation from the fundamental properties of human desires, needs and cognitions. Contrary to an increasingly popular but mistaken view within academic psychology, human beings are not analogous to computers in their ability to perform calculations and use rules or algorithms to solve problems with a set of convenient programs (Shaw and Bransford 1977). There are several major ways in which the computer metaphor fails badly when we observe real people behaving in the real world rather than college students performing on a console in some artificial environment. Many of these human "weaknesses" have survival value in both a biological and a psychological sense and they need to be taken into account when designing effective risk communications.

Personal invulnerability is a belief in the survival of self, in a kind of permanence, which transcends all manner of hazards, problems and difficulties (Thompson 1985). It enables people who are seriously ill or injured to comtemplate, and even help to bring about, recovery. It enables people who live hazardous lives in highly stressful situations such as battlezones, hospitals, prisons or the inner city to go about their business and remain productive and useful citizens. It enables smokers and drug addicts to believe that their habits are "safe" even though the medical evidence overwhelmingly indicates that they are lethal.

The personal invulnerability belief is a necessary assumption if human beings are not to be preoccupied with the evaluation of risk, which could only amount to a state of chronic anxiety and virtually perpetual stress. Hence the first major hurdle to be overcome in risk communication is a fundamental barrier to the recognition and acceptence of risk posed by the personal invulnerability belief.

A further, related human obstacle in the path of risk communication is the defence mechanism of *denial*. Long before Freud formally described it, the denial process must have played havoc with many innocent souls, perhaps reaching its epitome in the case of King Canute.

Denial can be seen in a wide variety of situations where habitual cigarette smokers who, when confronted with the evidence linking lung cancer and heart disease with smoking, will frequently argue that "it won't happen to me". The same attitude exists towards a host of risky behaviours such as driving too fast or recklessly, or while intoxicated with alcohol, eating unhealthy foods, the pursuit of activities such as hang-gliding, motor-cycle racing, or white-water canoeing. The human "intuitive statistician" is a very poor reckoner of probablistic and statistical information. One formal rule for the revision of beliefs is given by Bayes theorem in which posterior odds equal the prior odds multiplied by the likelihood ratio of the data. Humans do not alter their subjective probabilities as fast or as far as the evidence dictates, and are clearly sub-optimal in comparison to Bayes' theorem and may not even be Bayesians at all.

A further human characteristic which can reach sophist-icated levels is that of *rationalisation*. This process defends people against internally inconsistent or self-contradictory beliefs and performs a kind of cognitive dissonance reduction. A classic example of this occurred when an otherwise unknown Doomsday sect in Lake City, USA, announced the end of the world. The founder of the sect announced that a message had been received from the "Guardians" of outer space that on December 21 there would be a catastrophic flood which would submerge the West Coast of the Americas from Chile to Seattle. Only true believers would be saved, by flying saucers, at midnight on the appointed day. When the saucers failed to arrive and considerable tension was beginning to mount, the leader received a further message: to reward the faithful few, the whole world had been saved (Festinger et al 1956). Nobody likes it when their favourite theories and beliefs are contradicted by evidence. Rationalisations of various ad hoc kinds invariably come to the rescue, and scientists are no exception.

A universal process which enables the above phenomena almost free reign is that of *dissociation* (Hilgard 1986). In dissociation we observe detached domains of knowledge and beliefs within a single individual so that the same person may believe A and believe not-A in different circumstances or states. The processing of information in the form of belief-relevant evidence will therefore have varying and unpredictable impacts on an individual's beliefs, depending upon which cognitive sub-system the information connects with at the time of its presentation.

In *summary*, the above outline of psychological defences against threatening information should not be taken to imply that humans are never capable of rationality, because they most certainly are. But it is crucial that the designers of risk communication systems do not assume that scientific rationality is the norm and irrationality the exception. Systems should be designed on the opposite assumption - that irrationality is the norm - if they are to be of maximum effectiveness. The objective of successful risk communication should always be to override natural psychological barriers which are in place specifically to defend against threat.

The perception of risk

Perception is virtually never perfect, such as in the way that a photograph reproduces a scene. Perception is a highly selective, constructive and need driven activity which attempts to preserve the stability and constancy of the social and physical worlds. For the reasons given above, risk perception can rarely be expected to follow strictly logical principles or rules and it will often be "sub-optimal" in comparison with statistical or computational formulae. Researchers of subjective probability and risk have observed a number of pervasive biases and tendencies which should be given serious attention in developing risk communication systems.

Availability or vividness

The probability assigned to an event depends upon its vividness or availability (Nisbett and Ross 1980). Vividness is the emotional interest of information, its concreteness or *imageability*, and is dependent upon sensory, spatial and temporal proximity: the immediately available or accessible has the most impact, providing that it is vivid.

Information that is pallid, in the sense that is vague, unclear, abstract or difficult to understand or process, will often be ignored no matter how significant it might be for an individual's well-being. A typical instance of pallid communication was the health warning that was printed in tiny type on cigarette packets in Britain in the 1970s advising that smoking could be harmful to one's health. This warning was printed with the voluntary agreement of the manufacturers and, until recent years when the government has become a little more assertive, could easily be overlooked in a casual handling of the packet. Had the warning been heeded, people would quite literally have stopped buying cigarettes and put the cigarette manufacturers out of business.

Representativeness

Representativeness refers to the fact that judgements of probability are influenced by the similarity of the features of an event to the general category to which it is assigned (Kahneman et al 1982).

For example, if I tell you that I know somebody who is shy and wears glasses and ask you whether he is a librarian or a farmer you may well answer that he is a librarian. Yet this answer ignores the statistical fact that there are more farmers than librarians; the apparent "representativeness" of the description to the stereotype of librarians has had more influence that it warrants.

The representativeness heuristic includes the well-known "gambler's fallacy" in which some sequences of events are perceived more probable than others. Thus, in roulette, after the sequence red, red, red, a black seems more likely than another red, when actually the probability of obtaining a red remains exactly the same. These representativeness biases have obvious relevance to decisions about rare events like floods, volcanic eruptions, earthquakes etc. Such events may appear much less probable soon after a recent occurrence, so that people do not expect two 50-year events in one decade, let alone in one year, yet it is statistically quite possible for this to happen.

Conservatism

Conservatism, in psychology, refers to the human reluctance to change beliefs as much as the evidence requires. It can be a major problem in risk communication at a number of points in the process.

First, there is the delicate matter of deciding whether a complex and dynamic series of data sequences represent the genesis of a hazard. Secondly, having diagnosed a problem there is the equally delicate matter of deciding *what* kind of warning to announce and *when* to announce it. Being too early or too late both have obvious penalties. Conservatism may well mean that diagnosis is given later than it should be, and that the warning will therefore also be given too late. This would suggest that warning procedures need to be prepared well in advance and routinised through regular practice and rehearsal.

Two examples of risk communication

An example of message failure: the 1987 "hurricane" in southern England

In the early hours of 16 October 1987, southern and eastern England experienced a severe wind storm. Millions of trees were felled. Damage was inflicted on thousands of domestic buildings. Railways and roads were at a virtual standstill, and electrical power for a large part of London was cut off for many hours.

That morning the BBC (British Broadcasting Corporation) Breakfast Time television programme could not be screened in its usual format, and a news presenter was substituted to advise viewers about the storm and what actions were required in its immediate aftermath. The BBC managed to screen video sequences of the massive destruction wrought by the winds which included examples of cars literally squashed by trees. The news presenter repeatedly announced to viewers a message which essentially read as follows "DON'T DRIVE TO WORK: STAY AT HOME". Yet on the evening television news that day a somewhat dismayed BBC showed how busy the roads were as many London workers made their way home! Clearly the warning issued that morning had failed to deter many drivers from using the roads, thereby hampering the works necessary to restore them to normal usage.

Why did the message fail? Several characteristics of the BBC message deserve attention and they relate particularly to the vividness/pallidness concept discussed above. The first part of the warning ("DON'T GO TO WORK") was verbal only, and abstract, vague, and negative. None of these features promote vividness and therefore the instruction cannot be expected to be followed. It is impossible to visualise oneself not driving to work! One can only visualise oneself driving something; not doing something, cannot be successfully performed, almost by definition.

The second part of the message was equally flawed ("STAY AT HOME"). Although technically this is not actually negative, neither is it very positive. It is a directive which invites passivity and restricts sociability. It expects the viewer/listener simply to do nothing (except presumably to continue watching television!). When the most dramatic storm of the last 100 years has just subsided this is hardly a reasonable request. Clearly human curiosity will prevail and anybody who is mobile will quite naturally want to look at the effects, share experiences with friends and neighbours, and get involved in the aftermath of the storm which took place during the darkness between 1 am and 5 am.

With the wisdom of hindsight, how might the BBC choose to word such a message on a future occasion? Psychological insight and research would suggest that risk communications of any kind could be enhanced by including the following features:

(i)   use a multi-modal presentation, including for example verbal (acoustically and visually presented) and pictorial information (charts and diagrams);
(ii)   use a message that is as specific as possible;
(iii)   make the message "positive" rather than "negative";
(iv)   invite participative activity rather than passivity (even if you do want people to stay indoors; for example tell them to check visually their neighbours houses);
(v)   invite sociability rather than isolation.

Perhaps the following might be more effective than the version the BBC used: "STAY IN THE VICINITY OF YOUR HOME, PROTECT YOUR PROPERTY FROM FURTHER DAMAGE, SEE IF YOUR NEIGHBOURS REQUIRE ASSISTANCE".

Another Example: How to stop smoking?

A typical ineffective communication is that which can come in the form of medical advice from a general practitioner.

24

The context is the conventional one of the patient visiting his or her doctor with some respiratory problem such as a cough, and the following simple message is delivered: "STOP SMOKING". This may or may not be accompanied by some elaboration concerning the medical risks if the advice is not heeded. This advice, while being perfectly simple and sound, is extremely difficult to follow, and experience suggests that it is successfully heeded only very rarely. The message has all the characteristics of poor risk communication: it is verbal, abstract, non-specific, negative, and it invites passivity and unsociability.

An alternative and much more elaborate series of communications is required if the objective is successful long-term cessation of smoking. One example is provided by the multi-modal psychological smoking cessation programme devised by Sulzberger et al (1978). This is a "package" of procedures, known as the "ISIS Programme", requiring active participation, preferably in a group setting, with a wide variety of interesting techniques which make the objective to "STOP SMOKING" a concrete reality. The programme consists of a series of tasks which:

(i)   provide active methods for successfully reducing the desire to smoke;
(ii)   provide methods for rehearsing alternatives to smoking, of both a physical and mental nature;
(iii)   use mental imagery, relaxation, role-playing and meditation to enhance well-being;
(iv)   use group support and participation;
(v)   anticipate psychological defences and provide effective counter measures; and
(vi)   where possible, make the tasks *fun*!

Unlike the storm warning example given above, we can make direct comparisons between the two contrasting systems of smoking cessation using empirical methods. The following results are based on an evaluation conducted with 132 people immediately following participation in the psychology-based ISIS Programme, together with an evaluation 6 years later of the first 100 participants. These results can be directly compared with survey data on patients who have simply been told by their general practitioners to stop smoking.

A dramatic reduction in cigarette consumption occurs over the six-day ISIS Programme. Figure 2.1 shows this rapid reduction, from an average of 30 cigarettes per day to a fraction of one cigarette per day by the end of the Programme. This represents a massive 97% drop in daily consumption. In round figures, the 132 smokers were consuming a total of 200 packs of cigarettes per day before the Programme and only 5 packs per day immediately after it.

Eighty per cent of all participants reduced to zero consumption during the Programme and 100 per cent successfully reduced their consumption to a much lower level than previously. The drop-out rate of 4% was extremely low. Overall, these figures compare favourably with those obtained by the 34 programmes reviewed by Bradshaw (1973).

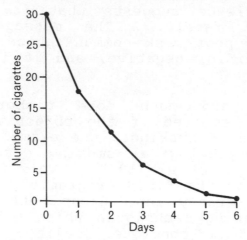

Figure 2.1: Reduction in cigarette consumption during the 6-day ISIS Programme.

It would obviously be gratifying if this high rate of abstinence could be maintained over the first few years following the end of the Programme. Unfortunately, all smoking cessation programmes, like drug abuse programmes for alcohol and heroin, must face up to the reality of relapse. Relapse rates for smoking cessation are particularly high during the first 3-6 months when the relapse curve levels off; a relapse curve averaged over 173 programmes obtained from Hunt and Bespalec (1974) is shown in Figure 2.2.

As indicated in this Figure, however, the ISIS Programme compares very favourably with this average curve and in fact shows significantly better results than the typical relapse curve. The abstinence rate for the ISIS Programme is significantly better than the average level reported in Hunt and Bespalec's comprehensive survey of available methods. Figure 2.2 is based on the first 63 people to enter the ISIS Programme who were contacted by letter or by telephone. The response rate of 87 per cent to this follow-up survey at 4-5 months was pleasingly high. Only eight people could not be contacted or failed to reply.

Of participants who were not smoking 4-5 months following the Programme, 65 per cent rated the Programme as "Excellent" and 35 per cent as "Very good". Less successful participants, despite their failure to cease smoking, gave the ISIS Programme high ratings: Excellent (24%); Very good, (57%); Good, (14%); Fair or poor, (5%). Clearly most participants enjoyed the ISIS Programme. A follow-up survey conducted six years after the Programme showed that almost 40 per cent of the participants were still completely abstinent. This figure contrasts starkly with the comparable result for smokers who had experienced only their doctor's warnings: less than 2 per cent abstinence only one year after the relevant visit to their doctors.

Thus the psychological programme is more than 20 times more effective than doctor's advice in changing smokers behaviour. These results clearly indicate that the ISIS smoking cessation programme provides a highly effective set of techniques for controlling cigarette smoking. This Programme appears to be a significant advance over many currently available methods. Its simplicity, brief duration and applicability to smokers from all walks of life should encourage its widespread application and it could be of national importance to the health of the community.

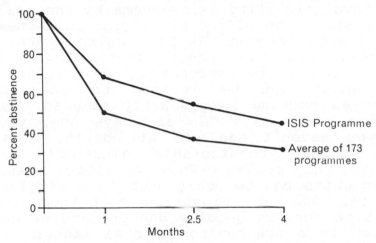

Figure 2.2: Relapse curve for the smoking cessation programme compared to the average results for 173 programmes surveyed by Hunt and Bespalec (1974). The difference is statistically significant.

The success obtained in smoking cessation encourages us to suggest extensions to many other social problems. Research programmes on the application of the same multi-dimensional approach to other areas are envisaged and further work is currently being planned. Alcoholism, heroin and drug abuse, obesity, stress management, interpersonal problems such as shyness, loneliness, anxiety, and aggression are all problems in urgent need of sensible and practical solutions. We believe that the methods on which we are currently working could help provide significant remedies to these enormous social disaster areas. The same psychological methods should also be given serious attention in the field of risk communications for natural hazards.

Conclusions: educating preparedness for disaster

Risk communications should only be designed in the total context of human psychology. This obviously requires resources and commitment beyond that which are usually deployed. But there is a growing awareness of the fact that if natural disasters cannot be prevented, many of their deleterious effects can be at least reduced, and even eliminated, if the public has been adequately prepared.

On the basis of psychological principles researched both in the laboratory and the field it is possible to suggest signposts for further developments in the disaster warning field. Preparedness programmes should be interesting, active, involve rehearsal, both imaged and actual, use group psychology and support, counteract psychological defenses, and whenever possible make the procedures enjoyable, and even fun!

The example of smoking cessation illustrates many of the psychological principles outlined earlier in this chapter. Personal invulnerability is overcome by the use of emotional imagery in which the effect of carcinogenic chemicals in the smoke is traced through the body using mental images of a minute person observing their effects inside the person's own body. Denial is overcome by describing many typical examples which can be related to each person's own experience as smoking is gradually reduced, for example an inner voice which says "Go on, have one, you deserve it because you haven't had one all day!". Many of these examples provoke considerable amusement amongst group members when they are so baldly described. Rationalisations and dissociation can be dealt with in a similar manner, and also by the use of relaxation techniques in which the contradiction between genuine dangers and doing nothing can be explored in a non-confrontational manner. Vividness is enhanced to a maximum by using highly concrete scenarios in which the barely possible becomes transformed into the highly probable, for example if you follow the correct procedures, you will successfully stop smoking (not lose your belongings, your roof, your house or your life).

I can think of no better example to illustrate many of these suggestions than the "Big Bird Get Ready For Hurricanes" programme described by Lynne Filderman in Chapter 12.

References

Bradshaw, P.W. (1973) The problem of cigarette smoking and its control. *International Journal of Addictions*. Vol 8, pp 353-371.

Festinger, L., Riecken, H. & Schachter, S. (1956) *When Prophecy Fails*. University of Minnesota Press: Minneapolis.

Hilgard, E.R. (1986) *Divided Consciousness: Multiple Controls in Human Thought and Action*. Wiley: New York.

Hunt, W.A. and Bespalec, D.A. (1974) An evaluation of current methods of modifying smoking behaviour. *Journal of Clinical Psychology*. Vol 30, pp 431-438.

Kahneman, D., Slovic, P. and Tversky, A. (1982) *Judgement Under Uncertainty: Heuristics and Biases*. Cambridge University Press: Cambridge.

Nisbett, R. and Ross, L. (1980) *Human Inference: Strategies and Shortcomings of Social Judgement.* Prentice Hall: Englewood Cliffs, New Jersey.

Shaw, R. and Bransford, J. (1977) *Perceiving, Acting and Knowing: Toward an Ecological Psychology.* Lawrence Erlbaum Associates: Hillsdale, New Jersey.

Sulzberger, P., Marks, D.F. and Hodgson, I. (1978) *The ISIS Smoking Cessation Programme.* ISIS Research Centre: Dunedin, New Zealand.

Thompson, J. (1985) *Psychological Aspects of Nuclear War.* British Psychological Society: Leicester.

3 Perceived Risk: Past, Present and Future Conditional

Colin Green

Abstract

To design an effective risk communication system it is first necessary to determine what beliefs and expectations the target population holds about the hazard, and their consequent behavioural intentions. Secondly, it is necessary to decide in what directions these beliefs should be changed if behaviours are to be more effective in coping with the threat. Thirdly, an effective alternative strategy must be devised to bring about these changes. Flood warning schemes are currently too often designed without recognising that meanings are given by the recipient, not by the originator, and that these meanings result from the recipients interpretation of a signal and to their expectations of the future.

Introduction: the need for a process model

The "public"- and all of us are members of the public for most of the time - is the subject of two divergent but concurrent myths. Members of the public are individually viewed as potentially omniscient, capable of selectively attending and reacting optimally to the most ambiguous message, and simultaneously as irrational and ignorant if they fail to so respond. The concept "panic" is an example of the second mythology: if the observer does not know why people are behaving in the observed manner, then that behaviour must be irrational.

For brevity, I shall use the term "flood warning" to cover both the informational aspect of the process and also the signal itself. If we are to develop adequate systems of flood warning these must be based upon a process model of beliefs; that is, of cognitions or, more loosely, of perceived risk. That is, we need to adopt the Kellian model (Kelly 1955), which is based on the premise that we use beliefs to some end, and that end is both to understand and to operate on the world.

Two key elements of this process model are that the beliefs an individual holds at any one time both have a past and imply a future (Green 1980a, 1980b). How the structure of beliefs is individually invented and elaborated, and by what means, is insufficiently understood (Kelly 1955); as are the ways in which new objects are integrated into the existing structures of belief (Green 1986). But beliefs serve both to group and to differentiate concepts and objects.

If, for example, we read that concern is being expressed about the risk from 2-4-7-D, E1011 or Muller-Thiery Syndrome, it is fairly certain that we will have no prior knowledge of these hazards since, as far as I know, they are all entirely imaginary. However, on the basis of their names, we might assume that they are respectively herbicides, food additives and a disease since their names are similar to those typical in these categories. Our beliefs as to the nature and extent of the risks from each are initially likely, therefore, to be similar to those beliefs which we hold about those categories or members of those categories of hazards with which we have, however incorrectly, associated these supposedly new hazards.

Beliefs imply a future because we hold them for some purpose: that of construing a hypothesis of the future and to explain the past. Beliefs imply expectations about what will happen and in turn these expectations influence the selection and interpretation of future signals.

A good illustration of the importance of expectations as determinants of behaviour is the story of the policeman who, during the 1977 Big Thompson Flood, told a group of people to leave the floor of the canyon because a flood was coming. When they hadn't moved after some minutes, he returned and told them that a dam had burst. Whereupon they left hurriedly (Gruntfest 1984). The expectations of a "flood" and of a "dam burst" were totally different. Further, predispositions towards actions, or behavioural intentions (Fishbein and Ajzen 1975), are selections of appropriate actions from the repertory of actions perceived to be available. This basic process model is outlined in Figure 3.1.

The feedback links in Figure 3.1 indicate that it is a learning model, and the corollary of this is that the more frequently expectations are confirmed, the greater the inertial effect of beliefs. This is a metaphor of beliefs as a flywheel; once beliefs have been elaborated it is very difficult to change them, particularly as these beliefs influence the selection and interpretation of new signals. Habermas (1979) and Kuhn (1962) have, in different contexts, elaborated similar models of inertial effects.

Kelly (1955) also introduced the concept of the "range of convenience" of a belief. If a belief is used to differentiate between, or group together, items or aspects of objects and actions, then the beliefs that are evoked will depend upon the items being considered. Other than for the purpose of completing questionnaires devised by thoughtful psychologists, the time we need such beliefs is when we have to choose what action to take.

Thus a belief is not very useful unless it helps in this determination of what is the best action. Consequently those beliefs which are useful depend upon a set of actions or behaviours which are perceived to be available. Although Milton remarked that "reason is choice", the foregoing is both a super-rational and ignores the link between beliefs and perceived action options; it is to assume that the domain of perceived available options is in some sense given. Clearly this is not the case, and beliefs imply options as well as options evoking beliefs. It also omits the learning process: that the array of action options cannot spontaneously evoke a set of beliefs, the structure of beliefs must be progressively "elaborated" (Kelly 1955). If we had to approach each choice de novo, choosing would be far too difficult.

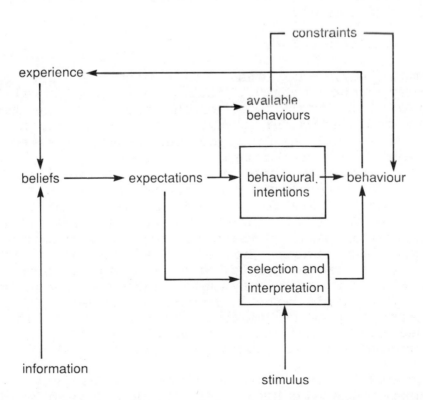

Figure 3.1: Basic process model for warning response

I have developed the argument at such a length for two reasons. First, because the purpose of warnings is to affect the time trajectory of people's beliefs and behaviours: to change their actions from what would have been their behaviour in the absence of warnings. Hence a process model is essential. Secondly, studying processes is rather difficult and most psychological studies give static views, which are descriptive but not necessarily causally descriptive.

To illustrate the difficulties, elsewhere I refer to the results of some psychological studies as analogous to Green's 2-factor theory of watch construction (Green 1986). Having hit a watch with a sharp blow with a hammer, it would be found that the fragments can be distinguished or separated into the categories or factors: transparent-opaque, and metallic/non metallic. In this example, luckily we already know that this description is inadequate to explain why a watch works. However, in exploring people's beliefs and behaviour we lack the equivalent prior knowledge. We may therefore be forced to infer what we can from the questionnaire equivalent of applying a sharp blow with a hammer: the statistical interpretation of the results may yield little more than the 2-factor theory of watch construction. As has been remarked, the physical scientists got there first and took all the easy problems.

Examples of flood hazard perception studies

I now have to be careful how I interpret the results of the various studies we have undertaken on the perceptions of risk and of flooding.

Beliefs and Expectations

For simplicity, beliefs concerning events will be categorised into those relating to the likelihood and severity of flooding; those which relate to the mechanisms, causation and nature of floods; and those which relate to the available and appropriate behaviours. These beliefs are, however, inter-related and interdependent. When we have asked people to compare different situations of hazard in terms of the individual's personal safety - that is from physical harm - we found that these judgements can be explained by the differences in individuals' beliefs as to the likelihood of a hazardous event occurring in each situation, and their beliefs as to the conditional probability of death should such an event occur (Green and Brown 1978). The range of convenience for these beliefs is limited to hazards with immediate effects: for other hazards like cigarette smoking and nuclear radiation, which people believe result in harm which is delayed, different beliefs underpin their judgements (Green et al 1983).

More generally, we have undertaken a variety of studies using populations who have been flooded (Green et al 1985); who live adjacent to areas which were recently flooded

(Penning-Rowsell et al 1984); and who live in a flood risk area where flooding has not occurred recently (Parker et al 1984). In these studies, we have looked at beliefs as to the likelihood of flooding in the future ; worry about flooding in the future; beliefs as to the risk to health and safety posed by flooding; behaviours which relate to beliefs that flooding is possible, conditional upon some circumstances (what we have called "revealed worry"); and judgements on the overall effect of flooding, should it occur, compared to other disasters which may befall one's property (Table 3.1). The problem from a flood warning viewpoint is that people do not worry enough about the risk of flooding; they tend to discount the risk and underestimate the potential severity of flooding in terms of its impact on their lives.

Beliefs as to the likelihood of flooding are conditional upon beliefs about the causation and mechanisms whereby flooding may occur. In this limited sense flooding is a non-random phenomenon. Areas at risk from sea flooding are likely to flood during winter storms when there is simultaneously a high tide. Similarly, properties at risk from inadequate storm sewer flooding are most likely to be affected in the summer, when thunderstorms are most intense. Parker and Neal (this volume) are examining beliefs as to the likely causation of flooding in particular areas and the related beliefs as to when flooding is likely to occur. These beliefs also imply expectations as to possible precursor events, or signals, that flooding might be imminent. In studies of revealed worry we have included some such possible precursors, but results of these studies are in terms of reported behaviours and not of signal value (Green et al 1987b).

Expectations of flood causation and mechanisms inter-relate with those of the character of the event itself, such as speed of onset and depth. In the case of dwelling fires we found that people believe both that they have a great deal of control over the risk, and that they have a high chance of surviving any fire (Green 1982). These beliefs would imply that people will endeavour to control and intervene in any house fire, and that their first choice of behaviour would not be to flee. This is exactly what happens in practice (Canter 1983). We would anticipate that expectations as to the development pattern and causation of flooding would similarly influence intended behaviours in floods. The anecdotal report of the Big Thompson Flood noted earlier is suggestive of the power of these expectations in influencing behaviour.

Harding and Parker (1974) explored behaviour expectations in Shrewsbury. More recently we have looked at actual behaviours on discovering a flood (Green et al 1987a), adopting the methodology previously used by Canter et al (1980) for the analysis of behaviour in fires (Table 3.2). Parker and Neal's current study explores in greater detail these issues of expectations as to behaviour on both warning and upon flooding, as opposed to actual behaviour.

Table 3.1

Ranking of events according to the relative degree
of distress and disruption likely to be caused by each.

	Rank	
	Median	Mean
Home burgled	3	3.1
Car Stolen	6	5.3
House and garden flooded	2	2.5
Burst water pipe in house	4	3.6
Dry rot in house	4	4.3
House fire - fire brigade required	1	1.8

Table 3.2

Uphill: Behaviour on Discovering Water Entering House

	(per cent of actions)		
	1st action	2nd action	3rd action
Tried to mop up water	2	6	3
Went upstairs	18	21	19
Tried to find out what was happening	6	13	10
Turned off electricity	7	13	0
Awaited rescue	1	2	9
Warned neighbours	4	0	0
Tried to keep water from coming into house	19	6	3
Tried to lift furniture etc. above water level	12	8	12
Left the house	0	6	3
Waited for the water to go down	0	7	30
Trapped by water	2	2	0
Rang for help/advice	12	0	1
Moved dependents/ pets upstairs	8	5	4
Moved necessities upstairs	1	2	3
Other action	4	7	0

Actual events are tested against these expectations. An event need not, however, lead to a revision of beliefs; alternatively it may be interpreted so as to conform to prior expectations. In those situations, for example where people believe that they are able to control the risk, they assign fault to those who suffered the accident should an accident occur. We found that when respondents were presented with a series of scenarios describing dwelling fires, there was a strong tendency to blame the occupier and ignore all data which might suggest that the house occupier could not control the risk (Green 1982).

Conversely, when tested against expectations, the event may be interpreted as failing to conform to those expectations. Expectations are not only descriptive but include normative elements: what ought to happen. If for instance the risk of fire is expected to be within the control of the household, then fires which result from factors outside their control, but within other people's control, ought not to occur. Irrespective of beliefs as to relative frequency of such events, these are the categories of fires which ought to be prevented (Green 1982), and indeed ought not to have happened at all. Here "ought" is always conditional on the perceived ability to do something. But what we found that was crucially important in our studies of dwelling fires was that our respondents considered it was more important to prevent those fires which ought not to occur than to prevent those fires which people believed occurred most frequently.

We know, formally, that those who build a dam must not in consequence allow any harm to occur to those living downstream of the dam. Dam failure is something that ought not to happen. If a failure does occur then the owners will not only be legally liable, but will have failed a moral duty. Courts will almost certainly find that there was a duty to warn. Intuitively however, it appears that those who live by a river, or by the sea, are perceived to have chosen to live there. Consequently, a flood does not in that case imply that there has been any failure by those who could have protected them since there, is no such duty to protect.

As practiced, benefit-cost analysis is based upon this view of property rights and moral duties: people will only be protected if that sum that they would be willing to pay to alleviate flooding is greater than the cost of doing so. An exploratory study we have undertaken, for flooding from inadequate storm sewers, indicates belief that such flooding is something that ought not to occur; it is perceived to have resulted from institutional failures whereby someone's sewage is tipped over the fence into somebody else's garden. Consequently, the consensus is that flooding from inadequate stormsewers ought not to occur, and interviewees believe that those who suffer should be compensated.

Appropriately, Littlechild (1986) has argued that following water authority privatisation in England and

Wales, legal remedies for damages should be available for those who experience flooding from inadequate storm and septic sewers. In the context of privatisation, there may well be different moral expectations concerning the "oughts" of behaviour from a private company to those which are allowable to a public authority. In the latter case, the presumption may be that the authority is meant to act to maximise the public interest as expressed through Parliament. This may mean that a wider range of behaviour is permissible than would be the case for an individual or private company where there is no such presumption of action in the public interest.

Warning intentions

Because beliefs have both a past and imply a future, warnings can operate in a number of ways. "Warning" is a convenient shorthand which designates the purpose of the message, although in objective terms what is involved is yet another signal competing for the individual's attention. At times, even interpretation of the purpose of a warning as being to warn may be generous because, the objectives of some organisations may be satisfied merely by the issuance of messages in and of themselves.

We can adopt either of two models for the warning process:

(i)   a conditioned response learning model; or
(ii) the process model.

In the former case, the presumption is that the stimulus (the flood) will evoke an unconditional response; that is, an instinctive response such as flight. Or, a learnt, or conditional response. In conventional conditioning theory terms, we seek to develop a learning process whereby the public comes to associate the conditional stimulus (warning) with the unconditional stimulus (flood), and behave in the same way in response to the warning as they would do when the flood itself occurs. The problem is, therefore, one of teaching the appropriate response behaviour and of developing the appropriate conditioning schedules, both so that people learn to associate the warning with the flood and the desired behaviour with the warning.

As a model, it is perhaps most useful as a framework for examining existing practices which frequently assume that the public has already learnt to associate the conditional stimulus with, and only with, a flood and has learnt the appropriate response. Equally, public awareness programmes might be appraised in terms of the criteria developed from the conditioning theory approach to learning (Skinner 1953).

Using the process model, the question becomes one of what beliefs warnings are intended to change. Warnings may be intended to change either those beliefs which the public has used to inform their expectations about flooding; or alternatively, to change the attribute values on their existing beliefs. As an example of the first case, we might wish to make salient the risk to life assuming that this risk is not universally considered. If the public already uses this belief in forming its expectations about flooding, then we may wish to change their opinions on the magnitude of the risk in a particular case.

In particular, warnings may be intended to do the following:

(i)   to change attribute values for beliefs as to the risk of flooding;

(ii) to change attribute values for beliefs about the severity of flooding; in turn these beliefs imply expectations about appropriate responses;

(iii) to increase the saliency and/or change attribute values about beliefs concerning those events, and signals, which would indicate the imminent or actual onset of flooding;

(iv) finally, to increase the saliency and/or change attribute values as to the effectiveness of alternative behavioural options.

This listing carries with it an implied expectation as to the nature of the current beliefs of those at risk. In particular, that those at risk: underestimate the risk; underestimate the severity of flooding; lack knowledge of the precursor events; and also misjudge or are unable to carry out, through lack of knowledge, the most effective responses to flooding. These assumptions may be wrong, and it follows that the design of a flood warning system needs to be based on the knowledge of the public's current belief structure as well as on what the warner would wish that structure to be.

The intention of the warning may be to operate in one or other of these ways, but we must remember that beliefs are independent and inter-connected, and that consequently it is unlikely that we will be able to change one belief without affecting others.

Beliefs as to the likelihood of an event may influence the selection and interpretation of an event or a signal which may indicate the imminent onset of hazardous events. Similarly, the interpretation of signals of a flood precursor depends upon the beliefs as to the mechanism and causation of flooding. Most signals have a variety of different causes, each with varying conditional probabilities, and signals are consequently ambiguous. The cause interpreted as being most likely may not be the correct cause. Thus, in an urban setting the most likely interpretation of the sound of breaking glass at 2 a.m. might be that it indicates a burglar or vandals, not that the house is on fire. Similarly to some of the residents of Uphill, the first sign of flooding was a damp patch spreading across the living room carpet from the hall doorway. This was variously interpreted as the boiler having burst or the bath overflowing, and not as indicating that flood water was seeping under the front door (Green et al 1985).

Individual disabilities, such as partial deafness, or environmental conditions such as a thunderstorm, will add to the ambiguity of signals (Handmer and Ord 1986). Warnings might, therefore, be designed to change beliefs as to the likelihood of an event in the hope that signals are more likely to be interpreted as indicating the onset of the event in question. For low probability events, this strategy is unlikely to be efficient, since such an interpretation is likely to be proved wrong most of the time, unless the signal is so unlikely to be associated with any other cause that no disconfirming experience occurs. Where a warning is man-made, it is possible in principle to select a warning system which is unique. Today, however, a siren sounding, for example, probably only means that a burglar alarm on somebody's car has been triggered accidentally.

In the same way, we might attempt to change people's beliefs as to the severity of the event since, the more important the event the more likely it may be that potential signals warning of that event are selected and interpreted as warnings. At the towns of Uphill (Green et al 1986) and Swalecliffe (Parker et al 1983), both of which have experienced sea flooding in the middle of winter, households reported having subsequently bought copies of tide tables: these were checked to see if an abnormally high tide was expected.

If we seek to increase the effectiveness of behavioural response then there are two possibilities: to increase the effectiveness of the behaviour which people currently expect to perform; or to change their preferred option. In the UK the general expectation of flooding is such that pre-flood evacuation is not a considered option. The two behaviours preferred are to attempt to keep the water out or to save valuable items (Harding and Parker 1974, Green et al 1985); the influence of experience on behavioural preferences is well known. Information could make the response more effective: advice, for example, to use polythene sheeting as well as sandbags; and to identify before a flood comes those points where water may enter the premises. Clearly, such advice would also need to be targetted as there are some floods or ground conditions where all attempts to keep water out of the building will fail.

The difficulty with providing information to the public is that it is easiest to provide the information when it is not needed: either well in advance of the flood, so that it is lost or forgotten by the time it is needed, or post-flood, after it is needed. However, developments in Information Technology, such as the French MINITEL system, might be useful. Here, instead of telephone directories, subscribers are offered a computer terminal giving access not only to a database of telephone numbers but also many other databases.

The parallel developments in remote interrogation and control of household electrical and telecommunication equipment also opens up the possibility of warnings or alarms to individual households.

However, the "information technology dwelling" will create its own problems. Flood warnings will be in addition to fire and burglar alarms, and a residence might also require warnings for one or many major hazards, that is, of incidents at chemical or nuclear installations and of dam failure. Each hazard would have a warning lead time and the appropriate behaviour will be different in each case. In the case of fire leave the house; leave the area in the case of a dam break and, probably, stay indoors and close all doors and windows in the case of a major hazard incident. The type of information overload problem experienced in aircraft cockpits and nuclear plant control rooms could then be expected.

Social context and changing beliefs

Social milieu

So far, this chapter has treated each individual as isolated and removed from any social or cultural context. A form of social context is necessarily implied, however, since unless beliefs are interpersonally communicable between individuals no communication is possible. Problems obviously arise when beliefs do not have such common meaning. Not surprisingly the work of psychologists focuses on the individual model, although attitude theory recognises the influence of social norms in affecting their behavioural choice (Fishbein and Ajzen 1975). Consequently one useful effect of warnings may be to change people's beliefs as to other people's beliefs and other behaviour in the expectation that they will then choose to conform to what they believe other people intend to do!

However, individuals operate in a social milieu and this influences expectations and behaviours. The importance of the milieu context was, for example, emphasized by the Summerland Fire where parents tried to collect their children before escaping the building (Sime 1979). Similarly in floods a very early action is for people to try to contact relatives, notably wives phone absent husbands, women phone mothers and mothers phone children (Green et al 1985).

Social culture and social roles are also important: one of the examples of this is that signals of a possible fire may not be acted on by a household group until the existence of the fire has been confirmed by the male dominant member of the group (Canter 1983). Similarly in hospitals all actions must be organised by a doctor. It is no use training nurses in how to deal with fires as they are too low in status: any untrained doctor if available will take over the fire fighting (Canter et al 1980).

More generally, anthropologists such as Douglas (1985) and Rayner (1984) have shown that different social groups differ in the way they organise their beliefs about the world and hence differ in their expectations. Overall, our problem in considering the design of warning systems is not to lose sight of the complexity with which we as individuals and members of society operate.

Changing beliefs and certainty of belief

In a simple model we might hypothesise that the ease with which beliefs can be changed depends upon the following (Fishbein and Ajzen 1975, Eagley and Himmelfarb 1978):

(i)   the conviction with which prior beliefs are held;
(ii)   the degree to which the signal can be interpreted as requiring a shift in beliefs; and
(iii) the judged reliability, or credibility, of the message and its sender.

The first two factors are equivalent to arguing that the ease of change depends upon the functional form of the confidence distribution about belief. Brown and Green (1978) showed how, in a Bayesian model, the degree of change conditional upon evidence depends upon the functional form of this confidence distribution.

Much of the literature on uncertainties or conviction of belief has argued that strength of belief and certainty of belief are identical concepts (Beach and Wise 1969, Wyer 1973). However, Polanyi (1958) argued that a belief as to a probability is incomplete: it must be assertive to be complete. Strength of belief and certainty of belief are therefore completely separate concepts. Figure 3.2 shows the variation in uncertainty between beliefs as to the threat to public safety posed by a number of hazards (Green et al 1985). It can be seen that uncertainty varies between hazards. This study also found that uncertainty was not solely an individual trait: that is, individuals varied in the degrees of uncertainty ascribed to the level of threat posed by different hazards. They could therefore be very uncertain about the threat from one hazard, but quite certain about that from another.

A second study suggested that certainty of belief may nevertheless be partly a personality trait. In this study a sample of students was asked to report how certain they would be that a dice or a coin was a fair dice/coin, conditional upon a given sequence of throws. For example, if a coin came up heads six times in a row it may be a fair coin, but at some stage one should conclude that it is not a fair coin. We found that given the results of a single throw about 40 per cent of the sample were "nearly certain" that the dice/coin was fair; most of the rest were "completely uncertain", and there were a few cynics who started by being pretty certain that the coin was unfair (Green and Brown 1980). A single throw is, of course, devoid of any informational content which would give any

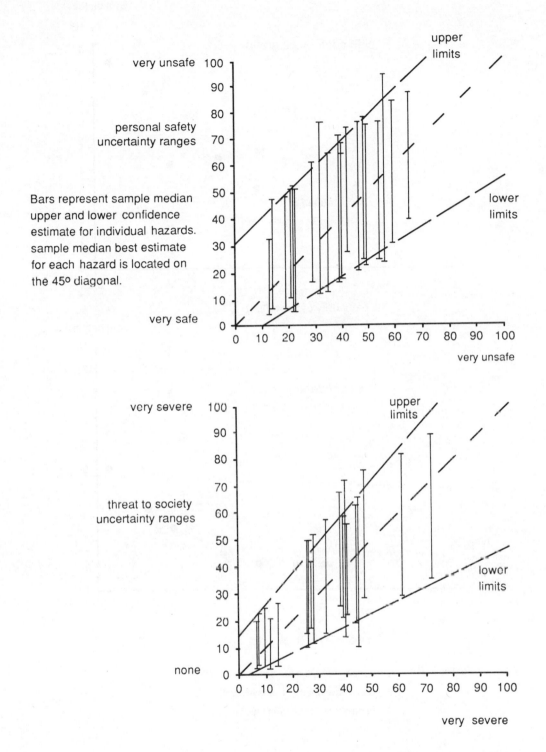

Figure 3.2: Beliefs as to the threat to personal safety and to society for a range of hazards.

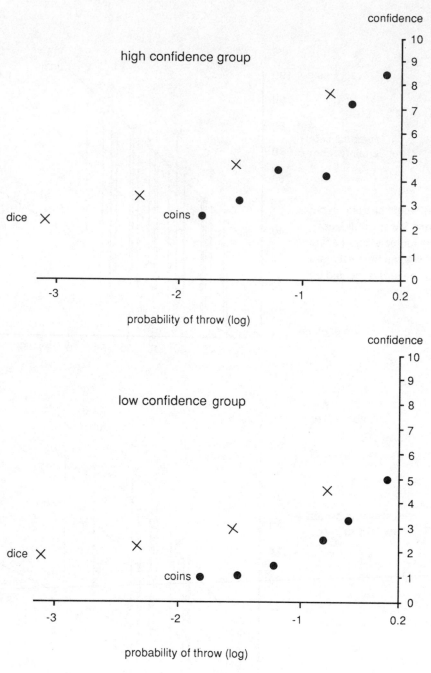

Figure 3.3:   Changes in confidence that the coins/dice
             are fair with number of throws.

clue as to the likelihood that the dice/coin was fair. Figure 3.3 illustrates how, for the simpler sequences of throws, certainties change with increasing numbers of throws. It is noticeable that those who started out "nearly certain" that the coin was fair remained more confident that the coin was fair than those who started out completely uncertain as to whether the coin was fair.

Taken together, the concepts of uncertainty and beliefs and the magnitude of the shift in belief implied by a particular interpretation of a signal are similar to Kelly's (1955) concept of the permeability of beliefs. A rich and complex structure of beliefs is, he argued, more permeable than a single simple, narrowly construed set of beliefs.

Sources of risk communication

A great deal of work has been done in regard to the perceived credibility or reliability of sources in various contexts. These range from work on public conceptions of which groups and professions are most suited to dealing with different types of social problems, to assessments of the likely validity of different possible informational sources in a particular context (Lee et al 1983). Put crudely, the three questions which the onlooker will use to judge the source are:

(i) do they know what they are talking about?
(ii) are they addressing the right problem?
(iii) and are they likely to tell us the truth anyway?

Lagadec (1980) reports that a French survey found that 61 per cent of those questioned believed that an accident on the scale of Three Mile Island had already happened in France, but that the facts had been concealed by the authorities; 80 per cent believed that if such a nuclear power plant accident did occur, it would be concealed by the authorities.

One clue as to the likely truthfulness of a source is the internal consistency of the words and deeds of that source. No credence is likely to be attached to civil defence advice in the event of a nuclear war that the population should stay at home, given that it would be issued by ministers on route by helicopter to underground command bunkers. On the other hand, the dumping of sandbags at street corners may not help much to minimise people's flood losses, but it does suggest that those in authority believe what they are saying. Similarly in a practice evacuation of a high rise office building in Canada, controlled by a public address system, occupants reported that they believed that it might in fact be a real evacuation because the speaker sounded flustered (Pauls and Jones 1980).

The "track record" of the source is also clearly an indicator. Although false alarms are frequently argued to result in a lowering of credibility (Breznitz 1984), this argument goes against classical conditioning theory (Skinner

1953). In a conditioning theory experiment, as in the famous "Little Albert" Study (Watson 1931), conditioning involves a schedule whereby the unconditional stimulus is presented prior to conditional stimulus. After a period, the response to the unconditional stimulus becomes associated with the conditional stimulus.

In the "Little Albert" study, Watson was able to condition Little Albert, an eleven month old baby, to fear white rats. Every time "Little Albert" reached out to touch the rat, the experimenter made a loud bang. Fairly soon, the child was terrified by the sight of the white rat - ethics committees have subsequently impeded the march of science. When the conditioned response is established, and the conditional stimulus (in this case the "loud bang") is no longer given, the conditioned response is gradually extinguished. The extinction rate is slower when during conditioning the unconditional stimulus (reaching out to touch the rat in the "Little Albert" case) is not always followed by the conditional stimulus (Skinner 1953).

But, for classical conditioning theory to apply, we require a learning period in which warnings are learnt to be associated with a subsequent flood. These warnings need not be reliable provided that at least some are followed by floods. More usually, the early learning period will be that warnings are not followed by floods. Here, one is tempted to extrapolate from the coin and dice experiment to see how quickly the beliefs of those who place and attach initial credibility or credence to warnings will weaken.

Consequences of warnings: coping strategies

Supposing that the warning is received and interpreted in the way in which the source hopes that it will be, what do we expect to happen then? We may expect the interpretation to act as a stressor; where the interpretation is equivalent to the appraisal (Lazarus 1971). The magnitude of the stress which results will be related to the demand compared to the individual's ability to cope (Holroyd and Lazarus 1982).

However, coping styles vary, being classified into active and emotionally orientated coping (Moos and Billings 1982, Pearlin and Schooler 1978). Emotionally orientated coping includes such strategies as denial and acceptance. The coping style which is adopted will influence the range of behavioural options on which the individual draws and response selected. We should not assume that everyone is going to run around filling sandbags: such behaviour might in fact suggest a hyperactive coper.

What the individual will do is to minimise their distress. They will only, therefore, attempt to minimise flood damage if this is the action which they consider most likely to minimise their distress. Lazarus and Launier (1978) have hypothesised that the style of coping adopted is a function of the appraisal of the threat: what are the stakes and

what are the options. Elsewhere it has been suggested that
personality descriptors, such as self-efficacy, affects the
choice of coping style (Moos and Billings 1982; Pearlin and
Schooler 1978): that those who feel less confident will be
less likely to adopt action orientated coping. Other work
(Rayner 1984) suggests that the choice of coping style may
be culturally influenced.

In exploring the worry induced by the risk of flooding, we
have constructed a list of questions for self-reporting
consisting of a series of behavioural options which people
might adopt when confronted by the risk of flooding (Table
3.3). Our rationale was that if people are worried, then
they will do something, and by constructing a series of such
possible behaviours, we hoped to construct a Guttman Scale
of revealed worry.

When we compared the derived Guttman scales of revealed
worry for a sample of respondents who were still at risk
from flooding, to their answers on a simple rating question
on the degree to which they were worried about the risk of
flooding in the future, which we termed "expressed worry",
we found a strange pattern. Although we already knew that
expressed worry was highly correlated to perceived risk
(Green et al 1983), it was found that while there was no-one
who scored low on expressed worry but scored high on
revealed worry, there was quite a number of people who
scored highly on expressed worry but low on revealed worry
(Bossman Aggrey 1986). When the items in the revealed worry
scale were examined it appeared that the items were heavily
loaded towards active coping, and hence biased against those
who adopted an emotional coping style or those whose ability
to cope actively was constrained by physical or financial
limitations. This hypothesis is being tested in current
work by attempting to derive independent scales of revealed
worry based upon active and passive coping items, and
comparing results on these scales with the results of using
Folkman and Lazarus's (1980) scale of Coping Style to
classify respondents.

The implications of active and passive coping styles are
several-fold. First, the source of the warning will have
its own cultural style of coping: a warning issued by a
religious group is likely to be quite different to that from
a police force. The latter are clearly orientated towards
active coping, the former more towards emotional coping,
although Noah may be said to be an exception. Secondly, the
issuer will tend to expect the recipient to adopt the same
coping style as would the source. If, as suggested (Mileti
1975), warnings contain behavioural advice it should be
orientated to both forms of coping style.

A third implication is that coping styles may be more or
less effective in coping with the stressor. In the event of
flooding, for which a warning aims to prepare the recipient,
one passive coping strategy is denial (Pearlin and Schooler
1978). Those studies (Burton et al 1968) which have
reported the redefinition of flooding, as either "high

Table 3.3

Worry About Flooding at Loughton

	per cent responding "yes"		
	Households who have been flooded	Households whose gardens have been flooded	Households potentially at risk
"We stay up all night when it rains"	31	6	6
"If we go away we arrange with neighbours how they can contact us in case of a flood"	68	46	15
"When it rains we check the level of the water in streams"	59	60	18
"We are afraid to go out when it rains heavily"	24	9	2
"When we go away on holiday or a visit we move important things above the possible water level"	22	6	2
"We are too worried to sleep at night when it rains heavily"	35	6	7
"When it rains heavily we move the car(s) to a safe area"	31	8	5
"We are afraid to go out when a thunderstorm is forecast"	27	9	2
"We would move to another area if we could"	26	0	3

water" or as being non-random events, are descriptive both of emotionally orientated coping, and of apparently successful coping. That such responses are described in a morally disapproving tone indicates both an action orientated coping style by the authors, and the assumption that the object of the individual is to minimise financial loss rather than personal distress. Fourthly, we might expect that a warning of an event to which the recipient foresaw no effective response, within the available behavioural options appropriate to their coping style, might increase distress. An active coper warned of the imminent impact of a meteor which will destroy the world might be likely to suffer distress or to engage in desperate if ineffective attempts to cope.

Treating a warning as a potential stressor whose appraisal evokes a coping response, also suggests answers to additional questions. If as a result of the individual's appraisal of the warning the coping demand is perceived to exceed the individual's capacity to respond, then stress (or rather distress) is the consequence. Any warning which results in an appraised demand within the individual's coping capacity will not result in distress. Hence, we may answer the question of whether false alarms cause distress by a resounding "sometimes" - depending on the nature of the warning and the person warned.

A second argument has concerned the effect of warnings which induce "fear". The suggestion from some studies (Krisher et al 1973) is that there is, at least for a given message, an optimum level of arousal. If the intensity of the stressor as specified by the warning is increased to this level then the likelihood of the adoption of the suggested active coping response is increased. However, too intense a stressor may result in a switch to emotional coping as the preferred strategy.

Conclusions

A warning is an attempt to intervene in an individual's dynamic system of complex inter-related beliefs and expectations. Therefore, designing risk communication systems to produce effective warnings, first requires knowledge of the prior structure of these beliefs and, secondly, a judgement on the desired form and direction of change based upon an assessment of what behaviours are potentially available to the recipient.

Thirdly, we need to find some appropriate stimulus for the alarm itself, and an effective way to enable the individual to learn to associate this stimulus with the desired response and to achieve the maximum reinforcement of the response.

The real test of the effectiveness of any flood warning system - or any risk communication and response system - is whether behaviours after the warning are more effective than they are after the experience of the hazard, in this case flooding. Warnings are in essence an attempt to convey the lessons of experience without the experience itself. In practice, I have considerable reservations about cases where flood warnings are judged to have been effective: it may be that this effect should have been attributed to prior experience of flooding.

References

Beach, L.R. and Wise, J.A. (1969) Subjective probability estimates and confidence ratings. *Journal of Experimental Psychology*. Vol 79, No 3, pp 438-444.

Bossman Aggrey, P. (1986) *A Path Analytic Model of the Subjective Severity of the Impacts of Household Flooding*. Flood Hazard Research Centre: Enfield.

Breznitz, S. (1984) *Cry Wolf: The Psychology of False Alarms*. Lawrence Erlbaum Associates: Hillsdale, New Jersey.

Brown, R.A. and Green, C.H. (1978) *Metrics for Societal Safety, N157/78*. Fire Research Station: Borehamwood.

Burton, I., Kates, R.W. and White, G.F. (1968) *The Human Ecology of Extreme Geophysical Events*. Department of Geography, University of Toronto: Toronto. (Natural Hazard Research Working Paper No. 1).

Canter, D.V. (1983) *Studies of Human Behaviour in Fire: Empirical Results and Their Implications for Education and Design*. Department of Psychology, University of Surrey: Guildford.

Canter, D.V. Breaux, J. and Sime, J. (1980) Domestic, Multiple Occupancy and Hospital Fires. In Canter, D.V. (ed) *Fires and Human Behaviour*. John Wiley: Chichester.

Douglas, M. (1985) *Risk Acceptability According to the Social Sciences*. Routledge & Kegan Paul: London.

Eagley, A.H. and Himmelfarb, S. (1978) Attitudes and opinions. *Annual Review of Psychology*. Vol 29, pp 517-54.

Fishbein, M. and Ajzen, I. (1975) *Belief, Attitude, Intention, and Behaviour*. Addison-Wesley: Reading, Mass.

Folkman, S. and Lazarus, R.S. (1980) An Analysis of Coping in a Middle-Aged Community Sample. *Journal of Health and Social Behaviour*. Vol 21, pp 219-239.

Green, C.H. (1980a) Fires, beliefs, expectations and interpretations. Paper presented at the *Third International Seminar on Human Behaviour in Fires*. Edinburgh.

Green, C.H. (1980b) Risk: beliefs and attitudes. In Canter, D.V. (ed) *Fires and Human Behaviour*. John Wiley: Chichester.

Green, C.H. (1982) Acceptable Risk - So What? Paper presented at the 20th International Conference of Applied Psychology. Edinburgh.

Green, C.H. (1986) Reason, choice and risk. Paper presented at the Collogue Internatinale de Recherche, Evaluer et Maitriser les Risques. Chantilly.

Green, C.H. and Brown, R.A. (1978) *Perceived Safety as an Indifference Function, N157/78*. Fire Research Station: Borehamwood.

Green, C.H. and Brown, R.A. (1980) *The Acceptability of Risk*. Final Report part 2, Contract FRO/028/68. Research Unit, School of Architecture, Duncan of Jordanstone College of Art: Dundee.

Green, C.H., Brown, R.A. and Goodsman, R.W. (1983) *The Perception and Acceptability of Risk, N7/83*. Fire Research Station: Borehamwood.

Green, C.H., Brown, R.A. and Goodsman, R.W. (1985) Injury or death by fire: how people rate their chances. *Fire*. (March), pp 44-48.

Green, C.H. Emery, P.J., Penning-Rowsell, E.C. and Parker, D.J. (1985) *The Health Effects of Flooding: a Survey at Uphill, Avon*. Flood Hazard Research Centre: Enfield.

Green, C.H. and Penning-Rowsell, E.C. (1986) Evaluating the intangible benefits and costs of a flood alleviation proposal. *Journal of the Institution of Water Engineers and Scientists*. Vol 40, No 3, pp 229-248.

Green, C.H. Penning-Rowsell, E.C. and Parker, D.J. (1987a) Estimating the risk from flooding and evaluating worry. In Covello, V.T., Lave, L.B., Moghissi, A. and Uppuluri, V.R.R. (eds), *Uncertainty in Risk Assessment, Risk Management, and Decision Making*. Plenum Press: New York.

Green, C.H. Tunstall, S., Emery, P.J. and Bossman Aggrey, P. (1987b) Evaluating the non-monetary impacts of flooding. Paper presented at the Annual Conference of the Society for Risk Analysis. Houston.

Gruntfest, E. (1984) Warning dissemination and response with short lead times. Paper presented at the International Workshop on Flood Hazard Management. Flood Hazard Research Centre, Middlesex Polytechnic: Enfield.

Habermas, J. (1979) *Communication and the Evolution of Society*. Heinemann: London.

Handmer, J.W. and Ord, K.D. (1986) Flood warning and response. In Smith, D.I. and Handmer, J.W. (eds), *Flood Warning in Australia*. Centre for Resource and Environmental Studies, Australian National University: Canberra.

Harding, D.M. and Parker, D.J. (1974) Flood Hazard at Shrewsbury, United Kingdom. In White, G.F. (ed) *Natural Hazards Local, National, Global*. Oxford University Press: New York.

Holroyd, K.A. & Lazarus, R.S. (1982) Stress Coping and Adaptation. In Goldberger, L. and Breznits, S. (eds) *Handbook of Stress*. Free Press, New York.

Kelly, G.A. (1955) *The Psychology of Personal Constructs*. Norton: New York.

Krisher, H.P. Darley, S.A. and Darley, J.M. (1973) Fear-provoking recommendations, intentions to take preventive actions, and actual preventive actions. *Journal of Personality and Social Psychology*. Vol 26, No 2, pp 301-308.

Kuhn, T.S. (1962) *The Structure of Scientific Revolutions*. University of Chicago Press: Chicago.

Lagadec, P. (1980) Societal challenges in risk assessment. In Conrad, J. (ed) *Society, Technology and Risk Assessment*. Academic Press: London.

Lazarus, R.S. (1971) The concepts of Stress and Disease. In Levi, L. (ed) *Society, Stress and Disease*. Vol 1. Oxford University Press: London.

Lazarus, R.S. and Launier, R. (1978) Stress-related transactions between person and environment. In Pervin, L.A. and Lewis, M. (ed) *Perspectives in International Psychology*. Plenum: New York.

Lee, T.R. et al (1983) *Psychological Perspectives on Nuclear Power*. Report No. 2. Department of Psychology, University of Surrey: Guildford.

Littlechild, S.C. (1986) *Economic Regulation of the Water Industry*. London.

Mileti, D.S. (1975) *Natural Hazard Warning Systems in the United States: a Research Assessment*. Institute of Behavioral Science, University of Colorado: Boulder, Colorado.

Moos, R.H. and Billings, A.G. (1982) Conceptualizing and Measuring Coping Resources and Processes. In Goldberger, L. and Breznitz, S. (eds) *Handbook of Stress*. Free Press: New York.

Parker, D.J, Penning-Rowsell, E.C. and Green, C.H. (1983) *Swalecliffe Coast Protection Proposals: Evaluation of Potential Benefits*. Flood Hazard Research Centre: Enfield.

Parker, D.J., Penning-Rowsell, E.C. and Green, C.H. (1984) *Whitstable Central Area Sea Defence Scheme: Evaluation of Potential Benefits*. Flood Hazard Research Centre: Enfield.

Pauls, J.L. and Jones, B.K. (1980) Building Evacuation: Research Methods and Case Studies. In Canter, D.V. (ed) *Fires and Human Behaviour*. John Wiley: Chichester.

Pearlin, L.I. and Schooler, C. (1978) The Structure of Coping. *Journal of Health and Social Behavior*. Vol 19, pp 2-21.

Penning-Rowsell, E.C. Parker, D.J. and Green, C.H. (1984) *Loughton Brook Improvement Scheme: Assessment of Potential Benefits*. Flood Hazard Research Centre: Enfield.

Polanyi, M. (1958) *Personal Knowledge*. Harper & Row: New York.

Rayner, S. (1984) Disagreeing about Risk: The Institutional Cultures of Risk Management and Planning for Future Generations. In Hadden, S.G. (ed) *Risk Analysis, Institutions, and Public Policy*. Associated Faculty Press: Port Washington, New York.

Sime, J.D. (1979) The Use of Building Exits in a Large-Scale Fire. Paper presented at the International Conference on Environmental Psychology. University of Surrey: Guildford.

Skinner, B.F. (1953) *Science and Human Behavior*. Free Press: New York.

Watson, J.B. (1931) *Behaviourism*. Routledge & Kegan Paul: London.

Wyer, R.S. (1973) Category Ratings as "Subjective Expected Values". *Psychological Review*. Vol 80, No 6, pp 446-467.

4 Education and Risk
Colin Wilson

Abstract

Public education about risk is often seen as a panacea for risk management. Many of the problems faced by educators generally also affect public education programmes. Such problems include the role of perception in learning, understanding the learning process, how information is processed, and the effectiveness of institutionalised learning. This chapter takes an educational perspective on risk communication, and outlines theories of learning, perception, information processing, models of communication, and models of educational systems of relevance to risk education. It examines in particular less formal educational models and their relevance to community risk education as opposed to education within the formal institutional system. It also takes a philosophical perspective on the role of education in social systems, and comments on the role of education in raising awareness and in the transfer of risk to less educated groups.

Introduction

Educating both hazard managers and the public about hazards which exist in daily life, and about various protective actions available, is considered with some ambivalence by risk managers. On the one hand, public education has been considered a peripheral aspect of the process, secondary to more important measures such as warning systems, information management, resource management and hazard response procedures. On the other hand, my experience with emergency managers who come to the Australian Counter Disaster College for training courses has been that there is a general regard for educational processes, particularly "public education", as both a catch all and a panacea: failing other solutions, it is frequently believed that a public education campaign will succeed.

As an educator, this places me in a dilemma. While I am convinced of the positive benefits of education, particularly if it is for the benefit of the community and the citizens within it, as opposed to simply "making the public follow our instructions" (as some emergency managers see its purpose), I am also aware of the fundamental problems involved with education in general: problems of context, learning, perception, communication and evaluation. Learning is essentially a change in behaviour resulting from experience; learning is change. For many this change is uncomfortable, and change may be resisted. The resolution of these problems is not easy, and I often wonder at the success of any hazard education programme given such seemingly insurmountable odds. But there appears to be no shortage of successful programmes dealing with a variety of topics on budgets ranging from millions to a few dollars.

Risk communicators involved in public education activities would probably benefit by becoming conversant with a number of models of learning, perception and communication which education has embraced. In many cases the theoretical underpinning provided by these models helps to ascertain the likely effectiveness of any planned learning activity.

Models of learning

There have been a large number of learning theorists who have had a considerable influence on teaching and educational practice. When discussing education about risk, a number of relevant theorists should be noted.

The *behaviourists*, such as Skinner (1968, 1972) or Pavlov (1927), regard learning largely in terms of stimulus-response activity, placing importance on both positive and negative reinforcement to promote desired behaviour. A behaviourist position would assume that the role of risk education is to bring about appropriate responses should a stimulus, a warning for example, be encountered. The appropriate response would be brought about through reinforcement, either positive or negative, or through punishment. One difficulty in attempting this approach in many community education programmes is that frequently the public's current behaviour is not accurately known, making relevant reinforcement difficult.

More often than not (for example community education programmes about road safety) current behaviour is labelled as inappropriate, the assumption being that the behaviour is aggressive, neglectful, anti-social and irresponsible. Consequently, there is a high degree of emphasis on punishment and chastisement, such as fines and general rebukes from authorities. This corresponds with the use of unpleasant or noxious stimuli in behaviour modification. The difficulty with the use of punishment to attempt to bring about appropriate response, is that often emotional side-effects accompany the punishment, identifying the punisher with the noxious stimuli. Another problem may be that it leads to suppression of the undesirable behaviour, but not its extinction. This leads to the idea that while we may change the behaviour, we may not change the underlying attitude. Bloom (1956), who is discussed later in this chapter, recognised the importance of affective or attitudinal objectives in education rather than just cognitive ones. A further problem is that in many cases punishment is not effective. Sears et al (1957) studied the effect of punishment on children's learning and concluded that punishment can often have the opposite effect to that intended. Aggressive children are likely to become more aggressive when overly punished. This is probably because punishment itself is often aggressive, and because the punisher is seen to approve of the punishment, thereby reinforcing aggressive behaviour.

It is worthwhile noting that hazard impacts such as floods can act as reinforcers in the behavioural sense. Skinner (1953) showed that behaviour reinforced intermittently at variable-intervals is the most difficult to extinguish. This is exactly the nature of flood events. Thus floods can positively or negatively reinforce appropriate or inappropriate behaviour. Inappropriate behaviour may be positively reinforced by a low magnitude event which causes little or no damage. Conversely, appropriate behaviour may be negatively reinforced by extreme events where few escape damage. Therefore, immediately after a flood it would be important to accurately ascertain community and individual behaviour, reinforcing and highlighting that which is appropriate, and attempting to counteract reinforced inappropriate activity.

The neo-behaviourists developed concepts relevant to this, and to risk education generally, through their study of social learning and role-modelling. The work of Bandura and Walters (1963) investigated the social context of learning. They emphasised the importance of role modelling, suggesting that most of our meaningful learning is achieved through example, more correctly termed imitation (or observational learning). This involves acquiring appropriate responses as a result of seeing a model. The distribution of model safety codes, or the erection of a model bushfire or flood resistant house in an area rebuilding after disaster, are examples of practical role-modelling in the context of risk awareness education. One important aspect is that negative models can also be copied, and negative role models are far harder to remove or modify.

Another relevant idea developed by the neo-behaviourists is the concept of learned helplessness. Essentially this implies that when someone is unable to overcome a repeated negative situation, behaviour will adjust so that there is no longer any desire to avoid the situation. A typical example would be children who always come last; eventually they accept coming last as inevitable and see themselves as losers. Someone who is repeatedly the subject of a particular risk, may eventually regard the risk as part of everyday life and reduce efforts to avoid or modify it. Education in this context is considerably more difficult than when the learner still believes that it is desirable to modify the situation.

At the community level, this may be one of the factors involved in the creation of a "disaster subculture", a concept discussd by Scanlon and others in this volume.

The *motivational theorists*, such as Maslow (1970) and Herzberg (1966), suggest that learning is largely based on motivation, particularly the influence of needs and drives, and arousal. According to the motivationists there is a range of needs, such as physiological and safety needs, which give rise to drives and therefore act as motivational factors. Knowles (1970, 1984) recognised that the best time for learning is when the need to know is present. Thus, ideally it would be more productive to target educational programs towards those who need to know, such as intending or recent residents in a floodplain, than simply to go for a blanket approach.

Arousal theory suggests that maximum learning takes place under optimum arousal conditions. Optimum arousal corresponds with maximum attentiveness. The difficulty with risk education may be that without sufficient arousal, and this is likely if the risk is not immediately apparent, learning will not be relevant. This would suggest that either the arousal needs to be created, or the learning needs to correspond with a period of high arousal, such as an actual event or conditions leading to an actual event. The difficulty with trying to create arousal is that vicarious experience is not likely to be as effective as arousal through direct sensory stimulation. Furthermore, it is likely that unless an actual experience occurs shortly after the vicarious experience of education, forgetting or suppression will occur. The practical implications of this might be that the learning about the earthquake risk, for example, is likely to be maximised a short time after a significant tremor because arousal will be high (it is important to note that arousal levels can also be too high: excitement is a poor learning state). Similarly, bushfire prevention programs timetabled for administrative convenience in the same week each year are likely to lose their effect unless arousal levels correspond. Educators who followed this approach would no doubt be hoping that their timetabled week did not correspond with a week of torrential downpours.

Instructional theorists influenced educationists away from the idea of learning as a simple stimulus-response process, and also highlighted the importance of the use of objectives to achieve clarity in purpose and to evaluate results. Bloom et al's (1956) taxonomy of educational objectives outlines a heirarchy of objectives in what he calls the psycho-motor, cognitive and affective domains (Figure 4.1). Essentially this means that learning involves physical skills, mental skills and attitudes, and that there are various levels of learning within each domain. Thus, while we transfer various facts or knowledge about say, taking out flood insurance, this may be wasted if we do not also pay attention to higher level cognitive processes, or to the attitudinal or emotional aspects such as its value or its sense of responsibility.

Gagne (1965) developed eight general categories of learning from simple signal learning through to discrimination and concept development. Of most significance is the idea that instructional goals need to be framed in terms of the type of learning involved in their attainment. This was developed by Romiskowski (1981), whose work suggested there are optimum methods for particular objectives. Therefore, if we wish to change attitudes towards risk, simply communicating facts may not be enough - we would also need to communicate effects, probabilities, and consequences in order to achieve an emotional response rather than just an ingestion of information.

The *cognitivists* developed models based on the intellectual processes involved in learning and the influence of organisation, decision-making, information processing and forgetting. Bruner (1965, 1966, 1974) and Ausubel (1963, 1968) stressed the need to develop concepts as an aid to both memory and to choices of action, rather than simply transmitting facts (although they differed about whether inductive or deductive processes were the most appropriate in concept formation). If for example we were to teach firefighters about safety procedures in fires, we could take one of two approaches. We could teach safety as a set of procedures to be followed, or we could teach it in the context of the concept of fire behaviour. Bruner and Ausubel would most likely argue that the latter is a better approach. Although simply teaching procedures may be satisfactory in certain circumstances, should unexpected circumstances develop the procedures would not fit the new situation. Someone who has the broader concept would be more likely to use adaptive behaviour.

Finally the *humanists*, such as Rogers (1951, 1969), who developed the phenomenological view, studied individual perceptions and personal uniqueness in the learning process, and challenged most of the models about learning, especially those of the behaviourists. Rogers suggested that each individual exists in a continually changing world of experience of which he or she is the centre. Under this model, the individual's main drive is towards personal growth, and the best vantage point for understanding behaviour, and therefore learning, is from the internal frame of reference of the individual. The primary implication for risk education is to challenge both the

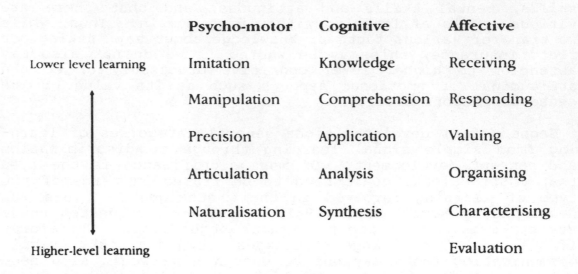

	Psycho-motor	Cognitive	Affective
Lower level learning	Imitation	Knowledge	Receiving
	Manipulation	Comprehension	Responding
	Precision	Application	Valuing
	Articulation	Analysis	Organising
	Naturalisation	Synthesis	Characterising
Higher-level learning			Evaluation

Figure 4.1: Taxonomy of educational objectives
(Bloom et al 1956).

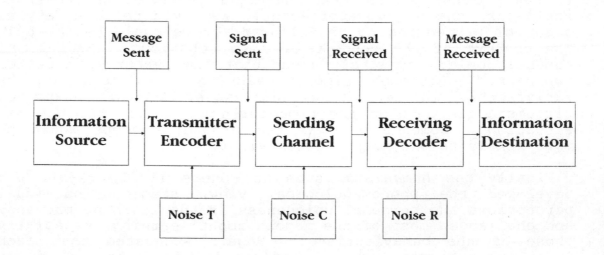

Figure 4.2: An "electronic" communications model.

assumption that authorities and educators are the best judge of what is meaningful and necessary for the public, and the assumption that the public is an amorphous mass with uniform needs capable of learning equal amounts in an equal time. Rogers sees education as facilitative rather than pedagogical, and takes the philosophical position that personal feelings ought to be respected, and that self-determination is everyone's right. It would be worthwhile keeping Roger's perspective in mind when looking at non-formal models of education later in this chapter.

Perception

The study of perception can be defined as the study of systems that relate input to output. A fairly simple view is of perception as a black box, where inputs are processed and somehow outputs result. The work of Rogers in regard to phenomenology is complemented by the vast range of work which has been done in the study of perception and learning.

Of most interest to educators are a number of perceptual principles which affect learning, and which would directly influence any education about risk. Essentially these are that perception is:

* *relative*. In other words our perceptions are influenced by other objects, viewpoints, concepts and experiences relative to those objects, viewpoints, concepts and experiences being studied.
* *organised*. We try to construct meaningful relationships or groupings concerning things being perceived.
* *selective*, and it has limits. We will therefore select only information of relevance when sensory information is complex.
* *based on expectations*. It will be constructed to fit the expected reality.
* *value laden*. Our existing values will directly influence our perceptions.
* *variable* between individuals and groups in the same situation. This is most significant since it implies that risk will be perceived differently by individuals even given that their situation is the same.

Information processing

Much of the work of the cognitive theorists examines how information could best be retained, and the influence of concept formation on memory and retention. They recognised the importance of the formation of principles and concepts for memory retention. Conceptualising about information leads to greater retention than simply trying to remember the information itself.

Essentially, information processing involves sensory input, processing using short term and long term memory, and output through action by muscular use or mental activity. Obviously this will vary greatly from individual to individual. We see and hear things differently, thus the sensory input will vary, our information processing capacities differ, and we have differing capacities in the ability to store and use memory.

In information processing it is important to remember that the amount of sensory data depletes considerably from input, through sensory information storage, then to short term memory, and finally to long term memory. Individuals have a capacity to ingest a large amount of sensory information, and to discard or ignore irrelevant information as they process it. Should sensory input be overloaded, or distractive from the main message, individuals will filter out factors of interest (which may or may not be relevant), or be unable to distinguish between relevant information (this probably gives rise to acronyms such as the KIS, Keep It Simple, concept in communication).

Both short and long term memory will fade through distortion, decay, suppression or interference. Distortion theory suggests that experiencing a number of similar events will lead to forgetting a specific event. A person who experiences a range of floods for example, may have difficulty recalling the specific details of one particular flood. Conversely, a unique experience is least likely to be forgotten because interference is not likely. Forgetting through decay (or fading) suggests that events that are not brought to mind or repeated frequently will not be remembered. Suppression theory suggests that people forget unpleasant events more easily (unless they are particularly remarkable). For example, most events we remember from our childhood are pleasant. Interference suggests that learning will be affected by either previous or subsequent learning, especially if there is a contradiction. This may be particularly relevant from the point of view of changing beliefs and attitudes about risk and hazards on the part of people with previous experiences.

Models of Communication

Effective communication means effective learning. Most models of communication have taken an "electronic" or "engineering" perspective, and concentrate largely on encoding, transmission and decoding systems (and problems), and the associated noise which interferes with effective communication. "Noise" is not only aural, but can be perceptual, visual, or psychological. There are many models familiar to educators and trainers, and a representative example from Woodson (1966) is outlined in Figure 4.2.

While such a model is useful because it draws our attention to the problem of noise and transfer problems involved with encoding and decoding, human communication is considerably more complex. For a start, communication involves many messages travelling back and forth, often at the same time, rather than just one message travelling in one direction. Human communication processes also concern action, interaction, perception, interpretation, feelings and social relationships. Rogers' work would suggest that effective communication involves taking a "receiver-centred" approach, and that until the communicator stands in the psychological and perceptual position of the receiver, effective transfer of information and ideas will not occur.

Some basic educational principles in risk communication are:

* The source of information must have credibility, and this may mean building a climate of belief between the public and those communicating the risk.
* The education program must form part of the normal environment of the audience.
* Any information must be consistent, repeated, and the context should not contradict the message.
* The message should have meaning for the recipient, in other words it must be relevant to their needs.
* When selecting the communication "channel", use those which are respected and used by the audience. This may not mean the usual or most obvious.
* The message must take into consideration audience habits, previous experience, literacy, and current knowledge, as well as factors such as level of arousal and the time which has passed since the last message.

Models of Education

Many of us regard education as synonomous with institutions. Most of us attend institutions until at least the end of our teenage years, or a little longer in the case of higher education, and then believe ourselves to be educated. The "real world" awaits us at the end of this process.

Three major assumptions are implicit about education in this view. Firstly, education is an intensive process conducted during a relatively short time span - the period of conventional schooling. Secondly, education teaches the basis of everything for later life. This is the "banking" approach to education alluded to by educators such as Paulo Friere (1972). Basically, it suggests that a front end investment will bring later rewards. It is an approach that is common to many training courses including those concerned with disaster preparedness. The third assumption is that an institution is the paramount setting for education to take place. Like any profession, teaching aims at self-perpetuation, and it is traditionally accepted that institutions are the proper places for learning. As a result learning has come to be regarded as somewhat divorced from ordinary living, and achieved in special places that are removed from life's mainstream. This is what Lundgren

(1983) suggests is the problem of "contextualisation" - the moment the workplace and everyday life are separated from the institution problems of context, interpretation and irrelevance unavoidably creep in. In addition, formal institutionalised learning can tend to see learning as the prerogative of the institution itself, the learner as a recipient rather than active, and with a possible overemphasis on credentials rather than learning outcomes.

This is not to say that institutions do not provide meaningful learning. Much of the criticism of formal institutions comes from radical educators like Friere, who may miss the importance of institutions to systems and societies as well as just the individual, and the scholarship which emanates from gatherings of learners in a formal setting. Rather it is to say that learning is not fully effective if the institutions are paramount. Faure (1972) proposed a broad spectrum of learning activities, which he basically categorised into three types - formal, non-formal and informal. His suggestion was that if educators tapped into all three types, then education would be most effective.

Formal education is the hierarchically structured, chronologically graded "educational system", running from primary school to beyond university, and encompassing many training courses in the technical and professional area.

The formal system is what we are accustomed to - the institutionalised educational system which runs structured courses with specified entry requirements. While having the advantage of tight organisation, efficient "throughput" and a rigorous academic tradition, it may suffer from remoteness from practical issues, inflexibility and a reactive attitude towards change. Examples would include residential short courses, and credentialled learning programs over a longer time frame such as tertiary qualifications, regardless of delivery method.

Non-formal education is any organised educational activity outside the established system. It may consist of workplace gatherings, community groups, consultations, resource provision or advice.

The non-formal system is still an organised activity, but is outside the formal institutional framework. These activities tend to be non-institutionalised, specific, short cycle and flexible. Typical examples are community education courses, advisory services, and field days. While lacking the organised framework of the formal system, they may be more efficient in some respects through their closeness to community needs and their learner-centredness. They are also far less resource intensive. Examples are: advisory services; displays; awareness programmes; extension consultancies; and technical services such as hazard mapping.

Informal education consists of our day-to-day learning experiences outside the other two types, and cannot be fully structured. Typical examples are reading a newspaper, or stumbling across an historical plaque. While these examples may appear trivial or unimportant, the unstructured approach forms the greater part of our learning and is an extremely powerful medium, as advertising demonstrates.

Networking is an important tool of the informal system, and the "word-of-mouth" cannot be underestimated in terms of strength and influence. One important distinguishing feature of informal education is the lack of direct contact between teacher and learner. Examples might include: information provision through data-bases and information banks; library lending systems; information pamphlets and notes; curriculum kits; marketing programs; planning and action guides; and publications and reports

Practical models

It is useful to compare the problem of communicating risk and potential education strategies, both for risk managers and the general public, with an example such as agricultural extension, which has in the last thirty years or so made extensive use of all three modes of education. Outlining the attempts and successes which have been made in agricultural extension may provide some useful practices for possible transfer into the risk management field.

Although there are some dissimilarities between the risk management audience and the agricultural audience such as size and interests, there are many similarities, such as distance, spread and breadth of understanding. There are also many vocations in both.

While maintaining its stake in the formal system through courses with credentials in areas such as farm management and agricultural science, the extension services offered by agricultural departments follow a more pure non-formal and informal mode. Rather than institutionalising the education of personnel through courses, the system has joined the land-manager "in the field". It is not usually staffed by certificated teachers and does not use them solely for the learning experiences it provides. It is just as likely to use fellow farmers as it is to use specialists. Its learning is not confined solely to the classroom, although short pedagogical courses are offered. The classroom is often the landowner's paddock or a neighbouring property. Its method might be a field day, a consultation, a farm visit, an advisory session on a problem or a practical demonstration. In other services, it follows informal methods, such as information systems (either hard-copy or electronic), media usage (paid and unpaid) and technical back-up to problems (e.g. testing).

The aim of these approaches is to solve problems - and the system is therefore more proactive in their solution, rather

63

than simply becoming reactive and waiting for enquiry. Programme structure is centred around critical issues and problems where the performance indicators are more identifiable, rather than being centred on a series of uncoordinated educational activities.

Faure (1972) made several key points which support a broad approach. There is no mention of any one organisation having responsibility. In agriculture, agricultural departments, second-tier businesses and primary producers have an integrated role in the delivery system, thus the gap is more readily bridged between the educational establishment and the business company. This assists its proactive role in change. Information and databanks are more easily integrated into the system, assisting this change process. The use of a broad range of personnel from technical specialist to management expert to fellow farmer contributes to information sharing.

By contrast, the isolation of the risk manager is often more than geographical. An effective, broadly based risk education system would achieve maximum ends by utilising each level of the educational delivery system, in a similar way to the agricultural model. A sample extension model for risk education utilising non-formal and informal techniques is outlined in Figure 4.3.

Risk Education in Formal Education

Schools can play an important part in developing community awareness of the needs and process of risk and hazard management. This can be achieved by hazards and risk education in the context of existing school curricula. The aims of a risk education process would be to achieve in children:

* an involvement in hazard and risk identification and mitigation;
* understanding of the social and environmental impacts of hazards;
* an ability to deal personally with hazards;
* positive attitudes, appropriate skills and behaviours in community disaster preparedness, prevention, response and recovery;
* awareness of their rights and responsibilities as citizens with respect to hazard management;
* awareness of the structures in society which deal with hazards.

Valussi (1984) examined the needs for a hazard and risk education curriculum in the seismic areas of Italy on the basis that school can play an important role in raising community consciousness about hazard and risk. He concluded that students had a limited perception of the hazards which faced them and attributed this to lack of educational action.

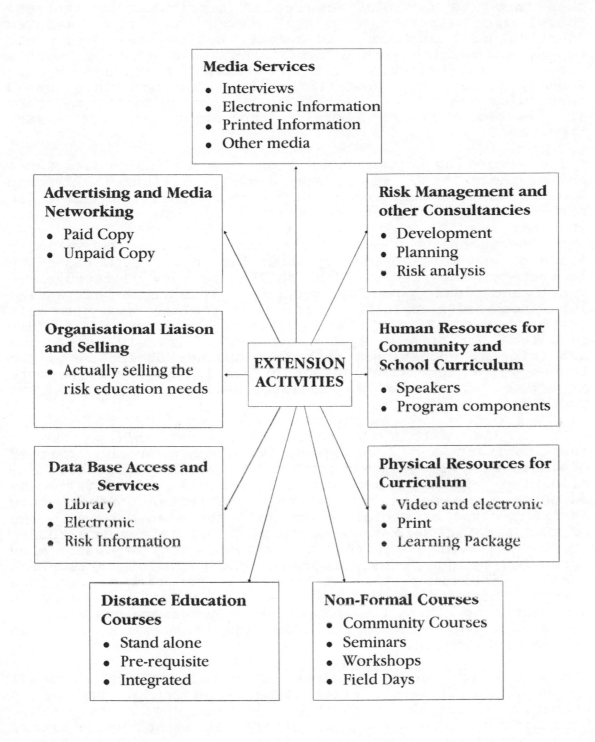

Figure 4.3: An extension model for risk education.

It is important to note however, two objections to a school based hazard and risk education. The first objection is that if hazard and risk education is to take place, it must take a contextual approach in school curriculum, rather than form its own distinct set of curriculum or content. There are already a large number of risk related "curriculums", such as road safety, health, sex, drugs and so on, with which such a curriculum would need to compete for school curriculum time. Unless risk and hazard education material contributes to existing school-based curriculum goals, it is likely to be ignored by the majority of teachers as peripheral, irrelevant or of lesser importance.

The second objection comes from more radical educational philosophers such as Friere (1972), Illich (1971) and Gramsci (1971), who argue that formal schooling serves to perpetuate and entrench the power of dominant class groups, who most use the educational system. Because those who use the educational system most are more likely to become more aware of and more advocatory about hazard and risk reduction in society, the risk could be shifted to less educated, less vocal and less powerful groups. This type of social imbalance as a result of formal schooling was the main reason behind Friere's and Illich's advocacy of a "de-schooled" educational system relying on largely non-formal and informal educational methods. Another objection is the tendency for formalisation and credentialisation to promote a degree of elitism in decision-making, limiting it to technical experts.

It is likely that the political process shifts risk to less dominant and less persuasive groups anyway, further emphasising Friere's objection to formal institution-alisation of education and its failure to assist less advantaged groups. There seems no guarantee however, that dominant class or social groups will not also make more use of and benefit more from non-formal and informal methods. It is worthwhile noting that attempts to evaluate many extension or non-formal programmes in terms of bottom-line change, including the agricultural programmes outlined earlier, have often foundered because of the difficulty in demonstrating that the educational programme caused the measured effect. As well, measuring behaviour change has proved problematic.

However, it can be concluded that reliance on a formal system for efficiency, effectiveness and social justice is probably also likely to fail. There is a reasonable possibility that populations who inhabit hazard prone areas, such as floodplains, will tend to use the formal institutionalised system less (Handmer 1984), and therefore stand to benefit most from non-formal educational programmes. A multi-strategy approach, utilising formal, non-formal and informal methods is most likely to bring rewards.

References

Ausubel, D.P. (1963) *The Psychology of Meaningful Verbal Learning*. Grune and Stratton: New York.

Ausubel, D.P. (1968) *Educational Psychology: A Cognitive View*. Holt, Rinehart and Winston: New York.

Bandura, A. and Walters, R. (1963) *Social Learning and Personality Development*. Holt, Rinehart and Winston: New York.

Bloom, B.S. et al (eds) (1956) *Taxonomy of Educational Objectives, Handbook I, Cognitive Domain*. Longman: London.

Bloom, B.S., Krathwohl, D.R. and Masia, B.B. (1956) *Taxonomy of Educational Objectives, Handbook II, Affective Domain*. Longman: London.

Bruner, J.S. (1965) *The Process of Education*. Harvard University Press: Cambridge, Massachusetts.

Bruner, J.S. (1966) *Towards a Theory of Instruction*. Harvard University Press: Cambridge, Masssachusetts.

Bruner, J.S. (1974) *Beyond the Information Given*. George Allen and Unwin: London.

Faure, E. (ed) (1972) *Learning to be: The World of Education Today and Tomorrow*. Unesco: Paris.

Friere, P. (1972) *Pedagogy of the Oppressed*. Penguin, Harmondsworth: Middlesex.

Gagne, R.M. (1965) *The Conditions of Learning*. Holt, Rinehart and Winston: New York.

Gramsci, A. (1971) *Selections from the Prison Notebooks of Antonio Gramsci*. (edited and translated by Hoare, Q. and Nowell Smith, G.), Lawrence and Wishart: London.

Handmer, J.W. (1984) *Property Acquisition for Flood Damage Reduction*. Final Report Australian Water Resources Council Research Project 1980/123. Canberra: Department of Resources and Energy.

Herzberg, F. (1966) *Work and the Nature of Man*. World Publishing: Cleveland, Ohio.

Illich, I.D. (1971) *Deschooling Society*. Calder and Boyars: London.

Knowles, M.S. (1970) *The Modern Practice of Adult Education*. Associated Press: New York.

Knowles, M.S. (1984) *The Adult Learner: A Neglected Species*. (3rd ed), Gulf: Houston.

Lundgren, U. (1983) *Between Hope and Happening: Text and Context in Curriculum*. Deakin University Press: Victoria, Australia.

Maslow, A.H. (1970) *Motivation and Personality*. (2nd ed), Harper and Row: New York.

Pavlov, I.P. (1927) *Conditioned Reflexes*. Oxford University Press: London.

Rogers, C.R. (1951) *Client-Centred Therapy*. Houghton Mifflin: Boston.

Rogers, C.R. (1969) *Freedom to Learn*. Charles E. Merrill, Columbus: Ohio.

Romiszowski, A.J. (1981) *Designing Instructional Systems*. Kogan Page: London.

Sears, R.R., Maccoby, E.P. and Lewin, H. (1957) *Patterns of Child Rearing*. Row Peterson: Illinois.

Skinner, B.F. (1953) *Science and Human Behaviour*.
    MacMillan: New York.
Skinner, B.F. (1968) *Technology of Teaching*. Prentice-
    Hall, Englewood Cliffs: New Jersey.
Skinner, B.F. (1972) *Beyond Freedom and Dignity*. Jonathan
    Cape: London.
Valussi, G. (1984) The Perception of Hazards in
    Geographical Education: Research Methods. in Graves,
    N.J. (ed), *Research and Research Methods in Geographical
    Education*. University of London Institute of Education:
    London.
Woodson, T. (1966) *Introduction to Engineering Design*.
    McGraw Hill: New York.

Section Summary II
The Psychology of Risk Communication

The three papers in this section provide a theoretical basis
for many of the empirical findings reported later in this
volume. The section has concentrated primarily on the
individual, the "micro" level of the risk communication
model set out in Chapter 1. Various problems, theories, and
approaches to changing beliefs, attitudes and behaviour are
canvassed. They deal with both "long-term" preparedness and
warnings requiring rapid response.

A dominant impression is that effecting real change to
beliefs, attitudes or behaviour is very difficult. Attitude
change alone (which is all that most studies attempt to
measure), will not necessarily affect behaviour as it is
subject to many influences largely beyond individual
control. Obtaining appropriate behaviour without attitude
change may be only partially effective; Wilson illustrates
this with the example of car driving and the associated
penalties.

Even the simple imparting of information, which we as risk
managers may regard as essential for people's well being,
confronts a series of psychological defences. These
defences may appear as defects in people's perception, and
as barriers to be conquered. Yet, given that people's main
objective may be to minimise stress, as Green suggests, such
defences are necessary armour: to enable people to cope with
threats they can do nothing about and to reduce feelings of
powerlessness or helplessness; to leave them free to
concentrate on the immediate problems and risks of day-to-
day living; to protect them from information overload; and
to enable them to deal with ambiguities and other problems

inherent in, or raised by the information, such as conflicts with other evidence.

Beliefs

Beliefs and the value systems which underlie our attitudes and have a substantial influence on our behaviour are characterised by resistance to change. Marks and Green described this inertia, aspects of which have been well documented since the 1940s (Hyman and Sheatsley 1947). People will tend to seek out information that is consistent with their beliefs and to ignore other material. Evidence is interpreted to fit in with expectations - as it is in much scientific endeavour (Amsterdamski 1975, Kuhn 1970; Gough 1988, offers a specific example of the interpretation of survey data). Information may be rejected or suppressed if it is thought likely to create emotional or financial difficulties for the people concerned, such as living in a high risk area and being unable to do anything about it, or admitting that your property is worth rather less than you thought because of publicity about the flood hazard.

Belief structures are extremely complex, and attitudes on one topic may be tied to attitudes or beliefs in areas apparently unrelated at first sight. In risk perception this may manifest itself in quite different attitudes to natural and technological hazards. In turn, these attitudes may be related to religious beliefs, questions of fairness and choice, and to attitudes towards nature, modern technology, authority, commercial organisations and government. Thus, following an evacuation order by the police, some people may comply out of deference to the authorities. Others, who may be convinced of the seriousness of the situation, may be reluctant to evacuate simply because the order came from the police. Green provides another illustrative example: people may believe that individuals choose to live by the sea or on a floodplain and accept the risk of flooding, but do not believe that the risk of being flooded as a result of a technological failure, such as a dam, is acceptable. In terms of warnings and preparedness programmes this suggests that success or failure may in part hinge on the relevant organisation's image for some quite different function.

Taken together, an individual's total set of beliefs constitutes his or her "world view" or outlook. "World views" act as powerful filters for all information, whatever its source. Tuan (1974), Buttimer (1984), and Douglas (1985) among others, have explored these issues in detail. Accepting this, we can see that each individual will have a unique world view, even if only slightly different from those held by others. Individual uniqueness is a concept developed by phenomenologists like Rogers (1969), who argue that the way people see the world and respond to it is a result of the interaction of their individual personalities and experiences.

The critical implication of this theorising for risk communication is that the public is not a uniform homogeneous mass and should not be treated as such. Chapters later in the volume describing case studies provide empirical verification of this point.

Barriers to persuasion

The risk communication message, which may be a vital warning, must generally compete for people's attention with a vast amount of other information.

Information is not a scarce commodity in modern industrialised societies. However, attention is scarce, and it is people's attention that we seek. In fact, information may be seen as being in oversupply (Smithson 1988). Members of such societies are generally proficient at screening out messages seen as not directly relevant to their needs. As the information supply increases, people naturally find that they are forced to become more selective and construct simplified views of reality (Perrow 1984); a process well documented for aircraft pilots, air traffic controllers, and nuclear power-plant control room operators.

Under such circumstances material about a relatively uncertain threat may scarcely be noticed. Risk perception studies over the last decade demonstrate that social risks and problems with careers, mortgages, families, traffic, neighbourhood crime, and toxic waste tend to dominate people's thinking where risk is concerned. Communications about floods and earthquakes for example, will generally be considered only after these more pressing daily concerns are dealt with. This is not to say that there are not occasions when people actively seek information on a particular topic. Then an information vacuum may exist - we return to this point below.

In addition, people are subject to a continual stream of often well presented commercial and non-profit advertising. Not only does this compete for their attention, but the process of habituation may mean that messages on a particular medium, for example television, are relatively ineffective. Through habituation we learn not to respond to trivial and unimportant stimuli:

> Paying too much attention to phantom threats is bad for two reasons....A state of high arousal should occur only rarely. Second, you may become so occupied with unreal dangers that you neglect the real dangers. (Buss 1978).

The process may be seen as the waning or disappearance of a natural response to a stimulus, such as the adaptation to aircraft noise by those living near airports (Quinnell 1981).

Assuming that the problem of competing information can be overcome, the risk messages have to survive the filtering process mentioned above as well as the specific psychological defences discussed in this section of the volume: denial, rationalisation, dissociation, and personal invulnerability. These processes all place limits on human information processing especially when risk are involved.

The converse of personal invulnerability, "learned helplessness", may also create problems for risk communication. People may feel that they can do little about their situation, so there is no point trying. For example, communications directed up the hierarchy in most organisations are severely inhibited by fear of punishment. It is largely for this reason that the apparently successful US Aviation Safety Reporting System is completely anonymous (Tompkins 1987)

We reiterate that generally these mechanisms do not indicate irrationality, but are effective means of coping passively rather than actively. Hazards research has largely ignored passive approaches.

Overcoming psychological resistance to persuasion

Clearly, the information must be seen to be relevant and credible. Message timing, mode of delivery, source and content will all have a bearing on successful communication - issues that are taken up in detail in Section V of this volume.

It appears that people are quite likely to ignore much information on risks, except when the desire to know is present. In his review, Wilson points out that arousal theory suggests that the best time to provide information would be during or immediately after an occurrence of the particular hazard. Salience would be high and the information seen as desirable. This is the "teachable moment" discussed by Filderman in Chapter 12 and elsewhere in this volume. At this critical period people have specific problems, which may be of an emotional rather than practical nature, and are seeking information to help solve them. The problem solving need should also be kept in mind when devising message delivery and content, as people are unlikely to be seeking information for its own sake.

The most common delivery mode for "official" risk communication is the mass media. Yet the successful ISIS anti-smoking campaign described by Marks, and points raised by other authors, suggest that personal contact is the more effective approach. In fact, a recent review by McGuire (1985) argues that there is little evidence that the mass media are effective persuaders. Personal contact, either at the individual or small group levels, helps to overcome some of the barriers to risk messages; in particular a reasonable degree of attention will exist - the receiver has to acknowledge the message. Importantly, it also provides the opportunity for instant feedback and for the message to be personalised; enabling, in theory at least, the message deliverer to focus on the individual concerns of members of the target audience. The approach is learner-oriented in the sense of informal education as described by Wilson. It has been extensively employed by religious and political groups (Brown 1963), but has been used little by commercial or risk communication authorities.

"Official" was emphasised above because a major mechanism for learning beliefs and behaviour appears to be role modelling - learning by example or imitation - much of which occurs without conscious effort. Risk information from official sources would appear to play a minor role. Buss (1978) discusses the major determinants of imitation for both the model and imitator. Quinnell (1981) examines the application of these to flood hazard management, and suggests that the:

> observed responses of competent, powerful or attractive models like civic leaders, police and others to flood risk may be critical in determining an appropriate response by floodplain residents.

The commercial world attempts to exploit this in "lifestyle" advertising campaigns, where the advertised product is associated with some desirable social situation (which has nothing to do with the product).

This relates to the need for the information to have a context or location within the individual's mind. Information without context is difficult to absorb. Consider the following passage:

> The procedure is actually quite simple. First you arrange things into different groups. Of course, one pile may be sufficient depending on how much there is to do. If you have to go somewhere else due to lack of facilities that is the next step...(Rummelhart 1977).

This extract would be more understandable if it had been preceded by a statement that it was about washing clothes. Also, in experiments subjects remember nearly twice as much of the passage when they are given such a statement before seeing the passage (Quinnell 1981).

Thus, in the absence of proper context or prior knowledge on the subject, warnings or messages intended to raise preparedness may be as incomprehensible as the above instructions for washing clothes. In this situation information may be placed in other contexts seen as relevant or not absorbed at all. Thus material on nuclear energy may be categorised with nuclear war. It may be necessary to compose messages to take advantage of contexts familiar to the target audience. This important point is expanded on later by Wilkins in Chapter 5.

The content of the message should be positive and say what to do as specifically and clearly as possible. This last point is to attempt to satisfy the "vividness" requirement of Marks. It should invite activity and sociability, rather than passivity. Telling people not to do something is likely to be less effective. The message should go beyond giving facts. Those formulating it need to consider the emotional and attitudinal aspects as well; for example, people may be seeking information for reassurance.

The message source must be perceived as credible. This point is returned to later in the volume, but is an increasingly difficult problem in societies where there is increasing distrust of government instrumentalities and large corporations. Credibility may be particularly problematic where technological, as opposed to natural, hazards are involved. The communicator may be seen as responsible for creating the risk and imposing it on a population who can see no benefit from the activity.

Concluding comment

This section has dealt with some of the processes in people's minds that are directly relevant to coping with information on risks. All three chapters acknowledge the importance of the social context - the subject of the next section. For convenience the social context can be termed the "macro" level or factors in risk communication, and the subject of this section the "micro" level or factors.

References

Amsterdamski, S. (1975) *Between Experience and Metaphysics*. D. Reidel: Dordrecht.

Brown, J.A.C. (1963) *Techniques of Persuasion*. Pelican.

Buss, A. (1978) *Behaviour in Perspective*. John Wiley and Sons: New York.

Buttimer, A. (1984) Perception in four keys: a commentary. in Saarinen, T. F., Seamon, D., and Sell, J. L. (eds) *Environmental Perception and Behavior*. Dept of Geography, Uni. of Chicago (Research Paper 209). pp 251-263.

Douglas, M. (1985) *Risk Acceptability According to the Social Sciences*. Routledge and Kegan Paul: London.

Gough, N. (1988) Children's images of the future: their meaning and their implications for school curricula. Presented at the *ANZAAS Centenary Congress*: Sydney.

Hyman, H.H. and Sheatsley, P.B. (1947) Some reasons why information programs fail. *Public Opinion Quarterly*. Vol 11(Fall), pp 412-423.

Kuhn, T. S. (1970) *The Structure of Scientific Revolutions*. (2nd edition). Univ of Chicago Press: Chicago.

McGuire, W.J. (1985) The myth of massive media effect: savagings and salvagings. *Public Communication and Behavior*. Vol 1, pp 173-257.

Perrow, C. (1984) *Normal Accidents*. Basic Books: New York.

Quinnell, A.L. (1981) Human information processing of flood risk. *Proceedings of the floodplain management conference*. Australian Water Resources Council. AGPS: Canberra. pp 303-315.

Rogers, C.R. (1969) *Freedom to Learn*. Charles E. Merrill: Columbus, Ohio.

Rumelhart, D. (1977) *Introduction to Human Information Processing*. John Wiley and Sons: New York.

Smithson, M. (1988) Personal communication. Department of Behavioural Sciences, James Cook University of North Queensland: Townsville.

Tompkins, R.K. (1987) On risk communication as inter-organisational control: the case of the aviation safety reporting system. Paper at *Colloquy on Natural and Technological Hazards*. University of Colorado: Boulder.

Tuan, Y.F. (1974) *Topophilia: a Study of Environmental Perception, Attitudes and Values*. Prentice Hall: New Jersey.

SECTION III
THE CONTEXT OF PERSUASION

5   The Political Amplification of Risk: Media Coverage of Disasters and Hazards

Lee Wilkins and P. Patterson

Abstract

Risk, and the assumption of risk, is a political as well as a scientific and technological problem. However, media coverage of hazards and risks often portrays the politics of the issue in a stereotypical dramatic fashion, relying on a series of culturally understood "scripts" to explain a series of complex social, scientific and political problems. Instead, literature from the hazards community suggests a taxonomy of risk and disasters in which politics plays a central role in mitigation and mobilisation strategies. Media coverage of many of these problems is probably most effective after rather than before event onset. Media stories, instead of relying on existing stereotypes, should adopt "schemas" from more traditional political coverage. These schemas should be applied to stories about risk and individual and governmental decisions regulating it. Only then can citizens of a democracy become well informed about the political choices that risk entails.

Introduction

In the late twentieth century, risk has become big news. For most of the past ten years, stories about risk - for example the Challenger explosion, famine in Ethopia, or the chemical leak at Bhopal, India - have topped the news agenda not for the day or the week, but for the year.

But, they are stories with a peculiar twist. Scientists, and many of those involved in the field of natural hazards, have insisted that the media has a responsibility to provide warning and mitigation information prior to event onset. Some studies (see for example Saarinen 1982, Ledingham and Masel-Walters 1985, Turner et al 1986) indicate that the media do provide such information. But others, primarily those who are involved in the field of risk and risk analysis, and those who deal with technological hazards, are more equivocal. Slovic (1985) has postulated the media play a significant role in "social amplification" - a process where a variety of cues exaggerate some risks, particularly low-probability events. Scholarly studies (see for example Nimmo and Combs 1983, 1985, Turner et al 1986, Wilkins 1987) support this view as well. Thus, most scholars agree that the media have some social responsibility to warn the public of impending dangers, whether natural or technological, but how the media interpret that responsibility has not yet been precisely described (Slovic 1985).

There is a more radical tack. When risky systems, particularly relatively low probability risk, become news stories, the "ideal"media activity may well begin *after*, not *before*, the event. The goal of such news coverage should be to raise salient issues at a time when people are more likely to pay attention to such information and to be willing to act on it. The mass media's role thus becomes one of political amplification: the framing of risks as political questions, that is defining risk as a series of choices between costs and benefits in which the public should have some say.

This chapter will meld three distinct areas of research within the framework of political amplification. First, a review of media performance in crises will provide some insight into the political story the media often tell about risky systems. Second, an overview of one fundamental problem in media coverage of risk coupled with a taxonomy of disaster and risk which shows how politics remains a central component of risk. Third, the chapter concludes with a proposal for how the media - through covering risk as politics - can improve their own performance.

Media coverage of disasters

Lippmann claimed that "the hardest thing to report is chaos" (1949, p215). As difficult as chaos is to report, it is even more difficult to predict. The typical role of the media in a crisis is to report on the aftermath - much like reporting that the sky has fallen after the fact rather than warning that the event is about to happen.

Several factors make disasters and risk difficult stories to report. First, disasters and risky systems are complex. Reporters and editors are often ill-equipped to cover the complexities of a disaster such as a disabled nuclear reactor, or a potential hazard such as the "greenhouse effect". Perrow uses the term "negative synergy" to explain complex and interactive effects of systems that even the designers do not understand (1984).

Secondly, disasters and risky systems require context. Crises are often the result of political and economic decisions as well as societal imperatives put into effect decades before the actual crisis occurs. Recounting this context takes time and space, a precious commodity in news.

Thirdly, it's a risky age. Any reporting of technology, and of the inevitable technological accidents, is affected by the human desire to feel safe in a highly unsafe world. Nelkin suggests that press coverage of technological developments "play on and probably encourages the public's desire for easy solutions to economic, social and medical problems" (Nelkin 1987, p51).

Given these difficulties most news stories about technological failure, therefore, are based on the often unarticulated cultural premise that society cannot abandon the benefits of modern technology, even when it fails (Perrow 1986). Faced with the problem of covering complex and unexpected disasters on an increasingly frequent basis, the media have fashioned several institutional strategies to cope with the unexpected (Patterson and Wilkins 1988). Schlesinger (1978) found that the BBC (British Broadcasting Corporation), "tamed" the world to meet the production needs of the medium. Tuchman (1978) calls it "routinising the unexpected" - the tendency of the media to report extraordinary stories in an ordinary manner.

Regardless of the label, when disaster strikes the media will rely on scripted behaviour to fit unpredictable events into the pattern called "news". The scripts include portraying the event first as melodrama, then as a mystery, and finally turning the story into a moral fable or myth.

Disasters as melodrama

From onset, the media will emphasize the dramatic nature of a disaster. Controversy, pathos and fear of the unknown will top the story, meeting television's visual imperative and the print reporter's need to humanise events. The television drama of Chernobyl was accomplished by juxtaposition of contrasting visual images or metaphors. Reports of children being forced to swallow iodine or forego contaminated milk followed reports of Soviet pronouncements of safety. Footage of atomic explosions was placed side by side with footage of reactors. All this created a drama: the conflict between risks assumed, sometimes unknowingly, for the benefits received.

Given the time and space constraints of the media, the melodrama of a disaster is often told through stereotypes. The chemical disaster in Bhopal, India in 1984, was played on television and in print as a series of stereotypes (Wilkins 1987). Among these stereotypes was the image of India as a backward, third world country in need of western technology - but unable to control it. Victims themselves can be a form of shorthand to allow the media to convey quickly the human tragedy of the disaster. Through this journalistic device, complex accidents are reduced to human suffering, as Bhopal and Chernobyl were often reduced to the dead - or erroneous reports of the dead - and injured. Such reports imply rather than articulate risk.

But the drama lingers for only the first few days after the event. For the story to continue at the top of the news agenda, it will usually evolve into a second genre - the mystery - in which government actions play a significant role.

Disasters as mystery

Soon after the event, media stories will begin focusing almost entirely on the search for the cause of the tragedy. In the case of natural disasters, such as earthquakes and tornados, the atmospheric and geological causes are known almost immediately, and this phase of reporting is rather perfunctory. However, in the case of a complex technological disaster or risky system the search for a cause is more prolonged.

But, the media as well as cultural imperatives demand there should be a tangible technological flaw or human error to blame for a disaster, what Ellul has termed the "technological fix" (Ellul 1965). This institutional and cultural constraint renders the journalistic search for a cause superficial, focusing almost entirely on short-term issues rather than long-term policy questions. The minimal analytic reporting conducted by a variety of news outlets after the Bhopal disaster focused on the technological problems at the plant, relegating the social, economic and political decisions that made the plant possible to a minor role. For instance, the economic demands by the Indian government to make the Bhopal plant labour intensive - thus forcing it to be constructed without a computerised warning system - were never mentioned in most media outlets and given only brief attention in *New York Times* investigations (Wilkins 1987).

Virtually all of the network television reporting of Chernobyl focused on similar technological questions: graphite moderation and lack of containment. The Soviet political decision making process or the economic imperatives that led to the design were not mentioned. In addition, television coverage failed to analyse the economics or ethics of the Soviet decision to locate plants near municipalities to obtain the added benefit of steam heat from the generator. Furthermore, these problems were isolated within a Soviet context; readers and viewers were never reminded that other countries, including the United States, had made similar trade-offs for similar reasons (Wilkins and Patterson 1987).

While the Challenger explosion was a drama for seconds, it was a mystery for months. First the media focused on the faulty "o-rings". Then the focus of the mystery shifted to "who allowed the potentially defective shuttle to take off", a question which was ultimately solved as a human failure within a too highly bureaucratised decision-making system. Challenger became a "whodunnit" in the media more often than an analytic look at the system that produced the problem.

Such a view, of course, omits any longer-term discussion of policy and politics. Indeed, once media reports fix on the "culprit", the institutional and cultural demands are met, and the media's role changes from investigator to propagandist. The story shifts from a mystery to a fable - an attempt to place the event within an existing cultural pattern.

Disasters as fables.

Although reports of faulty valves at Chernobyl or disengaged safety systems at Bhopal are important, disaster stories will remain salient to journalists only if they take on a more universal theme. While the initial reporting of the tragedy performs the important surveillance function, the moral play helps to correlate response to the tragedy (Lasswell 1958). Engler suggests that the moral plays can have social utilitarian value when he notes, "thousands will not have died in vain if multinationals now build safer plants" (1985, p488). Chernobyl, for instance, became a story of Russian secrecy and United States openness. Bhopal became a story of greedy American capitalism and the vulnerability of third world nations. And Challenger became a platform for the virtues of "responsible capitalism" and "altruistic democracy" (Gans 1979).

Reinterpretations of the cultural meaning ascribed to events also permeate disaster and risk coverage. The Bhopal and Chernobyl stories became not only a recounting of the events in India and the Ukraine, but also a recounting of the social extinction myth which has persisted in western culture at least since biblical times. Chernobyl and Bhopal help to reconstruct the myth, for in both instances it was deliberate government policy to assume a set of risks which underwrote the tragedy.

Thus, while the media play an important role in signalising a disaster, the truly long-range impact may be the effect coverage can have on policy after the story has developed into a moral play. Lasswell, in his formulation of political choice, noted:

> Politics is the study of the changing value hierarchy, the pyramids of safety, income and deference ... (and) the larger problem of discovering the actual significance which can be attached to them in redefining the value pyramid (Lasswell 1965, p158).

The moral play of traditional media coverage of disasters is relatively clear; corporate income and government safety appear as values in news reports; individual safety and the deference which underlies it are much less potent political forces.

The fundamental attribution error

While the foregoing tendencies may be ascribed to the failings of various institutions and the individuals who work for them, there is a more fundamental problem with reporting risk: the definition of news itself which mirrors a fundamental cognitive problem in the initial stages of risk analysis (Fischhoff 1984). Central to this error is "...the tendency to attribute too much responsibility to people for their actions and too little to the social and environmental constraints shaping those behaviours" (Fischhoff 1984, p15). This is what psychologists call the fundamental attribution error. The error arises when risky situations are "new", when the entire system is not subjected to analysis, and when the language used to express potential risk lacks precision.

By definition, news accounts of disasters or risky systems are apt to include the fundamental attribution error by focusing on the visible and dramatic aspects of a story. Car accidents, the product of a well known risky system, seldom become major news stories while Bhopal and Chernobyl did. The technological accidents became news because they were novel: Bhopal was the worst industrial accident in human history, and Chernobyl the worst publicly reported nuclear accident. The novelty itself means that the events lack context, both for journalists and for their readers and viewers. Without that context framing risk becomes exceptionally difficult (Altheide 1976).

Because news is event centred, it seldom includes models of the entire system. Expert analysis of risk relies on tools such as "fault trees" and "risk lists", and journalists have been urged to incorporate such a contextual frame in their reporting (Fischhoff 1985). Unfortunately, proper use of such tools requires training, and journalists - who are generalists by profession - tend to eschew both scientists and the often highly technical and equivocal language of science (Friedman et al 1985, Nelkin 1987). Further, journalists tend not only to simplify risks but also to dichotomise them (Sandman 1986). If there is no immediate risk, or more correctly no event-centred risk, then there is no story. What would be considered a "normal accident" (Perrow 1981, 1984, 1986) to the professional eng-aged in risk analysis, becomes the Challenger "catastrophe" on the nightly television report. Bhopal, however, does not become a symptom of a world-wide industrial disease.

Technical innovations in writing and reporting, such as the use of fault trees, could solve some of the immediate problems. However, they would not address the larger cultural milieu of science coverage, one which includes the notion of "selling science" or at least the concept of scientific progress (Nelkin 1987). As indicated above, scholarly studies of media reports on a variety of disasters (Quarantelli 1981, Nimmo and Combs 1985, Cochran 1986, Wilkins 1986, 1987, and Patterson and Wilkins 1988), indicated that media reports substitute a specific cultural and dramatic frame for what others have viewed as primarily a technical problem (Perrow 1984, 1986). The dramatic and stereotyped framework, because it omits most of the technical discussion particularly as it applies to risk, produces a skewed view of the problem.

Because the mathematical language of risk analysis is not readily translated into words and pictures free of cultural and emotional overtones (Douglas and Wildavsky 1982, Nelkin 1987), the analytical representation of risk itself becomes problematic in any journalistic endeavour. The pictures of Bhopal (Wilkins 1987) and Chernobyl (Wilkins and Patterson 1987) portrayed the risks of the two events as what Fischhoff et al (1981) have characterised as the "dread risks". These visual cues, close-ups of infants as they were buried or glowing clouds of animated gas moving from one place to another on the television screen, contained few qualifiers. Minimally, such messages lack context. Maximally, they may provide a vividly memorable portrait of pervasive and uncontrollable risk.

Thus, news and risk communication are, at some central levels, very much at odds with one another. News is event centred. But risk, particularly technological risk, is often systemic. Media coverage of hazards often relies on the conventions of storytelling, among them character, plot and drama. The assumption of collective societal risk, on the other hand, is founded in analysis. In short, traditional news is reactive and prescriptive, while proper risk communication should be proactive and preventive.

The issue for the mass media then, becomes one of equalising two functions of communication. News reporters need not only to learn how better to signal a risky event, but also how to educate the public to adapt to it.

A taxonomy of disasters and risks

Journalists are more familiar with some risks than others. While the Bhopal and Chernobyl disasters are unusual by any standard, tornados, hurricanes and some forms of techno-logical hazards - for example aircraft crashes and more minor chemical spills - are becoming increasingly common journalistic fare. In fact, a disaster continuum appears to have developed in terms of the media's ability to convey risks before a disaster, and to interpret causes after a disaster.

"Transparent" disasters and risks

At the far end of this continuum are those disasters which are "transparent": familiar and observable disasters with familiar causes, such as floods or tornados (Table 5.1). Because of their familiarity, reporting of these disasters will focus on "where", "when" and to "whom" the disaster happened. The risk of these transparent disasters is both quantifiable and forecastable. To some extent such disasters can be mitigated even before they occur. While news reports of these events may be based on the fundamental attribution error, it is less likely to dominate accounts of these known and somewhat quantifiable risks. Media reports of such disasters will more closely reflect "expert" analysis. The major political imperative of transparent disasters is preparedness, and often the media plays a role in helping a community to obtain assistance.

"Translucent" disasters and risks

Next on the continuum are "translucent" disasters: familiar and observable disasters with an unknown cause or an untimely onset, such as aircraft crashes and earthquakes. The focus of reporting on these disasters will be the on the "why" questions, since a familiar risky system has behaved in an unfamiliar manner, such as an airliner which crashes or a faultline which shifts.

If past media performance is any indication (see for example Wilkins 1985), the fundamental attribution error will permeate reports of translucent disasters to a significant degree. Translucent risks will be framed in terms of institutional or corporate preparedness, with specific institutions and sometimes individuals held responsible. Systemic analysis will be the focus of only a small portion of the coverage.

Thus, risks of these translucent disasters will be personalised in media amounts, and institutional analysis will be almost absent. Though translucent disasters can be mitigated - albeit expensively and litigiously - the ultimate mediated political question is the trade-off between maximum individual safety and maximum individual benefit, with little regard for the larger social issues such events often raise.

"Opaque" disasters and risks

On the other end of the continuum are the "opaque" disasters: those disasters which are neither familiar nor observable, such as nuclear plant meltdowns or the "greenhouse effect". Risk analysis has characterised "opaque" disasters as low-probability events. The focus of reporting in these disasters will be on the "how" question - trying to find out what forces interacted to cause the system to balk (see Kates 1985, for a discussion of "elusive" hazards) The risk of opaque disasters can be neither quantified nor forecast although experts attempt

Table 5.1

Taxonomy of risks and disasters

	TRANSPARENT	TRANSLUCENT	OPAQUE
SCIENCE			
FAMILIAR SCENARIO	yes	usually	rarely
FAMILIAR CAUSE	yes	sometimes	rarely
TRIGGERED BY	random natural forces	unknown forces human error	interactive processes
RISK QUANTIFIABLE	yes	yes	rough estimates
NEWS			
MAJOR NEWS QUESTION	what, where	why	how
INTERPRETABLE	yes	rarely	no
FUNDAMENTAL ATTRIBUTION ERROR	present and appropriate	present but requires added analysis	inappropriately dominates news stories
POLITICS			
SOLUTION PROPOSED	reconstruction	regulations	prohibitions or regulations
ROLE OF POLITICS	prepare	mitigate	obfuscate/ mobilise
ROLE OF INDIVIDUAL vs ROLE OF STATE	individual action effective; state supports	individual ineffective without state	trans-national action necessary
CENTRAL POLITICAL QUESTION	how effective is government	how expensive is safe	how fair is safe

such analysis, (Fischhoff et al 1981). Even attempts at mitigation are subject to a host of political, social and complex scientific forces.

Reports of such disasters, if indeed they even make the news agenda, will be enormously subject to the fundamental error of attribution. Bhopal thus becomes a contest between the Indian government and Union Carbide, while Chernobyl is reduced to a propaganda battle between two superpowers (Ellul 1964). In both instances, underlying political and social problems, which carry their own set of risks, were largely ignored - at least by the news media. This journalistic willingness to mediate the political reality (Nimmo and Combs 1983), prompted by long-held definitions of news and behaviour patterns, in turn, allows government a great deal of latitude in how it chooses to interpret various events.

A government's goal in "opaque" disasters may range along a continuum from diffusion of political debate on controversial issues to summoning an appropriate public response. In his best selling book *And the band played on*, AIDS reporter Randy Shilts notes that the state government of New York used a diffusion strategy during the early years of the AIDS epidemic in that state. This was in the hope of, among other things, averting general panic and placing a strain on state political and budgetary resources (Shilts 1987). On the other hand, government may wish to encourage some public actions, for example a reduction in fossil fuel consumption, as one possible mitigating influence on the "greenhouse effect". Government's goal, depending on the risk and the degree of political involvement, may be to obfuscate - the response to Chernobyl by the government of the United States - or to mobilise public opinion change, the United States' Environmental Protection Agency's publicly stated goal in dealing with toxic waste dumps (McClelland et al 1987).

But, the appropriate political goal for the public is less clear. A reasonable public goal, at least in a democracy, may be the thorough understanding of the collective trade-offs between risks assumed and benefits obtained, not only for the entire society but for well defined groups within that society. The fact that opaque disasters can be quantified or forecast in only the vaguest of scientific terms means the debate about them rightly moves into the political arena, where individual welfare can be balanced against society-wide benefits.

The political amplification of risk, and schema theory

The foregoing theoretical framework provides a pointed critique of the ability - or inability - of the mass media to convey risk information to the public. Such a critique is particularly noteworthy because it is founded on psychological theory - attribution theory - which was developed through the study of individual modes of

perception and cognition. If news about risk may be viewed
through the same theoretical frame, then it may be possible
to develop a predictive model about how mediated risk
information may be perceived by the public. Similar work,
also based on a psychological approach to cognition known as
schema theory, has already been applied to the larger issue
of political communication.

Schema theory, which was originally developed by
psychologists to explain how infants and young children come
to know and understand their world, has recently been
applied to political knowledge acquired through the news
media. A schema can be thought of, in the most simple
terms, as a primitive cognitive map - a guideline for
understanding a particular set of perceptions which enables
the individual to generalise from relatively incomplete
data. Elements in the individual analysis are not
restricted to acquisition of specific facts, but can also
include cultural understandings. In the early schema
experiments, for example, infants under the age of six
months failed to respond to pictures of a human face with
eyes and mouth transposed. Older infants reacted with a
wail - they knew something was wrong. In essence, they had
developed a schema for the human face.

Scholars now believe adults have a "broad array of schemas
that cover events that are likely to crop up in news
stories" (Graber 1984, p173). Such schemas exhibit a
limited number of dimensions, the most common being cause-
effect dimensions, the in-person dimension and institutional
dimensions. Other dimensions, for example human interest
and empathy and cultural dimensions, come into play in the
individual analysis of certain stories.

Individual schemas reveal a good deal of stereotypical
thinking. The schemas also appear to be a central element
in individual political belief systems, including strong
emotional commitment to certain symbols (Graber 1984, p173).
Schemas enable individuals to take specific news accounts
and generalise from them to larger political questions,
sometimes in one incomplete or stereotypical or emotional
fashion. But not all news is processed equally.

When people fail to learn or create appropriate schemas
for certain types of news, that news cannot be absorbed.
Socialisation of average Americans apparently leaves a
number of gaps in the schema structure. These gaps then
make it difficult to focus public attention on some
important problems. News about foreign countries and news
about science are examples. Even when such news is
presented in simple ways, much of the audience fails to make
the effort to absorb it because appropriate schemas did not
form part of past socialisation (Graber 1984, p206).

Assessment: towards improved media risk communication

The goal of risk communication should thus be to frame the risk debate, not as a scientific question, but as the political question which underlies various societal choices. Just as risk analysts have urged that risks be evaluated through use of a "decision tree", mediated reports of risk also need to emphasise the branching political and economic decisions which, ultimately produce the societal assumption of various risks.

What follows is an exploration of how the media might explain the risks and benefits of the various types of disaster, under existing or only slightly modified media standards.   This acknowledges that the fundamental attribution error is likely to remain couched with news reports and within the cognitive framework current research indicates most people apply to political questions.

"Transparent" disasters

For the transparent disasters, media portrayals of risk need to conform closely to the existing numerical analysis of various forms of risk. For example, it is possible to frame mitigation strategies for transparent hazards along more traditional political cause-effect schemas: insufficient government preparation results in an excess loss of life and property damage within a predictable time span.   Such reports would actually take advantage of the fundamental attribution error by *correctly* personalising the impact of events. For example, news accounts of a flood could link the loss of property and life with inadequate government preparation and failure to enforce floodplain regulations before the event.

Media reports utilising the human interest and empathy dimensions also could be aired and broadcast after disaster onset. The key here would be to draw parallels between those who lost lives or property through the disaster and those who did not, and to show how collective social choices have forced an unequal burden of risk on a particular population. An institutional schema could be employed as well, which would evaluate various agencies' mitigation efforts in terms of preparedness planning either before or after the event onset.

Media reports based on such schemas fit well within the traditional definitions of news while simultaneously acting in both a proactive and preventative manner. Using this concept, individual readers and viewers could fit the "simplest" form of hazards and risk into already existing political analysis schemas. The emphasis would be on the politics, not the science of the event. The goal would be an enhancement of the general level of social and political debate over risk-benefit choices, with an emphasis on the safety apex, as opposed to the income apex, of Lasswell's political value pyramid.

"Translucent" disasters

For the translucent disasters, where the goal is both mitigation and raising the salience of various risk-related issues, the media emphasis needs to be two-fold: that individual efforts can be effective; but that those individual efforts need to take effect within a larger political and cultural frame. In such a mediated explanation, mathematical risk analysis has little meaning. For example, cause-effect schemas could be used to urge individual acts of mitigation, such as the purchase of earthquake or flood insurance. Such news stories also could emphasise the human interest-empathy dimension.

Nevertheless, at least some news stories need to link individual activity to government programmes. While the individual undertakes mitigation activity through the purchase of insurance and other measures of preparedness, the chief means of government mitigation is through regulation. Thus, on the institutional level, the appropriate schemas to apply to risk stories would be agency effectiveness, government allocation of resources in various programmes, and the cost of various government programmes - if those costs are tied to benefits received.

However, the fundamental attribution error will render translucent disasters difficult for the media to report. While the schemas suggested have "positive" views in terms of disaster and risk mitigation, they are equally open to negative interpretation. For example, reporting the costs of various government mitigation programmes may be a way to enhance public perception of individual programmes and benefits, but only if government spending is not perceived as excessive and wasteful - another common institutional schema. Similarly, allocation stories may provoke a useful increase in public awareness, but only if the programmes described are not perceived as "expensive social programmes" with little individual benefit. Taken in this light, such stories may be most appropriate not *before* - but only *after* hazard onset, when the risk and its visible consequences are freshly in the public "funded memory" (Belman 1977). Mitigation of future similar disasters is the goal of such risk communication, not general preparedness for a variety of emergencies.

"Opaque" disasters

The media's role in reporting opaque disasters can perhaps best be characterised by the schemas that will not work to explain them. Chief among those is the notion of "selling science".

> The image in the press of the scientist as superstar of knowledge...(is) matched by another image - that of scientific knowledge as perhaps the most important resource of the nation (Nelkin 1987, p103).

When such an image dominates press reports, the average citizen translates it into a series of conflicting schemas. Among these are political notions about technological advances coupled with economic disruption, rising expectations, exhaustable resources, insufficient production and a cultural belief that Americans are unconcerned about the welfare of future generations. In the absence of appropriate schemas with which to process information - for example, concerning nuclear power - some people might process the information through a "nearby" existing schema - nuclear holocaust - thereby creating an inappropriate but believable individual interpretation.

Since public understanding of obviously complex issues is both simplistic and contradictory, reports about opaque risks should be couched not in numerical statements, but in a cultural and political context which frames hazard impact in terms of the structural inequities within society. For example, a structural inequity of the West is a dependence on Middle East oil which augments the need for nuclear power. Media reports of the opaque hazards of nuclear technology should deal with this fundamental fact. However, media reports of the opaque hazards are the most subject to the fundamental attribution error precisely because of humanity's limited understanding of the events. Such events translate readily into news, but not the sort of news which generally sparks political debate.

Concluding comment

Given this social and political choice, the schemas the media need to adopt are ones which raise issue salience while encouraging mobilisation. Some scholars have found that such behaviour results from stories which are issues laden (Patterson 1980) in the political sense and which build on a sense of individual efficacy (Burton et al 1978). Since current research indicates the average person is most sensitive to risks when they disturb the "status quo" (McClelland et al 1987), journalistic accounts of obscure risks are probably best tied to stories which emphasise the conflict between competing benefits and costs as well as the welfare of future generations. Such journalism is difficult to achieve.

But, the symbolic strategy (Carey 1969) of reporting these risks remains rather simple: it transforms science into a political debate. Only by emphasising the costs and benefits of various political choices - as portrayed by the inequities of assumed risk - can the public begin to develop the conceptual schemas which will encourage accurate information processing and hence increase knowledge and, for some, action. When it comes to risk, journalists need to make the trade-offs in the political value pyramid very plain.

Such reporting may have one lasting impact. Politics will mitigate more disasters, and manage more risks, than science ever could.

References

Altheide, D.L. (1976) *Creating Reality: How TV News Distorts Events*. Sage: Beverly Hills.

Belman, L. (1977) John Davy's Concept of Communication *Journal of Communication*. Vol 27, No 1, pp 29-37.

Bennett, L. (1983) *News: The Politics of Illusion*. Longman: New York.

Burton, I., Kates, R.W. and White, G.F. (1978) *The Environment as Hazard*. Oxford University Press: New York.

Carey, J.W. (1969) The Communications Revolution and the Professional Communicator. In Halmos, P. (ed), *The Sociology of Mass Media Communication*. University of Keele: UK. pp 23-38.

Cochran, F. (1986) KAL 007 and the Evil Empire: Mediated Disaster and Forms of Rationalisation. *Critical Studies in Mass Communication*. Vol 3, pp 297-316.

Douglas, M. and Wildavsky (1982) *Risk and Culture: An essay on the selection of technical and environmental dangers*. University of California Press: Berkeley.

Ellul, J. (1964) *Propaganda: the formation of men's attitudes*. Alfred A. Knopf: New York.

Ellul, J. (1965) *The Technological Society*. Alfred A. Knopf: New York.

Engler, R. (1985) Many Bhopals: Technology Out of Control. *The Nation*. April 27, pp 488-500.

Fischhoff, B. (1984) Judgemental Aspects of Risk Analysis (unpublished paper). Decision Research Inc: Eugene, Oregon.

Fischhoff, B. (1985) Protocols for Environmental Reporting: What to Ask the Experts. *The Journalist* (Winter), pp 11-15.

Fischhoff, B., Lichtenstein, S., Slovic, P., Derby, S.L. and Keeney, R.L. (1981) *Acceptable Risk*. Cambridge University Press: Cambridge.

Friedman, S.M., Dunwoody, S. and Rogers, C.L. (1985) *Scientists and Journalists: Reporting Science as News*. American Association for Advancement of Science: Washington D.C.

Gans, H.J. (1979) *Deciding What's News*. Vintage: New York.

Graber, D.A. (1984) *Processing the News*. Sage: Beverly Hills.

Kates, R.W. (1985) Success, Strain and Surprise. *Issues in Science and Technology*. Vol 2(Fall), pp 46-58.

Lasswell, H.D. (1958) The Structure and Function of Communication in Society. In Bryson (ed.) *The Communication of Ideas*. Harper and Row: New York.

Lasswell, H.D. (1965) *World political and personal insecurity*. The Free Press: New York.

Ledingham, J.A. and Masel-Walters, L. (1985) Written on the Wind: The Media and Hurricane Alicia. *Newspaper Research Journal*. Vol 6(Winter), pp 50-58.

Lippmann, W. (1949) *Public Opinion*. The Free Press: N.Y.

McClelland, G.H. et al (1987) *Improving accuracy and reducing costs of environmental benefit assessments: risk communication for superfund sites, an analysis of problems and objectives* US Environmental Protection Agency (Project Report) CR 812054-02: Washington D.C.

Nelkin, D. (1987) *Selling Science: How the Press Covers Science and Technology.* W.H. Freeman and Co: New York.

Nimmo, D. and Combs, J.E. (1983) *Mediated Political Realities.* Longman: New York.

Nimmo, D. and Combs, J.E. (1985) *Nightly Horrors: Crisis Coverage in Television Network News.* University of Tennessee Press: Knoxsville.

Patterson, P. and Wilkins, L. (1988) Reporting Chernobyl: Cutting the Government Fog to Cover the Nuclear Cloud. In Walters, Wilkins and Walters (eds.) *Bad Tidings: Communication and Catastrophe.* Lawrence Earlbaum Associates: New York.

Patterson, T. (1980) *The Mass Media Election.* Praeger: N.Y.

Perrow, C. (1981) Normal accident at Three Mile Island. *Society.* Sept/Oct, pp 17-26.

Perrow, C. (1984) *Normal Accidents: Living with High-Risk Technologies.* Basic Books: New York.

Perrow, C. (1986) The Habit of Courting Disaster. *The Nation.* October 11, pp 329 & 347.

Quarantelli, E.L. (1981) The Command Post Point of View in Local Mass Communications Systems. *Communication: Internat. J. of Communication Research.* Vol 7, pp 57-73.

Saarinen, T.E.(ed) (1982) *Perspectives on Increasing Hazard Awareness.* Institute for Behavioural Science: University of Colorado, Boulder.

Sandman, P. (1986) Explaining Risk to Non-Experts. At *Conference on Global Disasters and International Information Flow*: Annenberg Schools of Communication: Washington, D.C.

Schlesinger, P. (1978) *Putting Reality Together.* Constable and Co Ltd: London.

Shilts, R. (1987) *And the Band Played On.* St Martins Press: New York.

Slovic, P. (1985) Informing and Educating the Public about Risk. (Unpub). Decision Research Inc: Eugene, Oregon.

Tuchman, G. (1978) *Making News: A Story in the Construction of Reality.* The Free Press: New York.

Turner, R. et al (1986) *Waiting for Disaster.* University of California Press: Berkeley.

Wilkins, L. (1986) Media Coverage of the Bhopal Disaster: A Cultural Myth in the Making. *International Journal of Mass Emergencies and Disasters.* Vol 4, No 1, pp 7-34.

Wilkins, L. (1987) *Shared Vulnerability: The Media and American Perceptions of the Bhopal Disaster.* Greenwood Press: Westport, Ct.

Wilkins, L. (1985) Television and Newspaper Coverage of a Blizzard: Is the Message Helplessness? *Newspaper Research Journal.* Vol 6, No 4, pp 51-65.

Wilkins, L. and Patterson, P. (1987) Risk Analysis and the Construction of News. *Journal of Communication.* Vol 37, No 3, pp 78-90.

6 Economic Power and Response to Risk: a Case Study from India

Peter Winchester

Abstract

This chapter presents the results from a longitudinal case study of a cyclone and storm surge which occurred in south India in 1977. The findings reveal a clear and strong association between response to risk communication and socio-economic groupings in the population, and a clear difference in the perspectives of the government and the people. People's responses to the warnings were based: primarily on their assessment of what they could afford to lose and the penalties of a false alarm; partly on the "bounded" rationalisation of their past experiences with cyclones; and hardly at all on the seriousness or frequency of the warnings. There was also a positive correlation between reactions to a future hypothetical cyclone and socio-economic status. Evidence for this comes from the analysis of data from a stratified random sample of 202 households in the storm surge area (Winchester 1986).

Introduction

The assumptions of homogeneity of perception of risk, and responses to warnings, on which the forecasting and warning systems in India are currently based are misguided. They are misguided because they ignore the basic social and economic differentiations that exist within societies. The widely different perceptions of risks and the responses to warnings are based fundamentally on differential access to resources: relative wealth or poverty. This is most vividly illustrated in this case study, where most of the rich households left their houses and went to the "high ground" before the warnings of a severe cyclone and storm surge were given. The poor households stayed behind, not because they had not received the warnings, but because they could not afford to leave the area or take the risk of leaving - and thus losing - their few possessions.

The dysfunctions between blanket warning programmes and the assumptions of homogeneity resulting in varied and unpredictable responses, raise the question as to whether measures to reduce tangible damage and loss of lives might not be more effective if they were concentrated more on expansion of economic choice and self reliance (the "Thatcherite" approach), instead of relying on the development of technology and centralised disaster mitigation programmes (the "Welfare State" approach). We need to view risk communication within the socio-economic context of the target audiences, and to see that context as part of the whole disaster preparedness process including reconstruction.

In this chapter I will, first, briefly describe what occurred when a cyclone and storm surge struck the Krishna delta, South India, and the warning and preparation systems in use at the time. I will present my findings of how the people reacted and their reactions to a future hypothetical cyclone, and then contrast the problems of implementing warning systems from these people's viewpoint and that of the government. In conclusion, I will suggest how warning systems in this part of the world could be made more effective by using non-structural risk reduction measures.

The findings presented here are obviously area-specific, but it is hoped that they may have value in relation to risk communication in other parts of the world.

The cyclone and flooding of 19 November 1977

Geography of the strike area

The Krishna delta is situated about half way along the east coast of India in the state of Andhra Pradesh (Figure 6.1). The major landforms are floodplains, ancient channels, natural levees, ancient beach ridges and swales, mangrove swamps and tidal flats. About 30 per cent of the area is saline due to seasonal marine flooding on extensive areas of low lying land near the coast. This low lying land is also frequently waterlogged by flooding from watercourses and from excessive rainfall, due to poor soil drainage.

Geomorphology and flooding are the principal determinants of the settlement pattern; these are either nucleated so that more people live in relatively smaller but scattered sites in the highly fertile deltaic plain, or of the linear type which have developed along the boundaries between the deltaic plain and the natural levees (Nageswara Rao 1980). Population density is high, and in the case study area there

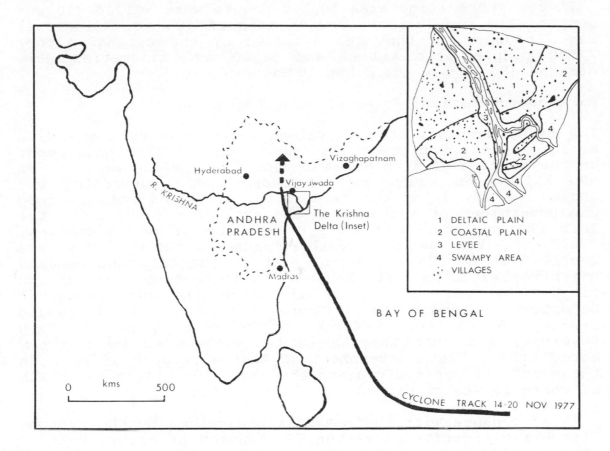

Figure 6.1:   The Krishna Delta and cyclone track of
              November 1977.

are 100 settlements at approximately 2.8 kilometre spacing
with an average population of 2,000 each.   In 1977 about
half these settlements were accessible by road for only 8
months of the year.

The population consists of farmers and landless labourers
(65 per cent), 10 per cent fishermen, 10 per cent animal
herders and 15 per cent artisans and shopkeepers.   The
principal crop is paddi (rice), harvested twice a year, the
cultivation of which accounts for about 90 per cent of the
employment in the area for 6 months each year and occupies
75 per cent of the available land.

The cyclone

The cyclone that struck on the evening of 19th November 1977
had started as a depression on the 13th November in the
south east of the Bay of Bengal (Figure 6.1).   The
depression had developed into a westward moving cyclonic
storm by the 15th November, changing direction from north-
westerly to north north-westerly on the 16th and developing
into a severe cyclonic storm by the 17th (Subbaramayya et al
1979).   The cyclone remained on that course until it struck
the coast accompanied by a storm surge 5 metres above high
tide level.

In the storm surge area 10,000 people were killed (10 per cent of the population), and an area of 600 sq. kilometres was flooded. In the area affected by the cyclone alone, 2,500 people were killed and 1,500 sq. kilometres were damaged (Raghavulu and Cohen 1979).

Risk communication: forecasting and warnings

The first warnings of the cyclone were given by the Indian Meteorological Department to the Andhra Pradesh government on the morning of 16th November when the cyclone was centred 900 kilometres south-east of Madras and approaching the coast. A day later the Meteorological Department informed the government of a change in the cyclone's course. On the 18th the cyclone, with an eye diameter of 60 kilometres, could be seen on the weather radar at Madras and was reported to be 235 kilometres east of the city and heading north westwards to a strike area 100 kilometres north of the city. By the evening of the 18th the Meteorological Department forecast that a "core of hurricane winds" would cross a 200 kilometre front on the morning of the 19th November, and that they would be accompanied by a storm surge of 3 metres (Government of Andhra Pradesh 1977). In the event the cyclone crossed the coast 100 kilometres north of where it was predicted.

In accordance with the measures prescribed by the Cyclone Distress Mitigation Committee (Government of Andhra Pradesh 1971), all the warnings from the Meteorological Department were passed on to the District Collectors in the coastal districts. These highest ranking government officials were responsible for passing on the warnings to the villages. However, contact by telephone was impossible in the more remote areas because the high winds had blown the lines down, but messages were broadcast on the radio at three hourly intervals; someone in every village has a transistor radio and the news spread rapidly. In many cases local officials were sent out on bicycles to the remote villages. The government could claim justifiably that warnings reached every village and hamlet, and that at least 90 per cent of the population had been warned at least 24 hours in advance, and in some cases 48 hours in advance, of the cyclone strike. This claim was later substantiated by my field interviews.

The high death toll could be attributed to a number of factors. One factor was undoubtedly the sheer size of the storm surge and its arrival at dusk. Another factor was the extreme physical difficulties encountered by people trying to evacuate the area; roads were swept away, trees blown down and the irrigation channels were flooded. One factor was not the lack of warning, although the government's political opponents claimed it was; they were on safer ground when they attacked the government for its failure to evacuate the exposed populations.

Table 6.1

Correlation between number of occupations,
landholding size and type of assets.

Occupation groups classified by number of occupations	Number of households	Landholding sizes[a] (in acres)				Asset types			
		>5	2.5-4.9	0.1-2.49	0	(A)	(B)	(C)	(D)
>3 (1)	18	11	6	1	–	17	1	–	–
<3 (2,3,4)	110	7	23	78	2	19	86	5	–
<2 (5)	36	–	1	35	–	2	10	18	6
<1 (6)	38	–	–	11	27	–	13	8	17
Totals	202	18	30	125	29	38	110	31	23

a/ The landholding size refers to the total amount of land held by
each occupation group and not the total number of landholdings.

Assets

(A) Income derived from hiring out, i.e. plough teams and bullock carts.
(B) Income derived from milch animals or equipment to carry on caste
occupation i.e. potter's wheel, fishing net.
(C) Consumer durables and jewellery which can be used to raise loans.
(D) Same as (3) but nil at time of interview.

Occupation groups/income

1 large farmers
2 small farmers
3 fishermen
4 petty traders; small cultivators; government officials
5 marginal farmers
6 landless

Occupation groups, wealth and losses

For the fieldwork surveys in 1981 and 1983 the 202 households interviewed were classified into six occupational groups. These groups relate to the main indicators of wealth or poverty: the number of occupations, landholding size and the types of assets (Table 6.1). In terms of relative wealth and poverty, occupation group 1 (large farmers) have incomes in the range of Rs25,000 - Rs50,000 per year (giving an approximate sterling equivalent, in 1981, of 1,750 - 3,000 pounds). Those in occupation group 2 (small farmers) have incomes from Rs15,000 - Rs25,000, occupation 3 (fishermen) Rs 7,000 - Rs25,000 and those in occupation 4 (petty traders/small cultivators /government officials) Rs5,000 - Rs25,000. The poorer groups (occupation 5: marginal farmers) have incomes of Rs5,000 - Rs15,000 per annum with occupation 6 (the landless) having only Rs2,500 - Rs7,500 per year (equivalent to 175 to 525 pounds sterling per annum).

Some of the large farmers could be said to be "rich", and apart from a handful of fishermen, they are the only group that can be so classified. Within all the other occupations there are variations; some are less "rich" or less "poor" than others. The landless and 50 per cent of the marginal farmers are definitely poor, and so are some people in the other groups, but it is not nearly as clear cut as is commonly stereotyped. The rich and the poor are not differentiated by where they live. Rich people, for instance the fishermen and some of the large farmers, live in the most exposed and dangerous places, in the so-called marginalised areas, and many poor households live in the most protected and lushest parts of the delta.

Research reported in Winchester (1986) shows that the scale of losses broadly follows the extent of wealth and ownership; loss of life was relatively higher among the poorest groups. Descriptions of these losses for typical members of these groups are given below. What is clear is that the poorer groups recovered slowly, and were critically dependent in this recovery on loans from either the banks or the richer villagers. The descriptions also highlight the diversity within the community.

Large farmer (Kapu) in the tidal flat (zone 4 in Figure 6.1). Ambati Balakrishnaiah lost nearly everything except his two children in the cyclone; however, he owned 6 acres of "patta" land and was able to raise large amounts of food for his immediate needs. Within a year of the cyclone he had acquired two milch animals and a plough team (two oxen) and a cart. He also remarried about 18 months after the cyclone.

By 1981, when first interviewed, he was still living in his octagonal concrete house, but he had built a separate kitchen and had taken over a large shelter for his plough teams and two milch animals, the materials for which had been provided by a voluntary agency. The shelter had previously been used as the village community hall for the post disaster food distribution centre and clinic. He had acquired another acre of patta land and was lending money to many of the poorest villagers.

At the time of the second interview in late 1983 he had just married off one daughter with a two acre dowry and was preparing for the marriage of his youngest girl, then aged 13. He thought that the worst risk to his way of life was a bad harvest; the nearest cyclone shelter was a kilometre away in Kammanamolu, but he thought that next time there was a cyclone warning he would leave and go to "high ground" with all his animals.

Small farmer (Gouda) on the edge of the tidal flat. Bellamkonda Narisimharao lost four of his five children and all his animals and farm equipment. His caste trade as a toddy tapper supplemented the income he had lost as a result of the destruction of the paddi crop. He owned two acres of high yielding land and so was able to obtain a crop loan (for a second crop) and loans for two milch animals.

By 1981 he had completely rebuilt his house, his remaining daughter had married and she and her husband were living in the parental house, as a joint Hindu family. The family by then had two plough teams, one cart and two milch animals, and this further increased to two carts and four milch animals by 1983. By 1983 there was also a grandson.

Fisherman (Pallecarlu) in the coastal flat (zone 2 in Figure 6.1). In the cyclone Visvanadhapalli Ammana lost his wife's mother, his daughter and a milch animal, together with his fishing nets and the boat that he partly owned.

By 1981 his wife had recovered from her mental breakdown but his father had died; he had a new boat and fishing nets, directly as a result of bank loans and voluntary agency intervention. He was still living in an octagonal concrete house on a cramped site but had built a separate kitchen and an animal shelter for his one milch animal (the result of another bank loan). His ownership of one acre of land (poor yielding) had helped him raise these loans. However, it is more likely that his diversification of assets into land, fishing, and animal husbandry had enabled his family to have recovered beyond its pre-cyclone position; a process largely dependent on the sustained presence of the voluntary agency and the intelligence of his wife.

Marginal farmer (Pallecarlu) in the coastal flat. Nagidi Busi lost assets in the cyclone but most of his large household survived. His one acre of poor land was not cleared for about a year, but because four adults survived and were not physically or mentally affected they were able to resume earning by labouring very soon after the cyclone, working first on rebuilding the tidal bund, then clearing the irrigation network and then working on the harvest of the second crop in May 1978.

By 1981 this household had acquired an acre of encroachment land and two milch animals through loans, mainly through their ability to pay them back as a result of their high labour power. By 1983 they had acquired a second acre of encroachment land and increased their milch animals to four. Their relative prosperity was mainly the result of decisions beyond their control. First the local irrigation network was marginally extended and their village of Nali benefitted. Secondly, it had been decided to allocate water for a second crop to the whole area around Nali for the first time in 14 years.

Landless (Harijan) in the inland part of the tidal flat. Palabathina Nagendram had lost almost his entire family, being left with his wife and his mother. By 1981 the concrete house into which he had moved in 1979 had almost collapsed, and he had built a small hut nearby for his family and newly born son and a teenage nephew who joined them after the cyclone.

The drastic loss of the labour power of his household had been balanced to some extent by the intervention of the voluntary agency; through loans the family had acquired a milch animal and some ducks. In 1983 the nephew migrated permanently, reducing the labour power of the household. But this loss had been offset to some extent by another milch animal, acquired through another loan, and the improved health of the family, which enabled them all to migrate temporarily to the mainland to work on the second crop around Nali.

Action taken by households

Most people were killed in the 1977 cyclone by drowning, either in their villages after their houses had collapsed or when they were trying belatedly to escape. Many did escape and the only survivors in the villages were those who went to the houses abandoned by the richer people, and 20 per cent of these houses survived the storm surge (Table 6.2). Many people fled to the schools and some of the temples, but these collapsed and became death traps. Most of the schools are built outside the villages on the poorest agricultural land, indicating the priorities given to education and agriculture.

The 1981 interviews revealed that nearly all the people in the villages stayed and waited for the storm, which they thought would be a cyclone with the usual flooding of low lying land. Fewer than 10 per cent, including the fishermen, thought that the cyclone would be so severe. No-one expected a storm surge.

Most people thought the cyclone would miss them, as many had done in the past. They rationalised their reluctance to leave by claiming that there was no-where for them to go, that there were no evacuation measures, that they could not take their possessions with them, and that if they left these possessions they would be stolen (see also Raghavulu and Cohen 1979). It is clear from the interviews that if the people had been warned about the storm surge, as opposed to just the cyclone, they would all have left their villages.

Possible actions in the future

The information about the people's reactions in 1977, when they thought the storm was only a cyclone, led me to ask what they would do in a future hypothetical cyclone. The reader will be aware of the difficulties in getting accurate information from people whose language you do not speak, particularly to hypothetical questions, but the replies were cross-checked with other sources.

Most people indicated that they would probably stay in their village in the event of another cyclone. This was because they were familiar with cyclones, and because they were afraid that their possessions would be stolen if they moved out (mainly animals, cooking utensils, food stores, fodder, and in some cases farm equipment and bullock carts), and also because it was too expensive to move for an event that might not happen (see below). The poorest people said they would flee to higher ground. Many said that they would again go to the rich people's houses. Their answers are summarised in Table 6.3.

After the 1977 cyclone the government implemented a programme of cyclone shelter construction. These circular buildings can shelter 500 people and are being built about every three kilometres along the coast. As well as the cyclone shelters the government has also built 25,000 concrete houses in the same areas. The provision of cyclone shelters and concrete houses has been largely ineffective; the issues surrounding their provision are discussed in greater detail in Winchester (1986).

In Table 6.3 the six occupational groups have been simplified into three groups to correspond broadly with the main indicator of wealth, i.e. land ownership. Large and small farmers own from 10 to 2 acres; marginal farmers and fishermen own less than 2 acres and the landless and petty officials have none (an average quality land holding of 2 acres can just feed an average household).

From Table 6.3 we see that less than 10 per cent of the large and small farmers would go to the cyclone shelters in either area: in the coastal areas they would prefer to get out of their villages and in the inland areas they would prefer to stay in their strong (non-concrete) houses. The reverse is the case for almost all the other occupations, who prefer to stay close to their possessions but not necessarily in the cyclone shelters. In the coastal areas, 90 per cent of the fishermen and marginal farmers say they would stay in their villages but did not much trust their newly built concrete houses, especially the flat roofs.

Table 6.2

Numbers of traditional houses destroyed and
people killed in the 1977 cyclone.

		Damage				
House type	Total houses in 1977	Number of houses destroyed	Number of houses damaged	Number of houses standing	Number of h/holds with >1 killed	Number of people killed
2t/4t (pucca)[a]/	38	20	4	14	12	16
2 pole (katcha)	80	62	16	2	20	44
1 pole/ hut	72	72	-	-	28	73
Totals	190	154	20	16	60	133

a/   2t/4t refers to two and four truss houses.

Table 6.3

Reactions to a future hypothetical cyclone:
response by Krishna delta households,
classified by occupation and topography.

			Response		
Classification of households[a]/	Topography	Number of house-holds	Stay in house	Go to cyclone shelter	Leave the village
Large and small farmers	Coastal[b]/	39	9	2	28
	Inland[c]/	51	40	7	4
Fishermen and marginal farmers	Coastal	44	6	33	5
	Inland	19	8	10	1
Petty traders and landless	Coastal	31	1	27	3
	Inland	18	6	11	1
Totals		202	70 (35%)	90 (44%)	42 (21%)

a/   see Table 6.1
b/   Tidal flat extending to 16 km inland
c/   Deltaic plain, levees and high ground

Problems connected with risk perception, warning and response

Problems from the villagers' perspective

Costs. A principal factor influencing people's decisions during the cyclone warning period was the cost of moving. This attitude was linked with their desperate need to reduce their debts or at least not increase them.

Most people saw their courses of action as *penalties* rather than opportunities. Costs of moving are high; only 30 per cent of the population owned traction animals and 15 per cent own bullock carts, so that hiring transport would have been difficult, even if the animals and carts had been available for hire. Many of the large farmers had left with their families on their own bullock carts for "high ground" before the cyclone. Transport costs would have been prohibitive to most households; the cost of hiring a bullock cart and two animals in the ploughing season was then 30 rupees per day; the costs of hiring them in a cyclone would have been about 100 rupees; in 1977 the income of a household with little or no land was 10 rupees per day which is less than their eating and clothing needs.

Erosion of traditional coping methods. People in cyclone areas have traditionally devised ways of coping with the relative unpredictability of the timing and severity of cyclones. These measures include: communal duties (the rich helped the poor after climatic disasters - droughts and cyclones); the preservation of common lands; and generally agreed varied agricultural practices.

By 1977 most of these coping methods had been destroyed by development and the commercialisation of agriculture as a result of the rapid development of irrigation in the 1930s and the associated rise of a monoculture. This development, coupled with a rapid population influx, resulted in the marginalisation of the majority of the population into the low lying and potentially dangerous areas on the coast. These areas had been stripped of their natural protective vegetation (mangroves) by the population expansion and need for firewood.

Until 1977 there had been no development programmes that in any way compensated the marginalised population for the loss of their common lands or for having to live on the low lying coastal strip. In the early 1960s a three metre high earth tidal bund had been built at about the same time that 20,000 acres of poor land had been given to the poorest in co-operative schemes (these collapsed due to lack of credit). At the same time, in the 1960s and 1970s, forecasting and warning systems and disaster preparedness schemes were being developed and refined. These did nothing to counteract the processes of impoverishment which eventually had such fatal consequences (Winchester 1986).

Coercion by the government. Since 1977 it has been easier for government to evacuate people from cyclone-prone areas by inducements (300,000 people in the south of the state of Andhra Pradesh in 1979; 200,000 people in the north of the State in 1981). Positive inducements include the prospect of a family receiving a concrete house or access to bank loans; negative inducements include the very real possibility of a household or a village being struck off the hand-outs register after a cyclone for refusing to obey the orders to leave. Both methods of inducement lead to over-dependence on the government and rising expectations.

Over dependence and rising expectations. The large government public works programme after the 1977 cyclone disaster - specifically, rebuilding the tidal bund, construction of new all-weather roads, cyclone shelters and concrete houses - has created both over-dependence on the government and rising expectations. An example of the dangers of such expectations can be seen in one village, where the villagers agreed collectively to reject the concrete houses they were offered, in the hope of getting better ones. But the offer was withdrawn after three years and the richer households rebuilt their houses leaving the poorest households without even the benefits of low-quality free houses.

The government's perspective

Penalties and rewards. There are high political costs for failing to warn exposed populations. As a result of the chaos after the 1977 cyclone the Andhra Pradesh government was forced to resign. There are also cost penalties in warning and evacuating areas when nothing happens. The major risk for governments is to "cry wolf" too often and for the people to cease to take any notice. Saving lives has a high political, but low economic significance in India, where labour is cheap. It is fortunate that in the case of saving lives, there is this coincidence of interests between the poorest and the government. Programmes that emphasise property protection are of less value for the poorest, because they have little or nothing to protect.

Greater political and economic penalties combined with the reluctance of many people to take warnings seriously has resulted in procedures where evacuation measures (i.e. forced exit) are implemented after the first warnings (Government of Andhra Pradesh 1981). Sometimes these are successful, and then the political rewards can be high. In 1981, the government successfully evacuated 200,000 people in the Godavari Delta, but the cyclone remained stationary for three days and eventually dissipated at sea. Previously in 1979 the government evacuated 300,000 people from a coastal area; the cyclone was a minor one in terms of wind and rain and had little effect. But the heavy rain that fell a few days later 200 kilometres inland created flooding in the relatively abandoned coastal areas, so the government could claim that they had saved thousands of lives.

Costs and risks. Two problems affecting costs are first, differing perceptions of a cyclone risk, and second, difficulties in prediction. Perceptions are governed to some extent by probabilities. The probability of a cyclone strike on any village is statistically very small and the risk appears small to the villager. When the probability of a cyclone strike is spread over a potential area of 500 sq. kilometres. with 1,000 villages and a population of 2 million, the risk then becomes a major problem for the government who will have to provide relief for perhaps 250,000 people and rehabilitation for 500,000.

Cyclone landfalls are difficult to predict, but predictions are becoming more accurate by the use of the Indian satellite link-up with Cyclone Warning Centres. In 1977 the landfall of the cyclone and the storm surge were predicted only 12 hours beforehand with an accuracy of plus or minus 100 kilometres; in 1979 the landfall was predicted 24 hours beforehand with an accuracy of plus or minus 50 kilometres, but the intensity of the storm had changed by the time it hit the coast.

The costs of warning and evacuation are negligible when compared to other expenditures. Warning and evacuation costs amount to about 10 per cent of budgeted relief programmes, which are themselves less than 5 per cent of the annual irrigation budget. Evacuation costs are also small compared with compensation for the loss of life (Rs 1,500 in 1977, Rs 5,000 in 1985, for each adult killed) . The total sum paid in compensation after the 1977 cyclone to those killed amounted to 5 per cent of the irrigation budget for the same year.

Summary and conclusions

This chapter has noted one Indian state government's approach to the problem of protecting people from cyclones and flooding. We have seen that in one crucial case the warning systems broke down because the government's assumptions of homogeneous response failed to acknowledge people's varied perception of risk and their subsequent actions in a widely differentiated society. We have noted a variation of response based on economic status and that the richest households had the widest choices in 1977, and that they would exercise those choices again in the future.

Two other conclusions are important. First, there is the dysfunction between government's perception of risk and the actual perception of the villagers , which indicates the need for a more sensitive approach to the priorities in designing warning systems for dangerous places. The approach could be based on an understanding of the correlation between damage potential, economic status, recovery potential, and response. We need to know more about the causes of differentiation within societies and how to alleviate them, as well as developing sophisticated forecasting and warning systems.

In the specific context of south India my suggestions for better warning systems would be to rely more on individual choice rather than centralised decisions and the development of organisational systems and management structures. That is not to say that these systems are not required, only that programmes are needed that place more emphasis on individual adjustments based on their choices, which in turn stem from economic strength. To leave people hopelessly poor leaves them hopelessly vulnerable.

Secondly, disaster mitigation as currently theorised is hopelessly wrong : "mismanagement" is a more appropriate term than disaster management. The over-emphasis on warning, evacuation and relief programmes, with particular reference to the developing countries, is well mirrored in an extract from a document by the Office of the Disaster Relief Coordinator (UNDRO);

> ... the formulation and enforcement of land use policies and plans, and appropriate building codes are key factors for the orderly establishment and safe growth of human settlements ... [This is] logically based on knowledge of existing natural hazards present and an analysis of disaster risks which may result ... referred to as "vulnerability analysis" ... through which it becomes possible to make rational decisions on how best the effects of potentially disastrous natural events can be mitigated through proper planning, as well as a system of permanent controls (UNDRO 1979: iii)

The use of words and phrases such as "responsibility", "systematised" "analysis", "mapping", "orderly establishment", "rational", "controls", all suggest the sort of rationality that the United Nations assumes (or would prefer to assume), either exists, or is possible to create. In coastal regions of India this is far from reality. In these areas which are physically remote from centralised control (as indeed is much of the rural Third World) it is impossible to implement planning controls and the orderly establishment of standards, and other methods relying on centralised control.

It is most important is to raise the economic status of the poor, so that they can react and respond to risk communication by making choices that safeguard both their property and their lives; rather than the present situation where they are powerless to react because of their economic impotence.

References

Government of Andhra Pradesh (1971) *Final report of the cyclone distress mitigation committee.* Office of the Chief Engineer, Major Irrigation: Hyderabad.

Government of Andhra Pradesh (1977) *Statement on Cyclone and Tidal Wave on 19th November 1977.* (By Sri Vengala Rao, Chief Minister of Andhra Pradesh). Government Secretariat Press: Hyderabad.

Government of Andhra Pradesh (1981) *Cyclone Contingency Plan of Action.* Revenue Department, Government Secretariat Press: Hyderabad.

Nageswara, Rao L.K. (1980) *Landforms and Land Uses in the Krishna Delta, India.* Unpublished Ph.D. thesis. Department of Geography, University of Andhra Pradesh: Waltair.

Raghavulu, C.V. and Cohen, S. (1979) *The Andhra Cyclone: A Study in Mass Death.* Vikas: Bombay.

Subbaramayya, I., Ramanadham, R. and Subba Rao M. (1979) The November 1977 Andra Pradesh Cyclone and the associated storm surge. *Indian National Academy.* Vol 45, Part A, pp 293-304.

United Nations Disaster Relief Organisation (1979) *Natural disasters and vulnerability analysis.* Report of Expert Working Group Meeting 9-12 July. UNDRO: Geneva.

Winchester, P.J. (1986) *Cyclone Vulnerability and Housing Policy: in the Krishna Delta, South India, 1977-83 .* Unpublished Ph.D. thesis. School of Development Studies, University of East Anglia: Norwich.

7 Social and Cultural Aspects of Community Vulnerability and Risk Communication

Yasemin Aysan

Abstract

All societies are vulnerable to a range of natural and technological threats. However, the type and degree of vulnerability varies greatly, not only between societies but even between households in the same community. Resource allocation in terms of risk reduction may not seem optimal to an outsider, but generally reflects local priorities and history.

Macro societal factors like the political economy, culture, religion, and socio-economic status are very important in vulnerability assessment. However, they should not be allowed to obscure smaller-scale factors. Thus, apparently homogeneous communities are frequently highly differentiated by class, strength of religious belief, age, access to resources, gender, education, family conflict, etc. It is frequently the poorest and weakest who live in the most hazardous areas.

Risk communication must recognise that it has to go beyond simply giving information if it is to have an impact. It has to address the underlying social and cultural factors constraining response. A prerequisite of this is an understanding of the community's vulnerability profile. These issues are explored using research in areas of Turkey and the Yemen Arab Republic which have been damaged by earthquakes.

111

Introduction

All societies possess some degree of vulnerability to a
variety of events, ranging from transportation accidents and
diseases to crop failure, earthquakes and floods. It is
very difficult to come to a global definition of
vulnerability, because different societies and groups within
societies are subject to different threats and are affected
in different ways. In several instances the same phenomenon
is perceived differently by various interest groups for
administrative, political, academic, religious or individual
reasons.   Out of these perceptions come different
classifications of vulnerable events, communities and
groups. Various methods of coping with risk follow.

There are very broad classifications which differentiate
between common social characteristics in the way certain
types of risks and coping mechanisms are perceived. These
classifications include, developed/developing countries,
rural/urban communities, and rich/poor societies.   For
example, while a high magnitude earthquake can have
devastating effects in Mexico City, the same magnitude may
not pose a serious risk in Tokyo.   Similarly, seismic
building regulations can be imposed as a means of reducing
future vulnerability in developed countries but in
developing countries lacking the necessary enforcement
bureaucracy and public support this would be a futile
exercise.

Accumulated field research reveals that even for the same
rural community the sources of risk are subject to change;
in a geographically and culturally limited area responses
are different and among a small group of people the impact
of the event is varied.   Yet, the aid-giving bodies'
perceptions of vulnerability, in terms of who is vulnerable
and what kind of measures should be taken towards mitigation
and rehabilitation, generally fail to allow for this
diversity.   In the majority of cases the definition of
vulnerability is limited to natural hazards and to their
threat to human life and property.   Consequently, the
policies of relief agencies aim at preventing the event, at
protecting life and property, and at replacing the material
losses with such provisions so that the impact of a similar
event might be decreased. After earthquakes for example, it
is assumed that once safe siting and safe housing are
provided, future risks are reduced to an acceptable level.
Yet, knowledge of other indigenous factors affecting the
vulnerability of the community, such as lack of technical
know-how, limited economic and material resources, cultural
and social priorities and other risks in relation to the
frequency of major hazards, could be equally important in
devising risk reduction programmes including those designed
to raise awareness.

In this chapter I examine the diversity of risk that rural
communities in developing countries have to face, the varied
impact of a disaster on different groups of the community,
and their responses to vulnerability.   Examples are drawn

from research conducted between 1982 and 1986 in the Gediz-Emet provinces of Western Turkey where a major earthquake occurred in 1970. Two additional small scale research projects undertaken in parallel complemented the major study, especially on the effects of disaster in the immediate post-impact phase. These examined the 1982 Dhamar earthquake in the Yemen Arab Republic and the 1984 Erzurun earthquake in Eastern Turkey. The conclusions highlight those community characteristics which would be relevant in devising risk communication programmes for similar circumstances.

Change of risk and local response to vulnerability

For rural communities in developing countries a relatively high degree of vulnerability is perhaps an inevitable part of everyday life. The way communities cope with these "daily risks" is not a simple "learning from experience" process but a complicated series of adjustments to change and variability. Where there are many forms of vulnerability and the resources to avoid them are limited, optimisation of these resources in relation to the local or household priorities becomes the key approach. This process can be defined as "common sense", which is an intuitive and experimental approach and arrives at locally appropriate solutions over a long period of time.

Traditional settlements and buildings in many disaster-prone countries are often criticised for their vulnerable siting and lack of risk consideration in the use of building materials. However, these buildings and settlements are usually built to serve a certain purpose at a given time, where the limited resources are optimised according to local priorities. Thus, many traditional settlements are located on high mountain slopes which often reflects an historic need for security and protection. Another important factor can be economics which requires the use of flat land for agriculture, hence the houses are built on slopes. In the Yemen earthquakes, settlements which were located on high mountain slopes for security, were the worst affected and the most difficult to reach with aid (Figure 7.1).

Gradually, in areas where security no longer remains a major priority and where the rural population is increasing rapidly, houses are inevitably built on lower slopes and flat land which are usually flood prone. In other words, while a certain type of vulnerability disappears another one is introduced as the needs of the community change.

Other factors like environmental considerations or technological change can create different kinds of risk. For example, in the mountain villages of the Gediz areas thick mud walls are commonly used to decrease vulnerability to the climate. Although these heavy walls increased vulnerability to the relatively rare earthquakes, and caused a lot of damage in the 1970 earthquake, they were necessary to reduce consumption of brushwood heating fuel during the cold winters: an annual event.

These few examples illustrate the changing priorities of communities living in rural areas and the delicate balance that they have to maintain for economic, physical and cultural survival at the cost of increasing vulnerability to one type of risk for the sake of avoiding others. Some of these problems may be solved if there is better understanding of safe building, or if the local materials and techniques can be improved through an education programme. However, improvement for communities with very limited resources is a matter of choice, each time optimising these resources according to their priorities.

Risk perception by government agencies, unaware or not interested in local conditions, will clearly vary from that held by the risk bearers. In such circumstances risk communication will be a one-way process. The messages are likely to be patronising and seen as irrelevant by the target audience; or worse, they may create antagonism between the communicators and audience.

Vulnerable groups in the community

The impact of events, acceptance of risk related information, and ability to undertake mitigation measures, displays variations among different groups even within apparently tightly knit communities. Such variations depend on age, sex, social status and values, education and experiences, wealth and power.

Socio-economic status

The class nature of the effects of disasters has been documented in a number of studies, and it is common that the most vulnerable sites and buildings of the worst quality are occupied by the poorest of the community (Westgate 1979, Maskrey and Romero 1988). In many cases this situation carries on after the disaster, the poorer victims benefiting less from aid and having less chance of recovering fully. The impact of an earlier earthquake in 1944 in the Gediz area, and the nature of rehabilitation, correspond well with this picture. This is perhaps due to very little outside intervention and the limited means these groups had to change the situation.

However, our study of the 1970 earthquake and its aftermath did not reveal a strong stratification linked with the pre-disaster state of the families and social structure. The reason was that the impact of the 1970 earthquake was stronger: families from all strata of the community suffered from the results of the event. In the Gediz-Emet area alone 144 villages were affected and the towns of Akcaalan and Gediz were devastated by the subsequent fires. A total of 1,089 people died, 1,265 were injured, about 17,000 houses

Figure 7.1: Traditional settlement in Yemen destroyed
by the 1982 earthquake.

115

were destroyed and 90,000 people were left homeless. The total earthquake damage was considerable, estimated at TL500 million (US$33 million).

Preparations for post-disaster reconstruction were much improved by the Turkish Government over the years and developed towards a policy of providing permanent housing, either contractor built or pre-fabricated. In the villages, single storey units of 42 square metres in area were built within a year on the original or relocation sites. Housing was provided for the families whose houses were badly or moderately damaged. Today, despite their low quality, these houses and the land they are built on fetch 15 times the original price. This greatly affects the economic status of the house owners. In addition, a male from each severely damaged house was given priority to become a worker in Germany. This resulted in 5,341 men leaving for jobs in Germany and earning 2-3 times the average income of a farmer in the Gediz area (Mitchell 1974, 1978).

Given all these factors, the questions of who lost and who gained, and how these issues were reflected in the changes that took place in society, became very complicated. Nevertheless, if class structure was not an important issue, families with members in Germany prospered more than those who remained behind. In fact access to this opportunity was not only determined by the degree of damage, but also by age and by social considerations - some men did not wish to leave their wives behind, especially if there were no grown up sons to protect them. The workers in Germany invest little in local industry, the money being spent to buy tractors, land or most important to build houses for future use.

There is no evidence that the wealthier pre-disaster families had a greater opportunity to work in Germany. Perhaps the families who were better off were more cautious about leaving their land and possessions and therefore remained in the area, though this is difficult to establish. If there is a question of economic vulnerability in the area the balance has probably changed to the advantage of those who lost their homes in the first place and received aid in the form of housing or jobs. This approach to aid may act as a disincentive to act on information about earthquake resistant building practices.

The aid given is not equally beneficial to all members of the community and one could say in developing countries the rich and more powerful have more access to it. However, our research in North Yemen, and in the Erzurum area of Eastern Turkey, revealed that the traditional social structures and cultural values prevalent among rural communities played a crucial role relative to vulnerability (Aysan 1984a).

Age, gender, social values and background

In the 1982 North Yemen earthquake the most affected parts of the settlement were the oldest sections, located on top of the hills and surrounded by walls. The houses were several storeys high and built of poor quality stone masonry. Vulnerability was high due to poor bonding, little timber framing, a low level of maintenance, and other technical reasons (Coburn and Hughes 1983). The majority of the people who lived in such areas were elderly or widows: these people became the most vulnerable in the community. They are also the least able to respond to conventional advice on how to modify the risk. With more people and less pressure for defence, new houses were built for the sons outside the walls, and as the old vernacular buildings completed their life cycles, the weakest of the community remained in them (Aysan 1984b).

In the immediate post-disaster period of the Erzurum earthquake in 1983 the situation seemed to be similar. The majority of those who were least able to take the initiative to build emergency shelters remained the most vulnerable: the elderly, the widowed women with young children, or women with husbands in the army or working abroad (Aysan 1984a).

The idea of social coherence expected in rural communities is perhaps not always applicable to all cultures and all situations. Due to very complex social values, customs, bloodfeuds and family conflicts, initial mutual help may be among the immediate kin only, or eventually fade away. Tribal discords can become stronger on the rumours of uneven distribution of aid. Purchasing of land by the state for relocation can create tension among land owners.

Age is another factor which differentiates not only the perception of risk by some people in the community, but also attitudes towards it. In all three cases, in the Yemen prior to the disaster, in Erzurum in the immediate aftermath of the disaster and in Gediz in the long-term post-disaster situation, vulnerability of the elderly was not dependent on their economic status but more on their social and cultural positions. In both countries elderly people were less concerned with safety and comfort and took a more fatalistic position regardless of their income level. Their response is best expressed in the words of more than one interviewee: "If it is God's will we will die; we are old anyway," which reflects both their acceptance of the prime importance of social values and their religious faith.

Preparedness programmes and warnings based on the assumption of homogeneous communities will founder in the face of such risk acceptance. The great diversity of risk perception, and other social and economic factors constraining receipt, interpretation, acceptance of and response to risk communication, needs to be considered in programme development. Vulnerable groups should be identified and targeted for special attention.

Post disaster recovery and vulnerability

The attitude of government in disaster-prone parts of the world has tended to be to cope with the disaster rather than to prevent it. This is true in the case of Turkey where the approach to reduce vulnerability is curative, providing permanent, technically safe housing, which provides future protection only for those who have already been badly affected by a disaster. The remainder, who could have been the victims, and therefore subsequently the protected, if the epicentre was elsewhere or if the intensity was higher, continue to live without the provision of safe housing.

Furthermore, there are almost no education programmes for improving building safety, or technical help to upgrade building standards, even in the most unsafe parts of the country. The timber framed buildings in the Gediz area could have withstood the earthquake better if the structural detailing was not poor, if the materials and maintenance were good, and if the siting was different (Anadol and Arioglu 1971).

If the measure of risk reduction is simply the provision of houses by the state the Gediz post-disaster housing programme is a successful one. But, such provision after a disaster has occurred is an attempt to provide a fairly simple technical answer to a more complex question of vulnerability. In the absence of changed attitudes physical safety, in the form of safe housing, does not guarantee social and cultural acceptance of the state's intervention. Social, cultural and economic needs very quickly outweigh the need for physical safety, hence the post-disaster houses - either on account of their location or their house form - remain empty and the vulnerable sites and forms continue. In the Gediz area the final rate of acceptance was high, although it was slow. In some villages state houses built in 1970 were only recently occupied, while others remained unoccupied (Ceylan 1983). The interviews revealed that the same "common sense" operated in such a way that the most advantageous conditions were chosen for rejection or acceptance:

* The provision of services like roads, electricity, and schools were factors which influenced the choice, in some cases resulting in rejection of the new.
* Site factors like climatic disadvantages, distance to arable land, water resources and small plot sizes were the other reasons for rejection.
* Although the house plans were not unacceptable they were too small for agricultural communities, therefore it was desirable to repair the damaged houses.

Thus, even when risk communication takes the form of the provision of new housing, failure to appreciate the role of other factors important in coping with the hazards of everyday living may lead to programme failure.

However advantageous, the state houses were not suitable for the rural communities. Therefore, those which were occupied were altered or extended to meet local needs (Aysan 1987). These changes varied from building barns and byres in traditional ways, to using new materials like breeze blocks, concrete and bricks to extend the living quarters. Nevertheless, traditional methods were not improved and new technologies were not necessarily safely used to make the buildings capable of withstanding future earthquakes. In other words, while many of the post-disaster risks were eased by state intervention, new forms of vulnerability were introduced into the area.

Long term implications of state intervention

To a Government, success or failure of a post-disaster programme is usually the degree of apparent recovery from the impact of disaster. Such an approach assumes that vulnerability decreases with disaster recovery and that such decreases can be maintained in the long term. This may be true for developed countries or in those urban areas where planning legislation and building codes can be imposed and are conformed to by society. However, in developing countries conformity does not always follow because priorities in local economies may not allow it. For example, in the relocated town of New Gediz the Municipality imposed building regulations and provided prototype timber and concrete house plans which fulfil their safety requirements. The prototype plans are controlled during construction but anyone can construct an extra staircase or an unsafe balcony. These later additions are themselves signs of economic recovery. For the families who cannot afford the cost of prototypes, there is no alternative but to live in the small state houses in unhealthy conditions, with the many social and cultural problems of overcrowding. On the other hand in Gokler, another Municipality, where control is very limited, people build in whatever style and material they can afford.

Cheaper construction may be more important than safety in many cases. The somewhat indeterminant risk from earthquakes is accepted in exchange for the benefits of a socially functional house. Of course the tradeoff is not simple: earthquakes may be seen as entirely within divine control. In any case concrete framing is not necessarily less vulnerable unless built according to specifications.

As local authorities raise their own budgets they are also under economic pressures. The population of New Gediz has doubled in 14 years, and consequently land on which to build has become very expensive (Germen 1978, Gurpinar 1978). The Municipality of Gediz, which controls building, sold marsh land at the outskirts of the town to cover the high cost of providing services. This land sale brought an income to the Municipality, but being not only earthquake but also flood prone, the new private development of three story houses is probably even more vulnerable than the oldest sections of the town.

After this time span economic recovery is evident in the area, perhaps helped by economic development during the 1950s, resulting from the introduction of agricultural mechanisation and artificial fertilisers, and by the state provision of services after the 1970 earthquake. However, the improved quality of the present physical environment seems initially to be largely due to the money coming from the workers in Germany, most of which is spent on building large two storey concrete framed buildings. Other than the plan types, neither the materials nor the construction type are similar to the indigenous ones. New building materials are widely available as transport has improved since the earthquake. It can be assumed that these buildings are strong enough to withstand earthquakes, although villagers claim that as they were not always supervised by the owner the builders cut corners in construction quality. However, the vulnerability issue related to new buildings mainly concerns the poor copies of them. A few such structures may be seen scattered in each village and these, with expanding aspirations and rising timber prices, are likely to increase in number in the future.

Forms, materials and techniques are all new and there is insufficient experience in their use, therefore misconceptions and mistakes are inevitable. With the lack of necessary skills among the builders, and a poor understanding of concrete framing, economic betterment did not necessarily help to decrease vulnerability to a desirable level, especially for those people who can just afford concrete but not the best means of construction.

To some of these people the appearance of economic prosperity may be more important than earthquake resistant design. Although, once again the tradeoff is not simple; apart from the question of fatalism the risk communicators may have simply failed to explain how to build safely. For example the message might have used unfamiliar concepts or channels, or may have been incorrectly targetted.

Those who were affected less by the earthquake continue to live in the traditional way, perhaps in greater economic competition since the disaster, with no aid received in material or technical terms.

Lessons for future risk awareness programmes

Several years after the event, "community vulnerability" had become a very complicated issue. The 1970 earthquake perhaps generated major changes, the outcome of which, directly or indirectly, will continue to affect the future of the communities in the Gediz region. Certain types of risks have remained from the past, others have disappeared over the years, or new ones have been introduced. The nature of the risk has changed, and the perception of risk has become more complex.

Although there is concern over earthquake risk among the members of the community, a number of factors accounted for their reluctance to act on these concerns by implementing safety measures. These factors are as crucial as understanding the vulnerability profile of the communities at risk when designing and implementing risk awareness programmes.

(i)   *Lack of technical information*: Intuitively almost all who experienced the earthquake knew that timber framed traditional houses collapsed with a greater margin of safety as opposed to the total failure of poor concrete framed buildings. But they had no technical understanding of structural principles to improve their dwellings even if they wished to do so. Any future reconstruction programmes should be designed to encourage community involvement in rebuilding to reduce future damage. The immediate post-disaster period is the best time for teaching safety measures to the public and to the builders.

(ii) *Aspirations for "modern" living*: The new building materials and technologies introduced to the area by the "guest worker" houses, and by increased contact with urban parts of the country since the earthquake, encouraged the tendency to build with alien materials and technologies. These are regarded as status symbols and aspired to as signs of "modern" living. Any housing programmes should anticipate these trends in building techniques and materials to ensure reasonable standards of safety.

(iii) *Other risks*: The risk of earthquakes and the safety measure to be incorporated in constructing houses were not the major concerns of the local families. Among various types of risks, economic problems and the future for children in terms of education and health had a higher priority. Incentives like subsidised building materials, housing loans or certificates for builders for attending training courses can be used to give housing safety a higher priority (Leslie 1987).

(iv) *Belief system*: More common than any of these relatively tangible issues is the traditional belief system which is the most powerful factor in affecting the attitude of rural people, particularly the elderly and the middle aged. For example, religion and the beliefs in faith were condensed in the often heard saying "If God gives us an earthquake..., if God wishes us to die... we will". The authorities have to work in full recognition and understanding of such attitudes.

(v)   *Construction process*: Prior to any technical training programmes it is necessary to define the target groups and their respective roles in building activities. For example, in the Gediz area the plan of the house is always plotted on the site by the master builder

121

followed by digging of the foundations by the family. The structural frame is again constructed by a group of builders but the walls are usually filled in by the members of the family. Men and women are involved in different parts of the decision making and in different parts of house construction.

(vi) *Perception of educational material*: The current pattern of communication between the house owners and the builders is verbal, improvising on the traditionally known types and standards. Hence, an understanding of architectural drawings and sketches is not very common. The exhibition in Gediz revealed this phenomenon that the perception of the physical aspects of building details and structural principles in relation to the impact of earthquakes was limited among the local people. Different graphic mediums were interpreted differently. While the photographs and three dimensional representations were easier to follow because of their familiarity with this medium from the newspapers and TV, the architectural drawings and settlement plans were not easily understood (Figure 7.2).

In particular sketches of houses which lacked any human figures or other familiar objects were not recognised even by the people who owned them. Local builders needed explanation and guidance on the drawings showing structural details of buildings (Figure 7.2). Explanations on real buildings or models proved to be the most useful medium. It was also felt by the team, although not tested, that human figures accompanying the drawings would help the people to comprehend the material better.

The difficulties of conveying the message simply by sending out wall charts or any visual material without the backup of real demonstrations and discussions on buildings, or continuous training, was evident in a campaign run by the Turkish Government. 500,000 wall charts containing visual and written information on "how to improve seismic resistance of rural houses" were distributed in 1972 to all villages and small settlements. These wall charts showed a sequence ending with a destroyed house, and would convey the wrong message for an illiterate person. A few were displayed in coffee houses - without any impact at all - but most simply perished.

(vii) *Timing and location*: The routine of work in rural areas has to be carefully observed prior to setting up training programmes or the distribution of material. If the programmes coincide with events like harvesting, ploughing, or planting the rate of attendance may be seriously affected. On the other hand, market-day, which draws villagers into a certain location in large numbers, can attract many people to a training centre or an exhibition, as was the case in Gediz.

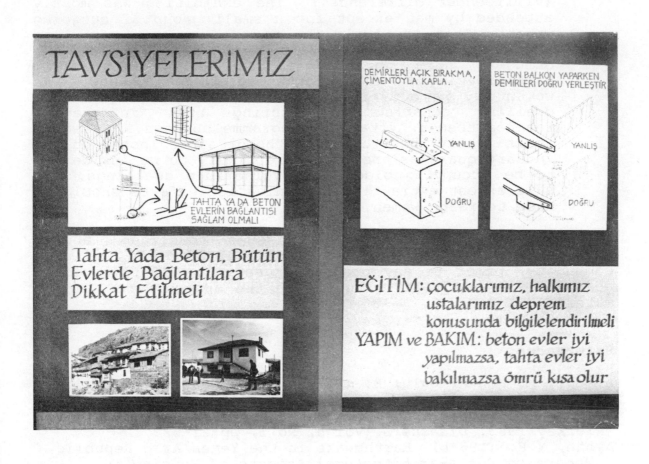

OUR RECOMMENDATIONS

Both concrete and timber framed houses must have strong joints.

Timber or concrete, attention must be paid to the joints in all houses.

Don't expose the iron bars, cover them in cement.

wrong

right

When building concrete balconies, please place the iron bars correctly.

wrong

right

EDUCATION: Our children, the public and builders should be educated about earthquakes.

CONSTRUCTION and MAINTENANCE: Concrete houses if not built properly, timber houses if not maintained properly, will not last for long.

Figure 7.2: Earthquake education material developed for Turkish villagers.

(viii) *Gender differences*: The exhibition was mostly attended by men except for a small group of outgoing women. This is partly due to the domestic work-load which keeps the women in the village but more to a cultural norm which restricts the females from participating in events attended by both sexes. As women may be actively involved in critical parts of dwelling construction ensuring that information reaches them is vital to programme success. As well, it is likely that they bare the greatest losses during an earthquake as they are more likely to be inside and to be occupying older more vulnerable dwellings. To this extent extra risk communication efforts should be made to reach women.

An understanding of the issues outlined above, particularly the social and cultural profile of the community, prior to any programme design is a prerequisite to targeting the right groups with the appropriate kind of material.

References

Anadol, K. and Arioglu, E. (1971) Gediz Depremi. *Mimarlik*. No 405, pp 45-55.

Aysan, Y.F. (1984a) The Erzurum Kars earthquake of Eastern Turkey 1983. *Disasters*. Vol 8, No 1, pp 21-32.

Aysan, Y.F. (1984b) Earthquake in the Yemen Arab Republic, *Papers on Socio-architectural Aspects of Housing in Earthquake Prone Areas of Turkey, 14-16 September 1983*. Building Research Institute: Ankara.

Aysan, Y.F. (1987) Homeless in 42m^2. *Open House International*. Vol 12, No 3, pp 21-27.

Ceylan, F. (1983) *User Adaptation to the State Houses in Four Villages: Evaluation of Post-earthquake Long-term Housing Activities in Rural Areas of Turkey*. Unpublished MA thesis, METU.

Coburn, A.W. and Hughes, P.E. (1983) *Dhamar Province Earthquake, 13 December 1982, Yemen Arab Republic*. Preliminary Report to the Central Planning Office, Joint Relief Committee. Martin Centre: Cambridge.

Germen, A. (1978) The Gediz Earthquake: Reconstruction between 1970 and 1977. *Disasters*. Vol 2, No 1. pp 69-77.

Gurpinar, A. (1978) *Post-earthquake construction of Gediz*, Seminar on construction in seismic zones. Bergamo-Udine, Italy, 10-13 May.

Leslie, J. (1987) Think before you build, experience after the Yemen earthquake. *Open House International*. Vol 12, No 3, pp 43-50.

Maskrey, A. and Romero G. (1988) Urbanizucion, Y. Vulnerabilidad, Sismica en Lima Metropolitana. *Predes Centro de Estudios Y Prevencion de Desastres*. Lima.

Ministry of Rehousing and Resettlement *(1970) Imar Iskan Bakanliginca Gediz de Yapilacak Deprem Evleri ve Hak Sahiplerine Uygulanacak Esaslar*. The Ministry: Ankara.

Mitchell, W.A. (1974) *Turkish Villages after an Earthquake: an Analysis of Disaster Related Modernisation*. Unpublished PhD. Dept of Architecture, University of Illinois.

Mitchell, W.A. (1978) *Post disaster recovery after seven year: old and new Gediz*. Paper presented to the Annual Meeting of the Association of American Geographers, New Orleans, April 10.

Westgate, K. (1979) Land-use planning, vulnerability and the low-income dwelling. *Disasters*. Vol 3, No 3, pp 244-248.

Section Summary III
The Context of Communication

The chapters in this section and parts of those elsewhere in the volume examine the context of individual and group decisions on risk. Essentially, they argue that context acts to limit choice and that it is as important to understanding risk communication as the psychology discussed in the previous section. Not only is the formulation, delivery and interpretation of risk messages affected, some would say determined, by contextual factors, but also the possible responses. The importance of context was raised initially in Chapter 1, where the risk communication model of Figure 1.2 illustrates its all-encompassing position.

To ignore or to improperly understand context is to invite programme failure. At worst, attempts to communicate information on risks may lead to attacks on the communicators by the target audience. The contributors show that context has many levels from the dominant national culture and socio-political framework governing how our society operates, the "community context"; through to the immediate environment of the target individual or household, the "local context". The influence of the different aspects of context will vary according to the particular risk or hazard. In the case of warnings there will also be factors specific to each event, the "situational context" (Handmer and Ord 1986).

Context is therefore subject to enormous variation and is different for each individual as argued by the phenomenologists quoted by Wilson in Chapter 4. A partial list of contextual factors would include:

* political economy and ideology, including the role of commercial organisations and trade unions
* culture, religious orientation, caste
* type of bureaucracy
* role of the mass media
* preparedness and experience
* degree of affluence
* community risk taking propensities
* social conformity, group cohesion, social and family networks
* building technology
* attitudes to gender
* "situational context", this is not discussed in detail in this section, but may be of crucial importance. The timing of the British windstorm of October 1987, for example, was a central factor in the very low injury level. At 3am on a weekday night most people are at home and asleep, and as such they are in a fairly secure environment. In addition, there would be little anxiety over missing household members as the household would normally be together.

This summary will outline the main themes within the discussion on context, before exploring the relationship between the contextual or "macro" level and the individual.

Risk communication and community context

History and the role of government

The process of risk communication includes decisions by government on what constitutes risk, and on resource allocation to publicise or otherwise deal with the problem. Decisions may result from lobby group pressure or political perceptions of what the electorate considers an "acceptable risk". They may also result from court decisions, from scientific evidence, and from the vested interests or ethical positions of those within the relevant bureaucracies.

It is important to recognise that decisions on risk are often the result of recent experience; science, economics, or equity may be adduced to justify a political decision taken in the wake of a disaster or "near miss". Rather than demonstrating political irrationality, such decisions are evidence of the social construction of risk.

Some information on all identified risks will be communicated, if only by informal networks within the scientific elite. However, as modern industrialised societies place considerable emphasis on equity and social justice, some information will generally be made public on most hazards.

The amount and type of information varies greatly between countries, from those with high levels of disclosure of information on risks, encouraged by statutes and a propensity to sue, such as the United States; to those with a relatively closed approach, such as Britain. Also, quite different risks may be emphasised: thus in Britain the national government has funded major campaigns on AIDS (Chapter 14) and Rabies; recent Australian programmes have concerned the danger of importing exotic animal diseases and a major anti-drug offensive; in Australian Aboriginal communities an anti-alcohol campaign is current. According to Wassersug (1989) the French government devotes considerable resources to persuading people of the benefits of nuclear energy. These examples provide further illustrations of the social and cultural construction of risk and risk communication.

Cultural and social values are not static, neither are any other factors in the risk communication process. Both Aysan and Winchester use historical analysis to show how the vulnerability of traditional communities has changed as they are drawn into the modern commercial world. The increasing amount of intervention by national governments and aid agencies to reduce one hazard, may increase exposure to another hazard and change the distribution of risk bearing within the community. This process is not confined to developing countries. Different risks are emphasised over time, according to the factors listed above, and for the same risk different approaches are considered appropriate; the shift from engineering works to land and people management for flood hazard reduction is illustrative.

The burden of change does not fall equally. Some sections of the community, generally the poor or less powerful may be left in an even worse position, or at least may be relatively worse off in that their position improves less than that of others. Thus, in our case studies it is the poorest farmers in India, and the elderly and certain groups of women in rural Turkey and Yemen who are especially adversely affected. As Aysan points out, other groups, such as the more traditionally minded, may not benefit from post-disaster recovery programmes, because elements of the programmes conflict with their beliefs.

The media as gatekeepers

Interestingly, in view of the weight of evidence for the importance of context in risk communication, Wilkins shows that in general, hazards and disasters are reported without context. Thus, after the Challenger space shuttle explosion the media were more interested in searching for someone to blame than in critically examining the system that produced the problem. This may be seen as part of the lack of interest in examining an important assumption underlying industrialised societies: that the benefits of modern technology are beyond question and outweigh the risks.

The tendency to ascribe to individuals responsibility for actions or problems which are the inevitable outcome of the system they operate within, is known as the "fundamental attribution error". Attribution to individuals performing the role of scapegoats is popular with the political and bureaucratic arms of government, as it shifts the focus of attention away from the "system" which created the risk. This is especially the case where the scapegoat is dead. For example, if an enquiry finds that the dead pilot of a crashed aircraft was responsible for the accident, then the various social requirements for a guilty party are satisfied (Tompkins 1987). This type of finding has the added advantage that no further action or retribution is required by the authorities.

The mass media are generally eager participants in this process - reinforcing rather than challenging the existing distribution and perception of risk. By concentrating on events and individuals they are unlikely to contribute to reducing the risks society faces, or to explaining why disasters happen. The shifts in vulnerability and the trade-offs between different types of risk discussed by Aysan and Winchester are generally not examined. The media are not alone here: other societal institutions, such as the courts, also tend to treat events in isolation (Partlett 1987). Occasionally this is not the case. Reports in the London newspaper, *The Independent* (21 November 1988), dealing with the 1987 fire at Kings Cross underground station, emphasised the way that the safety of the entire underground system had gradually been reduced as a result of government budgetary strategy and other factors.

However, despite all this criticism there is little evidence that the media play a major role in persuading people. That myths can persist despite conflicting evidence is illustrated by the robustness of the belief that television and other mass media have sizable impacts on the public's thoughts, feelings, and actions even though most empirical studies indicate small to negligible effects (McGuire 1985).

This raises the question of media effectiveness as risk communicators. Clearly, it is in doubt, although establishing effectiveness encounters difficulties explored in the next section of this volume. There is more agreement that the media play an agenda setting or gatekeeping role: they tell people not what to think, but what to think about (Oskamp 1984).

Nevertheless, Wilkins suggests ways of improving the media as a vehicle for risk communication and of expanding message content to include contextual factors. Both the behaviour of the different sections of the media and the capacity of the target audiences should be considered. This last point is particularly important, as mentioned in Section II; feeding people information when they lack the "schemas" or mental constructs necessary for absorption may be a pointless exercise.

In addition, the media play important indirect roles in setting the context for risk communication. For example, for reasons unrelated to risk or emergency management they may establish or destroy the credibility of an agency with responsibilty for issuing warnings, raising disaster preparedness, or involving the public directly in decisions on risk.

The broadcast media offer an important, and in some cases the only, avenue for rapid dissemination of warnings. Authorities with responsibility for warnings need to ensure that the necessary links with the appropriate media are in place before the event.

Local context: heterogeneity of the target audience

The target audience will frequently operate in a different context to that of the risk communicators. At the most general level both groups would usually be under the same national political economy, although in Europe this is often not the case. In either circumstance, the message senders would typically be highly educated members of scientific, bureaucratic or commercial organisations. The message receivers, on the other hand, may have completely different backgrounds, belief systems, attitudes to risk, and as discussed in Chapter 1 are quite likely to use a different language for expressing risk. One possible important exception to this dichotomy might be risk information provided by trade unions to their members.

These frequent, enormous differences between the senders and recipients of risk communication messages highlight the need to tailor messages to the target audience.

However, the target audience is not a homogeneous mass. The case studies reported by Winchester and Aysan show that even small rural communities are likely to be highly differentiated. A possible theoretical basis for this was set out in Section II. Typical differences may result from: gender; age; socio-economic status (including caste); education; health; religious belief; blood feuds and family conflict; and the personalities and experiences of individuals and households. Many of these factors are not necessarily independent.

This summary will consider socio-economic factors, and then briefly highlight the importance of gender and religious orientation as factors emerging from the preceding chapters.

Socio-economic status may be viewed broadly as a question of access to knowledge and resources: the bases of power and the facilitators of action. It is important to note that status varies both within and between communities; the following comments may apply to either situation. Assessment of the impact of status on risk communication and response may be complicated as people in different socio-economic groups may have different religious or political orientations.

Access to resources may be limited by cost. Thus, a community's poorest will frequently occupy the most hazardous locations, because the lower rent or property prices are all they can afford. As noted below, such households will frequently be headed by women. Although cost is important, other factors may keep people in particularly hazardous locations or out of a community's most desirable and safest areas. Bourne (1981) points out that at least one third of all households in a competitive housing market have little or no choice: a point reinforced by O'Riordan later in this volume. Affluence will generally widen the range of available options, although choice is restricted for a range of reasons in addition to cost, including: discrimination; the psychological stress of leaving familiar environments; kinship ties; and through immobility resulting from physical handicaps.

Hazard reduction programmes based on raising awareness will have little impact on such people, who may or may not be fully aware of the hazard, but unable to afford to do anything about it (Handmer 1984). Response to warnings of life threatening events may also be inhibited. Winchester reports that the poor in his case study site would not respond well to a cyclone warning because they could not afford to: even evacuation was seen as too expensive by the poorer villagers.

At the other extreme, developers and those who stand to profit from the hazardous area may attempt to discredit or trivialise the information. They may also attempt to circumvent or terminate the risk communication process. The 1984 furore over flood maps in Western Sydney is salutary (Handmer 1985).

What is not so obvious is the way community-wide hazard education programmes may benefit only certain groups, as suggested by Wilson in Chapter 4. Improvements to national health, widely attributed to healthy lifestyle, anti-smoking, health promotion campaigns, disguise an important distributional effect. Macken (1986) argues that the benefits of these campaigns are restricted to the middle classes.

Many target groups will be differentiated by *gender*. Failure to take account of this in distributing information concerning earthquake resistant building practices in Turkey, meant that the material reached only men. It did not reach women who traditionally build the walls of dwellings. Later in this volume Brown shows that women wanted different risk information to men and preferred different media. This type of risk communication variable also raises ethical questions, as females frequently bear a greater risk than males to certain hazards (Rivers 1982). This may be because they are more likely to occupy especially vulnerable housing as in Aysan's examples and in certain Australian floodplains (Handmer 1984); and social custom in rural areas may mean that women are more likely to be indoors and thus trapped in collapsing buildings during earthquakes. Another gender related issue is discussed by Goldhaber and deTurck (1988). They found that a sign warning against diving into shallow water had the desired affect on females, but appeared to have actually encouraged risk taking behaviour by males.

Religious beliefs and the associated morality may affect different aspects of risk communication. Strongly religious schools or communities, for example, may refuse to distribute information on AIDS. In terms of response to warnings, consider the difficulties posed by the comments reported by Aysan,"if it is God's will we will die... we are old anyway." This may be more powerful than the "learned helplessness" mentioned in Section II, because it may be based on theological dogma. Warning and preparedness programmes would need to convince the risk bearers that steps to improved safety are indeed within their control.

The individual and a changing context

The addition of multi-level and multi-faceted context to the individual psychology examined in Section II, begins to give an indication of the complexity of risk communication. The number of factors involved suggest that accurate programme evaluation would be very difficult.

The importance of contextual factors varies according to the community, the individual, the risk or hazard, and the specific circumstances. As is evident, the factors are continually interacting with each other and with the target audience(s). These interactions will frequently be two-way. In many cases the feedback will lead to changes in some aspect of the context; in turn the context may change the risk perception, or other aspects of the psychology, of the targeted individuals. The gradual accumulation of experience of, and evolution of attitudes and behaviour towards, some environmental hazard illustrates the model. The risk message is part of this process.

The risk communication model of Figure 1.2 should be viewed as having all elements constantly interacting, with the interactions changing all elements. Change would normally be gradual, but may be rapid, for example in the aftermath of a major disaster. The model involves process and is dynamic rather than static.

References

Bourne, L.S. (1981) *The Geography of Housing.* Edward Arnold: Toronto.

Goldhaber, G.M. and deTurck, M.A. (1988) Effectiveness of warning signs: gender and familiarity effects. *Journal of Product Liability.* Vol 11, pp 271-284.

Handmer, J.W. (1984) *Property Acquisition for Flood Damage Reduction.* PhD Thesis, Department of Geography, Australian National University: Canberra.

Handmer, J.W. (1985) Flood policy reversal in New South Wales. *Disasters*. Vol 9, No 4, pp 279-285.

Handmer, J.W. and Ord, K.D. (1986) Flood warning and response. In Smith, D.I. and Handmer, J.W. (eds) *Flood Warning in Australia*. Centre for Resource and Environmental Studies, Australian National University: Canberra. pp 235-257.

Macken, D. (1986) In sickness and in wealth. *The Age*. Melbourne. 31 May, pp E1-E2.

McGuire, W.J. (1985) The myth of massive media effect: savagings and salvagings. *Public Communication and Behavior*. Vol 1, pp 173-257.

Oskamp, S. (1984) *Applied social psychology*. Prentice Hall.

Partlett, D.F. (1987) *Forecasts, Warnings and Legal Liability: High Pressure and Gale Warnings for Weather Forecasting*. Centre for Resource and Environmental Studies, Australian National University: Canberra (Working Paper 1987/7).

Rivers, J.P.W. (1982) Women and children last: an essay on sex discrimination in disasters. *Disasters*. Vol 6, No 4, pp 256-267.

Tompkins, R.K. (1987) On risk communication as inter-organisational control: the case of the aviation safety reporting system. Paper at *Colloquy on Natural and Technological Hazards*. University of Colorado: Boulder.

Wassersug, S.R. (1989) The role of risk assessment in developing environmental policy. *International Environment Reporter*. (January), pp 33-43.

SECTION IV
ASSESSING SUCCESS

8 Evaluating the Performance of Flood Warning Systems

Dennis Parker and Jeremy Neal

Abstract

After demonstrating the growth in the use of flood warnings, and recent instances of warning system failure in Britain, this chapter addresses some of the problems of evaluating the performance of flood warning systems. Various possible performance indicators are discussed, and some of the factors influencing the utilisation, and limiting the usefulness, of these indicators are evaluated. Several examples are given of these evaluations, based on preliminary research findings from the Severn Trent Water Authority area in Britain.

Introduction: the growing dependence on flood warnings

There appears to be growing dependence on flood forecasting and warning as an important type of risk communication in Britain. Reliable statistics are currently unavailable but the value of property in floodplains is almost certainly increasing and it is possible that the number of people living in flood prone areas is also steadily rising. In addition, water authorities are currently implementing plans to reduce the number of properties not covered by a flood warning service. This growing emphasis on flood warnings is not just a feature of Britain. For example, in the United States the rapid development of the east-coast barrier islands has placed millions of people within the hurricane surge zone, and as in India and Bangladesh flood forecasting and warning systems are constantly being extended (Rangachari 1986).

The British approach to flood hazard reduction comprises a combination of structural engineering measures, such as flood embankments, and non-structural adjustments, especially floodplain development controls and flood forecasting and warning services (Penning-Rowsell et al 1986, Handmer 1987). Sea flooding is a major threat to life and property, especially along the east coast, where a storm tide warning service was established following the 1953 flood disaster in which over 300 people died. A similar storm tide warning service is currently being established on the south and west coasts.

British rivers are generally short in length and this reduces flood warning lead times to between 2-10 hours. The heavily urbanised catchments are so flashy that a 30 minute warning lead time is not uncommon. Nevertheless, on many rivers the Water Authorities have established a flood forecasting and warning capability based on rainfall-runoff models. Additionally, experiments are being made to extend flood warning lead times by using weather radar which permits flood routing models to be driven by data on rainfall duration and intensity rather than on river flow. The potential annual value of a flood warning service in urban areas in England and Wales, based on weather radar, has been estimated to be between 1.22 million and 3.0 million pounds sterling (National Water Council and Meteorological Office 1983).

Recent flood forecasting and warning failures in Britain

It is self evident that forecasting and warning systems sometimes fail. This was dramatically demonstrated by the problems the Meteorological Office had in warning the British public of the severe storm accompanied by hurricane-force winds which devastated southern England on 16 October 1987.

While a number of floods have been successfully forecast in the recent past, there have also been notable failures. The York city flood warning system proved unsatisfactory during the 1978 flood when the police failed to warn those requiring warning. As a consequence, and following public pressure, remedial measures were taken such that during the 1982 floods in York the warning system apparently performed well, perhaps partly because the public had experience of how best to respond.

The December 1979 river Stour floods caused more damage than would have been the case had Wessex Water Authority been able to make more accurate flood forecasts and had the Christchurch police warned all those at risk (Parker 1987). Similarly, in the same flood event in Blandford Forum in Dorset, local people claimed to have received no warning. Wessex Water Authority has now taken remedial measures.

The December 1981 floods on the Somerset coast which caused approximately 10 million pounds damage were not forecast and the seriousness of the tidal surge only became clear after the sea had overtopped coastal defences. At the time the storm tide warning service was under trial and it appears that liaison between the Meteorological Office and Wessex Water Authority was less than satisfactory.

No warning was given of the floods of 23 August 1987 in the upper Trent catchment because it was believed that a flood warning service was unnecessary. The flood that washed away the railway bridge at Glanrhyd near Newport in north Wales, also in 1987, was not forecast sufficiently well to allow British Rail adequate warning, with the result that a train driver and three passengers lost their lives.

These known failures are probably but a small sample of the problems with the performance of warning systems, especially flood warning systems. Failures are not uncommon, and these problems can seriously undermine the efficacy of our severe weather warning systems in Britain. Indeed, further research may well reveal that serious failures of flood warning systems are much more common – possibly even more common than successes – than has hitherto been recognised. The problem is a global one as the many documented instances of warning failures testify (e.g. Handmer 1988).

Evaluating system performance

Given the reliance now placed on flood warning services in Britain and elsewhere to save lives and reduce property damage, it is important to evaluate the performance and effectiveness of the service. There are a number of ways in which the performance of flood warnings might be assessed and each has its strengths, weaknesses and difficulties (Penning-Rowsell and Handmer 1986).

Extent of coverage

At the crude end of the range of evaluative criteria is the proportion of flood prone properties within a region served by a flood warning service. Data on the number of properties served by flood warnings are relatively easily assembled and this is one of the "level of service" indicators currently used by the water authorities in England and Wales. While this performance indicator is useful at a strategic planning level, it provides no measure of the quality of the service provided, and takes no account of warning system failures. It is possible, for example, that the quality of warning services is declining while they are being extended to cover more properties.

Damages avoided

A more sensitive indicator is the loss avoided by a flood warning service. Clearly, it is much more difficult to assemble data systematically for calibrating this indicator, and a system of near-continuous monitoring of loss avoidance is needed to optimise the flood risk communication process. A further problem is that it is necessary to identify not just the material savings directly or indirectly attributable to flood warnings, but also the less tangible benefits such as reduced anxiety and stress attributable to the presence of an effective and efficient flood warning system.

We now know much more about assessing indirect flood losses such as traffic disruption costs and industrial production outages (Parker et al 1987). However, research in Britain indicates that in some circumstances, even when direct physical flood damage is high, residents rate the intangible flood effects of anxiety and ill-health as being more important (Green et al 1983, Parker et al 1983)). Thus, while it is now relatively simple to estimate direct and indirect flood damages avoided, other important classes of loss present problems. Given that direct physical damages are relatively easy to assess (e.g. Chatterton et al 1979) it is quite likely that attempts to measure performance will concentrate on this category of loss and may miss out precisely those impacts which are more important to flood victims. Thus, giving a misleading measure of performance.

Consumer satisfaction

A third approach to performance evaluation of flood-risk communication is to determine the level of satisfaction of flood warning recipients with the warning service they receive. Consumer preference and customer satisfaction is increasingly being seen in Britain as the most important indicator for the utility industries, including the water authorities which issue flood warnings. Customer satisfaction is seen as an important counter to accountability criticisms especially where monopoly services are concerned, and it matches the current increasing market orientation of public services.

However, a debate has developed among those concerned with evaluating the delivery of services such as local government and police services about whether public evaluations of service delivery are accurate and valid measures of performance (Angrist 1976, Dean 1980, Percy 1986). At one level it is clearly dangerous for government agencies to ignore public views and evaluations of service.

Some empirical evidence shows that there is relatively strong congruence between public and police reports of victimization incidents (Parks 1981). Other empirical evidence suggests that the public frequently have erroneous perceptions of local services and two studies of the police service in the United States suggest there is little in the way of statistically significant relationships between "objective" measures of performance evaluation and public evaluations (Stipak 1979, Brown and Coulter 1983). However, it is possible that the "objective" measures of service delivery used in these studies (e.g. crime levels, response times) bear little relation to those attributes of a police service which the public value most. This is a central problem affecting our ability, first, to evaluate consumer satisfaction meaningfully, and secondly, to design flood warning systems which will work effectively.

Public evaluations of flood warning services present several problems. First, for most people - even those living in floodplains - floods are infrequent events perhaps being experienced only once or twice in a lifetime. The comparison with being a victim of crime is perhaps therefore a useful one. Thus, the basis on which the public has to assess the performance of a flood warning service is usually limited to only a small number of incidents. It is, for example, unlike the fairly continuous basis which people have for assessing the performance of the normal day-to-day weather forecasting system.

Secondly, floods of widely differing severity affect flood prone areas. Public satisfaction with warnings given during a small flood is not necessarily a sound guide to public satisfaction with warnings given in a major flood. Thirdly, there is plenty of evidence to suggest that the public frequently misperceives the flood risk. They also misunderstand flooding mechanisms, and the purpose of, and degree of protection afforded by, flood alleviation projects (Parker and Penning-Rowsell 1982, Penning-Rowsell et al 1986).

The pre-Thames barrier evaluation of the effect of widespread television, poster and leaflet publicity about London's flood warning system undertaken in 1979 is a good example. Despite the massive publicity effort fewer than 10 per cent of those interviewed correctly associated the sound of sirens with the one hour warning. As few as 4 per cent would have taken the correct actions of staying put rather than attempting to go home (Greater London Council 1979). It is tempting to ascribe these findings to the "stupidity" of the public, but it is more likely that the flood warning system was not designed on the basis of a sound understanding of how the public perceive the flood risk and what people are most likely to do following a warning.

Finally, where the public are ill-informed about flood risks, the possibility exists that high levels of public satisfaction with a warning service may reflect complacency or under-estimation of the danger of flooding, and over-estimation of the effectiveness of the warning service.

Examining failures

A further method of risk communication performance evaluation is to identify, categorise and record flood warning "failures", and perhaps to compare these with occasions when the flood warning service apparently performed "adequately". An advantage of this "failure" approach is that the failures may be categorised according to where in the entire flood forecasting and warning system the fault or faults occurred, and this can aid system improvement.

This approach immediately raises some tricky questions about the operational definitions of "failure" and "adequate performance". System performance might be measured according to the number of flood victims who receive an official flood warning within a given time before flooding of their property commences. "Total system failure" would then be defined as the failure to deliver a flood forecast to any flood victims within a given time and area, or the failure even to forecast a flood. "Partial system failure" would relate to the proportion of flood victims not receiving a flood warning. "Adequate performance" might be achieved when, say, 95 per cent of flood victims within a given area receive a flood warning within a given period prior to flooding commencing, and so on. Further categorisation would include cases where warnings are issued but floods do not occur.

The problems with this approach lie in obtaining information after the event when other urgent clean-up tasks are pressing but, more significantly, in the wide range of possible measures of performance which flood victims might use. In the above explanation, failure is related only to receipt or non-receipt of flood warnings and warning "lead time". But there is a wide range of possible attributes of flood warnings which may be just as important or more important to flood victims, such as predicted depth of flooding.

Comments on performance measures

The above four ways of approaching the evaluation of the performance of flood forecasting and warning systems are not the only ones available. For example, Penning-Rowsell and Handmer (1986) list a range of possible measures, including "hydrological/engineering/technical" measures such as comparisons of the flood forecast (say timing and depth) against what actually transpired, or the proportion of "false" forecasts issued. There is also a range of other possible economic measures of performance including a full cost-benefit analysis.

This range of possible performance measures demonstrates that we must be very careful about interpreting what performance measures actually tell us. For example, it is possible that a particular improvement in a flood warning system might be economically efficient whilst at the same time not serving to increase consumer satisfaction. Similarly, technical improvements to warning services may result in no additional consumer satisfaction. The number of "false" warnings may not be a good measure of performance at all since the research reported below suggests that at least some people would rather be warned than not warned at all, even if there is no following flood.

Customer perceptions and evaluations of flood warning systems

If we are to use customer satisfaction as an indicator of the performance of flood warning systems then we need to understand more about the following:

(i)   how the public forms perceptions about floods and flood risks;

(ii) what the public knows about and how the public perceives the responsibilities of authorities involved in delivering flood warnings;

(iii) what attributes of flood warning services the public regard as being the most and the least important; and

(iv) how the public derives their rating of their satisfaction with flood warning services.

Through research on decision theory and bounded rationality, a great deal is already known about cognitive limitations and public perception of floods and flood risks, especially the difficulties which the public experience in handling probabilistic information (Slovic et al 1974). Our knowledge is growing of the factors which influence individuals' response to flood warnings (Handmer and Ord 1986). However, less is known about the last three items in the list above.

Figure 8.1 is a version of Percy's (1986) theoretical framework of influences on citizen perceptions and evaluations of service agency performance, applied to flood warning services. The model is an attempt to clarify the important influences and elements within the cognitive processes by which people perceive the performance of flood warning agencies.

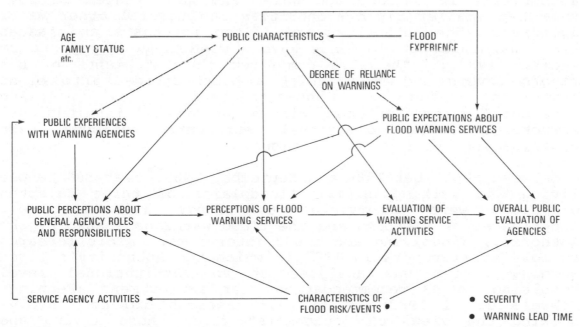

Figure 8.1:   Factors influencing public perception of flood warning system performance (Percy 1986).

Importantly, the model in Figure 8.1 postulates that the public's level of satisfaction with the performance of flood warning services is related to a range of factors. First, there is the individual's overall direct and indirect experiences with water authorities and others involved in the warning process such as the police and local authorities. Experiences may well be related to factors other than flood warnings. In Britain, water authorities make charges for water supplies as well as making flood forecasts, and an individual's experience with water charges - especially if there are customer disatisfactions with the level of water charges - may thus affect his or her performance evaluation. Thus, what Percy (1986) calls the "total service environment" is likely to be important in evaluations of the performance of any one aspect within that environment.

Secondly, there is the individual's understanding of the role and responsibilities of the various agencies involved in flood forecasting and warning. Here there may be misunderstandings and misperceptions. Thirdly, there are the individual's expectations of the flood warning service. This is likely to have a major effect on evaluations of performance, especially where expectations are high or low and where what happens in practice varies greatly from what was expected. Closely related to expectations is reliance - or the degree to which the individual has come to rely on the warning service.

Flood warning performance in the Severn-Trent Water Authority Area

Severn-Trent Water is one of the largest of the ten water authorities in England and Wales and was created in 1974 from two smaller river authorities and several other water agencies. The Authority makes flood forecasts and issues flood warnings but does not have a mandatory duty to do so (Parker 1987). The area comprises the catchments of the rivers Severn and Trent which are sub-divided into eight divisions based on sub-catchments, thus allowing considerable local autonomy within the overall institutional structure. The divisional structure reflects past organisation, policy and practices.

Between September 1986 and September 1987, over 500 people living and working on the floodplains of three selected divisions were interviewed to obtain data on their experiences of flooding and the flood warnings issued by the Authority, (involving about 650 interviews). This research follows earlier work in 1983 in which the Authority's flood warning system was analysed at an institutional level resulting in 53 recommendations for improvement (Penning-Rowsell et al 1983). The 1983 research did not involve seeking the views of "customers" (i.e. those living and working in floodplains), but the latest research builds on one of the recommendations - that the views of floodplain users should be sought in order to evaluate further the performance of the flood warning system.

During the recent period of research there have been a number of floods and numerous flood alerts and warnings. In particular the Upper Severn catchment was severely flooded in November 1986 and January 1987 by floods with an estimated annual probability of occurrence of 5 per cent (return period of about 20 years). In August 1987 the Upper Trent catchment suffered floods with an estimated annual occurrence probability of 1 per cent (return period of about 100 years).

In the following sections of this chapter, the flood warnings of the Severn-Trent Water Authority are examined using the performance criteria set out above.

Evidence of actual and potential system failures

To begin by evaluating the research results overall: Table 8.1 provides data on the number of "failures" to warn floodplain users of floods within the three Water Authority divisions, based on the sample of floodplain users interviewed. Here, the measure of "failure" is a crude one and comprises whether or not someone who was flooded received a flood warning. Thus, this measure takes no account of whether the flood warning was regarded as being useful by the respondent. There were 154 cases, from a total of 513 responses, in which floodplain occupants were flooded but received no warning. Of these 154, 65 are in the Upper Trent division. There are also 39 cases when a warning was issued but flooding did not occur, nearly nine-tenths of whom are in the Upper Severn division.

Table 8.2 gives the warning lead times experienced by those respondents who could recall this accurately. In 19 cases the warning lead time is negative in that the warning was received after flooding had commenced, and in 18 cases the warning was received as flooding commenced.

An intuitive evaluation of the performance of the three divisions reveals some marked contrasts. These are closely related to historical institutional factors, which also help to explain some of the overall results. This evaluation suggests that the warning system is in a condition to fail either totally or partially in two out of the three divisions and that these failures are likely at different stages within the flood forecasting and warning process (Figure 8.2).

Upper Severn division The Upper Severn division has a history, over the past 40 years, of repeated major flooding. Although some towns and farmland are protected to some extent by flood embankments and other structural measures, flooding still presents a serious problem. In consequence the Water Authority has continued to operate a relatively highly organised flood forecasting and warning system inherited from its predecessor agency.

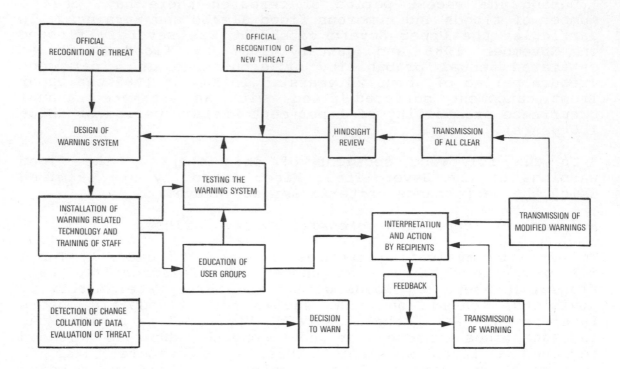

Figure 8.2: Foster's (1980) idealised model of warning
system design and evaluation.

While this system is designed to provide warnings for the
various urban areas within the catchment, the system is
perhaps most closely attuned to the needs of farmers and
landowners who suffer the most frequent and usually the most
severe flooding. The warning system relies on a network of
flood wardens who receive information from the Water
Authority, in some cases via the police, and who then
disseminate the warnings to neighbours further along the
information dissemination chain (Harding and Parker 1974).

This system appears to work well especially within the
farming community in which "neighbourliness" is strongly
developed. Here, then, the Water Authority divisional staff
well appreciate the risk of flooding and its potentially
serious effects on the community. The forecasting system is
thus well developed and local people cooperate relatively
effectively to minimise the flood danger: the system appears
to perform well.

Upper Trent division In the Upper Trent division, however,
Water Authority staff do not believe that there is much need
for a flood warning system. The history of this division is
that during the time of the previous Trent River Authority
much was done in the way of structural works to provide
towns and floodplains with a high standard of flood
protection – often originally to a 1 per cent (100 year
return period) standard. Thus, divisional staff believe

Table 8.1

Performance of the flood warning service in three
Severn Trent Water Authority Divisions 1986 - 1987.

Were you flooded?

Were you warned?	Upper Severn		Upper Trent		Avon		Total
	No	Yes	No	Yes	No	Yes	
No	76	75	0	65	19	14	249
Yes	34	214	0	0	5	11	264
Total	110	289	0	65	24	25	513

Table 8.2

Reported lead times by warned respondents.

Reported flood warning lead time (hours)	Frequency of occurence	Per cent
-6.00 to -10.00	10	7.5
-0.25 to -5.00	9	6.8
0.00	18	13.5
0.02 to 5.00	49	36.8
6.00 to 10.00	26	19.5
11.00 to 20.00	17	12.8
more than 20.00	4	3.1
	133	100.0

Notes: 36 cases warned but not flooded.
94 missing cases.

147

that while there is a threat of residual flooding, there is little call for a well developed warning service; although they have issued warnings in certain circumstances in the past. Indeed, during the 1983 study we encountered a belief amongst some divisional staff that it was preferable to avoid any suggestion of developing flood warning services further within the Upper Trent area, lest people come to rely on them. This belief was still present in 1987.

There is also a feeling that to inform the public of the residual flooding problem - now probably increasing as catchment urbanisation and other factors lead to declining protection standards - would be to spread alarm unnecessarily. Thus, the views prevalent within this division are a legacy of history and previous practice but they do not accord with those of Severn Trent Water Authority's headquarters staff who believe that there is a strong case for establishing a more comprehensive flood warning service for the Upper Trent catchment.

This case was dramatically underlined by the severe flooding of 23 August 1987 during which at least 80 residential and industrial properties were flooded in Stoke-on-Trent and Uttoxeter. Road communications throughout the region were disrupted and the motoring organisations received over 2,000 calls for assistance. Although the Water Authority was able to monitor rainfall and stream levels, no flood warning was issued. This must be counted as a "total system failure" due in large part to the belief within the division that the flood warning system should not be extended.

Avon division In the Avon division, where the flood threat is similar to that in the Upper Severn, divisional staff believe that there is value in a flood forecasting and warning system. However, our knowledge of this area indicates that difficulties are being experienced in establishing and maintaining a warning dissemination system which is likely to be successful in the event of a flood being forecast.

The principal difficulty in this division in 1987 was a general problem identified in the 1983 research. The Authority is able to forecast floods and issue warnings to the police. But liaison with the police, who normally shoulder the burden of disseminating flood warnings to the public, is proving problematic. This is because some parts of the Avon catchment fall within police areas which deal mainly with another water authority and the police appear reluctant to liaise with Avon division. Also, the police do not appear to want flood warnings from the Avon division. Apparently the police take the view that, if received, these warnings will not be acted upon. Finally, there is concern within the Avon division that the police will either under- or over-react to any flood warnings received. Thus, in some parts of this division, the warning dissemination system is not well assembled and partial or total warning failures are more than likely in the event of a flood being forecast.

Customer satisfaction with the flood warning service

In an attempt to measure customer satisfaction with the Severn Trent Water Authority flood warning service, all those interviewed were asked to rate, on a four point scale, how satisfied they were with the current flood warning service (Table 8.3).

The results indicate that, of the 495 cases included, the highest levels of customer *satisfaction* are found in the Upper Severn division where 81.9 per cent were either "completely" or "quite" satisfied with the warning service provided. The highest levels of customer *dissatisfaction* appear in the Avon division where 32.6 per cent are either "not very" or "not at all" satisfied with the service they receive, and where as many as 65 per cent of respondents proposed changes to the current service.

The results from the Upper Trent division are significant. Despite the fact that all 64 respondents had been flooded without a warning (Table 8.4), this division records the highest proportion of "completely" satisfied customers, although the proportion of "not very" satisfied and "not at all" satisfied customers is also high at 28.2 per cent. In this case, the data appear to support the importance of consumer reliance and expectations on their performance evaluations (Figure 8.1). Reliance on the flood warning service is lower in this division than elsewhere, and thus expectations are lower, and this appears to be one reason why lower levels of satisfaction are not recorded.

The interpretation of these results should recognise, first, that overall the responses are heavily biased towards the Upper Severn division, where most flood warnings were issued during the research period. Secondly, the results from the Upper Trent division suggest that many respondents are apparently satisfied with no service, possibly because their reliance on the service is low because there has been no service in the past.

Changes consumers require to warning services   Table 8.5 summarises the first, second and third mentioned changes which respondents suggested would lead to an improved flood warning service. The first three desired changes seek to extend warning lead times, to predict the maximum flood depth, and to provide more information in warning messages. However, the next most frequently mentioned improvements – "make sure we get a warning" and "a flood warning system would be useful" – suggest that flood victims would rather receive a warning than not receive one, even if flooding does not follow. The need to provide a warning in daylight hours is also significant. This response comes mainly from farmers who find it difficult to take actions such as finding and moving stock at night, and points to the need for targeted warning systems.

Table 8.3

Satisfaction with the flood warning service in
three Severn Trent Water Authority Divisions

Division	Satisfaction level (percent)					Reliance* (mean)	Changes needed (% yes)	No.of valid cases
	Comple-tely	Quite	Not very	Not at all	N.A.			
Upper Severn								
residential	31.6	47.4	8.8	3.5	8.8	3.44	26.8	57
agricultural	30.4	52.4	8.4	7.4	1.3	2.41	43.8	309
industrial	26.3	52.6	10.5	10.5	0.0	2.68	47.4	19
overall	30.4	51.5	8.8	7.0	2.3	2.56	41.4	388
Upper Trent								
residential	0	00.0	0.0	0.0	0.0	4.00	0.0	1
agricultural	48.4	22.6	22.6	6.5	0.0	3.40	36.7	62
industrial	0.0	00.0	0.0	0.0	0.0	4.00	0.0	1
overall	46.9	25.0	21.9	6.3	0.0	3.42	35.5	64
Avon								
residential								0
agricultural	25.8	38.7	9.7	22.6	3.2	2.96	65.5	31
industrial	16.7	50.0	25.0	8.3	0.0	3.00	63.6	12
overall	23.3	41.9	14.0	18.6	0.0	2.52	65.0	43

Note: *Reliance   1 = "completely"
                        2 = "considerably"
                        3 = "not very much"
                        4 = "not at all"

Table 8.4

General satisfaction levels of flooded respondents
in three Severn Trent Water Authority Divisions.

Division	Satisfaction level (per cent)					No.of valid cases
	Comple-tely	Quite	Not very	Not at all	N.A.	
Upper Severn						
Warned	35.6	51.9	8.2	4.3	0.0	208
Not warned	18.6	47.1	14.3	20.0	0.0	70
Overall	31.3	50.7	9.7	8.2	0.0	278
Upper Trent						
Warned	0	0	0	0	0	0
Not warned	46.9	25.0	21.9	6.3	·0.0	64
Overall	46.9	25.0	21.9	6.3	0.0	64
Avon						
Warned	27.3	63.6	9.1	0.0	0.0	11
Not warned	30.8	23.1	7.7	30.8	7.7	15
Overall	29.2	41.7	8.2	16.7	4.2	28

Table 8.5

Changes required to the Severn Trent Water Authority
flood warning system (recorded comments).

Repondents who felt that changes could be made in order to improve
the current service. Comments in the table represent all those
mentioned more than once.

	Frequencies			
COMMENT	First	Second	Third	Overall
Extend warning lead times/issue warnings earlier	31	5	0	36
Predict the maximum flood depth	6	9	12	27
Provide more information in the warnings	13	6	2	21
Provide a constantly updated information source	6	7	3	16
Give the warning during daylight hours	2	14	0	16
Make sure we get a warning	15	0	0	15
A flood warning system would be useful	11	0	0	11
Provide an answerphone service	3	3	4	10
Refer to river levels at a known land mark	2	5	2	9
Include details of the rate of rise	0	5	4	9
Include information on the state of roads	4	2	2	8
Provide written instructions on what to do	7	0	0	7
Provide at least two hours notice	0	6	0	6
Predict the size of the flood	2	0	3	5
Anything would be an improvement	3	0	0	3
The water authority should issue the warnings	3	0	0	3
Clean out the river	3	0	0	3
Land liable to flood is away from the farm house	0	3	0	3
Issue warnings in the summer months	0	3	0	3
Get the warnings out as quickly as possible	2	0	0	2
Return the control of warnings to the police	2	0	0	2
Give details of help available during the flood	0	2	0	2
Issue warnings in plenty of time for livestock to be moved	0	2	0	2
Existing threshold levels are too far apart	0	2	0	2
Make flood warnings more localised	0	2	0	2
Risk a false warning rather than issue no warning	0	0	2	2
Those who need to move stock must get a warning in daylight hours	0	0	2	2
We keep cattle inside during the winter	0	0	2	2
The levelling station should be kept maintained	0	0	2	2
Others (other comments recorded once only)	47	38	29	114
TOTAL	162	114	69	345

Flood losses avoided by the flood warning service

The flood losses avoided by the Severn Trent Water Authority warning service appear to be less than expected and there are difficulties in using data on flood losses avoided to evaluate warning system performance.

For those respondents who received a flood warning from the Severn Trent Water Authority, and who were subsequently flooded, Table 8.6 shows the direct and indirect flood losses avoided. These losses were avoided as a result of actions taken both prior to the warning being received, which are thus not attributable to the flood warning, and also after the warning was received. The results show that the estimated flood losses avoided during the 1986-87 study period owing to damage-reducing actions taken by individual land and property owners totalled 1,508,749 pounds sterling. However, only 19.8 per cent of this estimated avoided loss was due to the official flood warning system.

For those warned, the estimated losses avoided which were not attributable to the flood warning were 729,475 pounds, and those attributable to the flood warning were 298,450 pounds. For those not warned, the estimated losses avoided just due to prompt actions, without warning, were 480,824 pounds.

Taking the Upper Severn division, where there is a relatively high level of satisfaction with the flood warning service (Table 8.3), approximately three quarters of the losses avoided are not attributable to the service itself but to the vigilance of the floodplain occupants, most of whom are farmers (Table 8.6). We must therefore ask whether this satisfaction with the flood warning service here is due solely to what the system provides or whether it is not also related to the total losses avoided, from both "official" and "unofficial" warnings.

It is not easy to determine whether these data indicate that the official flood warning system is performing satisfactorily or unsatisfactorily - there is therefore a problem with this performance measure. For example, while there have undoubtedly been savings from the warning service, these savings appear to be limited. It is quite possible that the warning service is not providing the right kind of warnings to permit recipients to make greater savings. One possible means of further evaluating the warning system in terms of loss avoidance might be to compare reported savings with those savings which would be reasonably expected given different warning lead times. This is being pursued in further research.

Conclusions

Evaluating the performance of flood warning systems is a complex problem. As this paper demonstrates, the problem is amenable to a variety of approaches but much research

Table 8.6

Damage reduction by warned respondents: proportion attributable to flood warnings in three Severn Trent Water Authority Divisions.

Mean reported warning lead time (hours)	Attributable to flood warnings	Directs avoided (£)	Indirects avoided (£)	No.of valid cases
Damage reduction				
UPPER SEVERN				
	Yes Total	273,700	2,400	60
4.89	Mean	4,558	40	
	No Total	728,725	55,300	74
4.45	Mean	9,847	747	
residential				
	Yes Total	200	0	2
0.00	Mean	100	0	
	No Total	2,820	0	2
11.50	Mean	1,410	0	
agricultural				
	Yes Total	273,500	2,400	57
4.87	Mean	4,798	480	
	No Total	712,605	50,300	67
4.31	Mean	10,635	739	
industrial				
	Yes Total	0	0	1
-7.00	Mean	0	0	
	No Total	13,300	5,000	5
3.56	Mean	2,660	1,000	
AVON (agricultural cases only)				
	Yes Total	22,350	0	4
5.67	Mean	5,587	0	
	No Total	750	0	1
missing	Mean	750	0	

Note: A minor sign against mean reported warning lead-time indicates that the warning was received after flooding commenced.

remains to be done, not least in interpreting precisely what different performance indicators actually reveal about flood warning systems.

The "failure" approach looks promising, providing that a more subtle index of failure can be produced which utilises those attributes of flood warnings which consumers regard as important. The "consumer satisfaction" approach will remain problematic until more is known about what factors determine satisfaction, and it may well be that consumer satisfaction is not the most appropriate measure of performance where flood warnings are concerned. The "loss avoidance" approach is feasible where avoided-losses attributable and not attributable to flood warnings can be isolated - otherwise it is misleading - but more research is required to compare the loss avoidance achieved with the theoretical maximum loss avoidance.

The research on flood warnings within the Severn Trent area suggest that warning system failures will occur in parts of at least two out of the three divisions studied, either because of historical and institutional reasons or because of inter-agency liaison problems. In the other division the consumer satisfaction with the flood warning service appears to be high, but this may not be entirely attributable to the flood warning service. It appears also to be related to the degree of success individual floodplain occupants are experiencing in reducing losses, irrespective of the warnings they receive. Consumer satisfaction may turn out to be lower here in more extreme events with which they have, by definition, less experience of coping.

Our results suggest that the degree to which floodplain occupants rely on flood warnings is a most important influence on their levels of satisfaction. We can now see that many improvements are needed in the warning service, and that providing earlier warnings is a top priority, and that providing some warning is more important than worrying too much about "false" warnings.

Overall, the research findings have several lessons for risk communication in general. However, these lessons probably only apply to warnings of extreme events which are characterised by gradual rather than very sudden onset. First, those who are most readily activated to take avoidance actions are also likely to be those who have built up the most experience of extreme events through living and working in frequently affected hazard zones. These people are also those who are most likely to have developed their own environmental cues to the onset of extreme events and procedures for avoiding damage. It could perhaps be suggested that these people do not require an "official" warning service, but here we recognise that in these instances warnings may offer vital confirmation rather than a first alert.

Second, customer satisfaction with a warning service may not necessarily be the basis on which to design and invest in warning systems. Relatively high levels of public satisfaction may well reflect low expectations and are no guard against a disaster. In this sense warning services may well exhibit the characteristics of "merit goods" in that they should, perhaps, be provided for the good of the public at risk, even where the public appears to place a low valuation on them and is relatively satisfied without them.

Acknowledgement

The authors wish to acknowledge Severn Trent Water Authority which provided the contract for the research reported here.

References

Angrist, S. (1976) Subjective social indicators for urban areas: how useful for policy? *Social Forces*. Vol 9, pp 217-230.

Brown, K. and Coulter, P. (1983) Subjective and objective measures of police service delivery. *Public Admin. Review*. Vol 43, pp 50-58.

Chatterton, J.B., Pirt, J. and Wood, T.R. (1979) The benefit of flood forecasting. *Journal of the Institution of Water Engineers and Scientists*. Vol 33, No 3, pp 237-252.

Dean, D. (1980) Citizen ratings of the police: the difference contact makes. *Law and Policy Quarterly*. Vol 2, pp 445-471.

Foster, H.D. (1980) *Disaster Planning: The Preservation of Life and Property*. Springer Verlag: Berlin.

Greater London Council (1979) *London tidal flood warning system - Report on surveys associated with exercise floodcall 1978*. Greater London Council: London.

Green, C.H., Parker, D.J. and Emery, P.J. (1983) *The Real Costs of Flooding to Households: The Intangible Costs*. Middlesex Polytechnic Flood Hazard Research Centre: Enfield.

Handmer, J.W. (Ed) (1987) *Flood Hazard Management: British and International Perspectives*. Geobooks: Norwich.

Handmer, J.W. (1988) The performance of the Sydney flood warning system, August 1986. *Disasters*. Vol 12, No 1, pp 37-49.

Handmer, J.W. and Ord, K.D. (1986) Flood warning and response. In Smith, D.I. and Handmer, J.W. (Eds) *Flood Warning in Australia*. The Australian National University, Centre for Resource and Environmental Studies: Canberra.

Harding, D.M. and Parker, D.J. (1974) Flood hazard at Shrewsbury, UK. In White, G.F. (Ed) *Natural Hazards, Local, National, Global*. Oxford University Press: New York.

National Water Council - Meteorological Office (1983) *Report of the Working Group on National Weather Radar Coverage*. NWC: London.

Parker, D.J. (1987) Flood warning dissemination: the British experience. In Handmer, J.W. (Ed) *Flood Hazard Management: British and International Perspectives*. Geobooks: Norwich.

Parker, D.J. and Penning-Rowsell, E.C. (1982) Flood risk in the urban environment. In Herbert, D.T. and Johnson, R.J. (Eds), *Geography and The Urban Environment*. Wiley: Chichester. pp 201-239.

Parker, D.J., Green, C.H. and Penning-Rowsell, E.C. (1983) *Swalecliffe Coast Protection Scheme: Evaluation of Potential Benefits*. Middlesex Polytechnic Flood Hazard Research Centre: Enfield.

Parker, D.J., Green, C.H. and Thompson, P.M. (1987) *Urban Flood Protection Benefits: a Project Appraisal Guide*. Gower Technical Press: Aldershot.

Parks, R. (1981) Comparing citizen and observer perceptions of police-citizen encounters. Paper presented at the *Annual Meeting of the Southern Political Science Association*. Jackson MS.

Penning-Rowsell, E.C., Parker, D.J., Crease, D. and Mattison, C. (1983) *Flood warning dissemination: an evaluation of some current practices within the Severn Trent Water Authority area*. Middlesex Polytechnic Flood Hazard Research Centre: Enfield (Geography and Planning Paper 7).

Penning-Rowsell, E.C., Parker, D.J. and Harding, D.M. (1986) *Floods and Drainage: British Policies for Hazard Reduction, Agricultural Improvement and Wetland Conservation*. Allen and Unwin: Hemel Hempstead.

Penning-Rowsell, E.C. and Handmer, J.W. (1986) *Evaluating flood warning effectiveness: the conceptual, methodological and practical research problems*. The Australian National University, Centre for Resource and Environmental Studies: Canberra (Working Paper 1986/6)

Penning-Rowsell, E.C. and Handmer, J.W. (1986) *Flood forecasting and warning: a survey of institutions and policies*. The Australian National University, Centre for Resources and Environmental Studies: Canberra (Working Paper 1986/25).

Percy, S.L. (1986) In defense of citizen evaluations as performance measures. *Urban Affairs Quarterly*. Vol 22, No 1, pp 66-83.

Rangachari, R. (1986) *Flood Forecasting and Warning Network on Interstate Rivers of India*. Government of India, Ministry of Water Resources Central Water Commission: New Dehli.

Slovic, P., Kunreuther, H. and White, G.F. (1974) Decision processes, rationality and adjustments to natural hazards. In White G F (Ed) *Natural Hazards, Local, National and Global*. Oxford University Press: New York.

Stipak, B. (1979) Citizen satisfaction with urban services: potential misuse as a performance indicator. *Public Administration Review*. Vol 39, pp 45-52.

9 Evaluating Communications about Nuclear Energy: the Case of Sizewell "B"

Jennifer Brown

Abstract

Risk communication is a burgeoning field of research drawing from many disciplines among which psychology is clearly of central importance.

This chapter reports the findings of an attitude survey of a representative sample of the population living within a 30 kilometre radius of the Sizewell A nuclear power station. The site, owned and operated by the Central Electricity Generating Board (CEGB), has been the subject of a protracted public inquiry into proposals to build an additional nuclear station of the pressurised water reactor (PWR) type.

The CEGB undertook a series of detailed consultations with local people about nuclear energy in general and the PWR in particular. This chapter describes these as well as an evaluation of the various modes of communication used, and presents a series of recommendations based on the study's findings.

Introduction: aims and context

The context for this chapter is that of communication research characterised as analysing "who says what to whom, how, and with what effect" (Lee 1986, p 150). Here the "what" specifically refers to nuclear energy, and the "who" is the Central Electricity Generating Board (CEGB) as the originating source of risk information. Most particularly the chapter will focus, first, on the "how", as measured by a series of evaluations of CEGB communication techniques, including exhibitions, guided tours, talks and information dissemination, and, secondly, on the impact these communications have on the "whom" (i.e. the general public living within a 30 kilometre radius of an existing CEGB nuclear power plant subject to a planning proposal for an additional reactor).

With regard to context, in January 1981 the CEGB made a formal application to the Secretary of State for Energy to build a pressurised water reactor (PWR) at Sizewell in Suffolk. The government instigated what turned out to be a long running public inquiry with hearings lasting from 11th January 1983 to 7th March 1985. Not only was there intense local press coverage of the issues discussed during the inquiry, but there were also frequent national newspaper and television news stories and documentaries.

In an effort to reach local people more directly the CEGB instituted various types of information dissemination. Against this background, the Board commissioned a research group within the Department of Psychology at the University of Surrey to evaluate the impact of these different forms of communication. This was done, first, by conducting a quantitative survey of 701 individuals living in a 30 kilometre radius catchment area from the actual and proposed reactor site, and secondly by a detailed evaluation of the CEGB's communication media.

Three interrelated issues in particular will be addressed:

(i)   Why communicate information at all?
(ii) What are the processes involved in the transmission of information?
(iii) What recommendations can be made once the evaluations have been undertaken?

The work reported spans five years, and covers a considerable variety of topics related to risk communication and response. The public's understanding of the term radiation and radioactive waste is described in Brown and White (1987); theoretical issues about communication are covered by Lee (1986); and descriptions of children's knowledge and attitudes are provided in Brown et al (in press).

Rationale for providing information

There are a number of reasons why information about potential hazards is communicated to the public. Four have been characterised by Covello et al (1986). There are, first, reasons related to information and education; second, joint problem solving and conflict resolution (public participation in decision making); third, behavioural changes and protective action; and, fourth, reasons related to disaster warnings and emergency information.

The first of these is considered non-directive but purposeful activity to inform the lay public about potential hazards. This is a pre-requisite for public debate and participation. The last two are generally more directive and are often aimed at individual health or natural hazard warnings. The motives for the non-directive type of communication are usually couched in terms of sound democratic principles, but with a touch of realism. Cvetkovitch et al (1987) point out that the desire to communicate to the public is a response to the "right" of citizens to know about the possible hazards they face, but also it is a pragmatic recognition of the need to give information in the aftermath of disasters such as Seveso, Bhopal or Chernobyl.

With respect to the communication of information about nuclear energy, it is the general educative and participation rationales that are involved. These are elaborated further below.

Communication of information about nuclear energy

The rationale for providing information is based on the key concept of democratic participation in decisions, and on educational objectives. Both mean that government is pressured to provide clear, unambiguous information on nuclear power for the public at large.

Democratic participation

The government in the United Kingdom makes both explicit and implicit statements on this issue in policy documents, parliamentary debates and through Select Committees. These tend to be broad, all-encompassing statements. The Royal Commission on Environmental Pollution, chaired by Sir Brian Flowers (1976), in a section entitled "Public Assessment of Nuclear Power" pointed out that nuclear development raised major issues of unusual range and difficulty which are political and ethical as well as technical in character. It was the belief of the Committee that these issues could only be fully appreciated and weighed in the light of "wide public understanding".

From the 1986 report of the House of Commons Environment Committee on nuclear waste (the Rossi Report), comes the following:

> There is a need to provide more information and to help
> the public understand the issues (Para 233)
> The industry must make positive efforts to give as much
> information as possible to the public, regardless of
> the identity of those asking for it... (Para 234)

The recommendations of this committee included the suggestion that the nuclear industry should review its approach to informing the public and should be more open and forthright.

One could also refer to planning legislation. The Skeffington Report (Ministry of Housing and Local Government 1969) aimed to achieve better decisions from the planning process by basing them on fuller discussions with information coming partly from the public. The *Town and Country Planning Act 1968* refers to the need for adequate publicity and to peoples' right to comment on plans. The implication is that effective information is a pre-requisite for participation, which is itself a right the public should guard carefully.

Educational objectives

Various bodies are concerned to enhance the image of science generally, and thus promote scientific awareness among the public. The Royal Society is prominent in this sphere. In a report called *Public Understanding of Science*, published in 1985, it argued for a better science education for all. Generally it was felt that a better public understanding of science could be a major element in promoting national prosperity, the rationale being that a strong economy depends on science and technology which needs skilled scientific personnel. Hostility and indifference to science, which appeared to be more common in Britain than amongst our industrial competitors, "weakens the nation's industry" (p9).

Science is also seen as important on a personal level. The report argued that since almost all public policy issues have scientific or technological implications, everybody needs some understanding of science. Personal decisions such as those concerning diet, vaccinations, hygiene and safety at home or work were cited as being helped by an understanding of science.

The basis of this understanding should be a "proper" science education, reinforced by more science in newspapers and on television. Children were specifically mentioned as a group towards whom considerable effort should be expended on communicating scientific ideas. Moreover, scientists should learn to communicate with the public more effectively and to this end should consider it their duty to "explain science simply" (p 6).

Assessment: obligations and problems

The various nuclear agencies in Britain have a mandate to provide public information about the science and technology of nuclear energy. The United Kingdom Atomic Energy Authority (UKAEA) has an obligation to produce information for the public, deriving from the *Atomic Energy Act 1954* which states that:

> The authority shall have power to distribute information relating to, and educate and train persons in matters connected with, radioactive substances.

Both the CEGB and the UKAEA publish information leaflets, mount exhibitions and provide a special service for schools. The UKAEA additionally makes films for distribution to schools. There is a huge budget for the provision of information (over 3 million pounds sterling in 1983).

All of these obligations and initiatives call for a more informed citizenry who can contribute to national prosperity, make better personal decisions and play a role in planning decisions.

But there is a dilemma. Essentially, we have to ask: "is there such a thing as neutral information?" The ethical issues concerning communication of risk information have been addressed with respect to our own research by Lee (1986) and elegantly elaborated by Earle and Cvetkovich (1987). Space precludes an extended discussion of these issues here, but our view in conducting this research is a recognition that for people to participate in decisions about potentially hazardous technology, information must be geared to their needs and agendas. However, a recurring attitude amongst the scientific or engineering communities is one of "correcting the misperceptions" of a technically illiterate and irrational public. Unless evaluations of material originating from these professional sources are undertaken, these assumptions will continue to be perpetuated and the gap between "expert" and the lay public will continue to widen.

The process of information transmission

The availability, flow and receipt and retention of information about potential and/or actual hazards takes place within a complicated network of transmission. Cvetkovitch et al (1987) note that several levels of decision making and interpretation are involved, many of which are not under the direct control of the originating source: in our case the electricity utility.

Other researchers (Covello et al 1986, Slovic et al 1982) point out that the news (and entertainment) media not only act as transmitters but also as translators of information between the risk communicators and the public. The news media have been criticised for exaggeration, overemphasis on the human drama, selectivity and biased reporting. In some cases the media will persuade people to act in such a way as to conform to news norms. For example, Three Mile Island film crews asked people to move indoors so they could show deserted streets (Lagadec 1985).

Scientific and technical information is diffused through a series of filters from the expert to the lay public. Such a process has been described by Moscovici and Hewstone (1983). They propose that consumption of news in scientific fields variously takes place in classrooms, living rooms and work canteens, and derives from television, films, and casual chats. Moreover, during its diffusion, scientific knowledge not only becomes detached from its parent method or discipline, but is transformed by the particular communication channel. In addition, individuals respond selectively to the information, in order to serve their own particular goals and purposes.

This process of selectivity is accompanied by an approximation principle. In dealing with information of this type, non-scientifically literate individuals find the concepts or details unfamiliar. In an attempt to reduce uncertainty or ambiguity, they anchor the unknown to its nearest plausible approximation. Ryder (1982) and Brown et al (in press) give examples of this approximation principle at work with reference to children's understanding of nuclear energy. For adults, Slovic et al (1982) point out

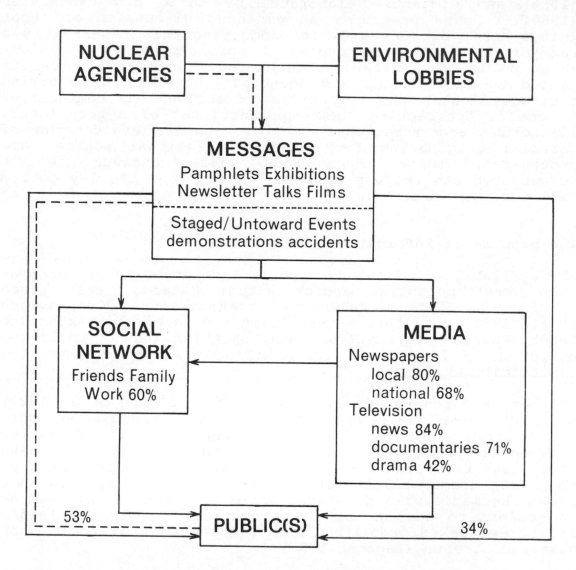

Figure 9.1: Transmission and filtering of information about nuclear energy. Percentages refer to the proportion of respondents in the Sizewell area (total = 701) receiving information via particular sources. The dotted line is the route studied in detail.

that nuclear energy is particularly prone to such a process because of its association with the vivid and imaginable dangers of nuclear war. (See also Chapter 6 of this volume).

For the purpose of the present discussion a summary diagram illustrates the transmission network (Figure 9.1). The originating sources of messages about nuclear energy tend to be the principal pro-nuclear organisations and their antagonists, namely the various nuclear agencies and the environmental lobby. Their messages may be directed through talks, leaflets or exhibitions. Results of our survey conducted in March 1985 in a 30 kilometre radius of the Sizewell site indicated that 53 per cent of the 701 respondents did receive information from the CEGB directly and 34 per cent from an environmental organisation.

However, the survey did indicate, overwhelmingly, that most people obtain information from their local or national newspapers and from television. Interestingly, nearly half (42 per cent) claim their information comes from watching television drama or films.

Finally, the issue of the proposed power station was evidently a matter of local concern and 60 per cent claim to have gained information from discussions with family, friends and working colleagues.

It is beyond the scope of the present chapter to tackle the complexities of the impact of these differing sources of information on peoples' understanding of nuclear energy. Rather, attention is turned to one particular route: that of CEGB generated messages and the impact these had on targetted groups.

Evaluating CEGB information at Sizewell

The CEGB undertook extensive consultations with the local public around the site of the Sizewell nuclear reactor concerning the proposal to build a Pressurized Water Reactor.

CEGB information evaluated

The Surrey research team conducted an audit of the various methods that the CEGB had used to communicate information to local people about nuclear energy in general, and the PWR in particular. What follows is a description of those methods, and the reactions of various groups who were exposed to them.

(i)   The CEGB *Newsletter* was first published in January 1983 and was received free by some 11,000 local people and by 2,500 others on a mailing list. Its main aim was to keep people informed about the proposals to build another nuclear station at Sizewell.

(ii) The *exhibition*, mounted as a permanent display in 1982, forms part of the Information Centre at Sizewell which was opened in 1980.

(iii) There were two *information offices*, serviced by the Information Centre, one at Leiston and the other at Ipswich. Monitoring the numbers of visitors was erratic but at its height the Ipswich office recorded 196 visitors in one month in 1983.

(iv) *Talks* are run by a panel of volunteers from the CEGB's station staff. Speakers are invited by clubs, societies, schools, colleges and other groups. In the 12 months up to September 1985, 54 talks were given locally by members of the speakers panel.

(v) Between three and four thousand members of the public *visit* the Sizewell "A" station every year.

Research methods

We undertook research in four modes:

(i) interviews were held with key informants (CEGB personnel, environmental lobbyists, local and county council officers, and journalists);

(ii) evaluations were made of specific communications, including recipients of the Sizewell Newsletter, visitors to the exhibition, and to the "A" station, the information shops and those attending the talks;

(iii) surveys were undertaken of the public in Suffolk to measure awareness of , and attitudes towards, nuclear energy; and

(iv) finally, a content analysis was made of selected communications (press releases, public meeting transcripts, and letters sent to the Public Inquiry).

Summary results

The most significant overall findings from the surveys are, first, that members of the various publics differ in their attitudes, prior interests, and abilities to cope with the technical information presented in the various modes of communication. Second, the issues of most public concern changed during the course of the Sizewell Inquiry ; and third, much of the public's information about the nuclear issue is gleaned from the media and less frequently through direct CEGB sources. We found, also, that the distance people live from the station was not directly related to what they felt or knew about nuclear matters. More crucial was their social or economic involvement with station personnel. Finally, we found that information was not always clearly presented, and that conflicting messages were being communicated to the public.

Detailed results of the evaluation

The research objectives in conducting an audit of the various modes of communication were several. We wished to provide an account of the information requirements of the intended audiences. In others words, what were the issues that those in receipt of the information actually hope to hear about or have clarified? Next, we were interested in the audiences' level of understanding and their overall satisfaction with the manner and style of presentation. Finally, we attempted to assess the impact of the different modes of communication in terms of the degree of reassurance they achieved and also to measure any changes of opinion concerning nuclear energy. These aspects are discussed in turn.

Information sought by the public

In general, members of the public seeking information from the CEGB wished to hear about health, safety and radio-active waste. The groups who had some degree of technical interest or knowledge (students, teachers or those on the Sizewell Newsletter mailing list) were more likely to express interest in design, financial costs and technical details from the Public Inquiry. Those attending the talks were most likely to want to hear about waste issues, and those visiting the station wanted details of the process and reactor design (Table 9.1).

Groups of local teachers, the Young Farmers, Young Wives and those on the local Sizewell Newsletter mailing list did emphasize local impacts more than other groups. The Young Wives focussed on health related issues more than any other group.

Satisfaction with forms of information

Of the communication media used by the CEGB, the Newsletter was the most negatively rated in terms of style and of presentation (Table 9.2). It was least often thought to be interesting, factual, open, explanatory, effective or persuasive and most often to be complacent, patronising and biased. The talks were judged by most of those attending to be interesting, explanatory and factual. For the most part, only the films were thought to be too long compared to the other forms of information. Those attending the talks or dropping into the information offices were the most likely to report being satisfied with answers to their questions. Visits to the power station itself were also rated positively and resulted in the acquisition of some technical knowledge by the Young Wives and Young Farmers groups.

Comprehension and reassurance

Both the visits to the station and exhibition stimulated visitors into wanting more information. The power station visit itself proved most demanding, as people only partially understood the talks. People having at least some technical awareness (i.e. through school or college study) reported greater appreciation of the concepts, while overall groups from the Young Wives, Young Farmers, and Women's Institute were significantly less able to cope with all aspects of the information that was provided for them.

Table 9.1

Interest in nuclear power issues before receipt of information.

	TALKS		POWER STATION VISIT			EXHIBITION			NEWSLETTER	
	Women's Institute	Teacher Students	Young Wives	Young Farmers	Poly-Technic Students	School Pupils	Youth Training Scheme Trainees	University Students	Local	Mailed
Prior Interests	%	%	%	%	%	%	%	%	%	%
Health	90	80	89	48	48	86	85	38	69	60
Safety	76	80	84	57	76	71	68	50	61	66
Waste	95	90	58	52	67	86	68	33	-	-
Process	33	40	58	61	62	62	47	58	-	-
Design	14	30	16	48	81	48	24	63	-	-
Costs	19	50	16	22	24	48	18	63	23	39
Local impacts	48	20	16	30	19	33	44	13	56	55
Inquiry	19	30	0	30	10	29	35	17	21	30
Anti case	19	10	5	13	14	19	27	21	19	39
Number of respondents	21	10	19	23	21	21	34	24	87	101

Table 9.2

Perceived presentation style of the various modes of information.

	TALKS		EXHIBITION			NEWSLETTER	
	Women's Institute	Teacher	School pupils	Youth Training	University Students	Local	Mailed
Style	%	%	%	%	%	%	%
Interesting	67	80	100	56	46	38	51
Factual	43	80	76	74	33	25	42
Biased	19	10	33	44	17	32	36
Explanatory	48	90	71	53	33	13	30
Patronising	5	10	0	6	8	25	20
Simplistic	24	0	19	15	38	10	25
Complacent	0	10	0	0	0	26	19
Reassuring	-	-	-	-	-	14	19
Balanced	29	50	43	12	21	12	17
Technical	29	10	62	62	13	16	15
Worrying	-	-	-	-	-	20	12
Reliable	19	40	14	6	4	7	16
Persuasive	14	44	24	27	21	8	14
Open	29	30	43	12	17	3	13
Impersonal	-	-	10	15	0	14	10
Effective	24	50	48	35	21	11	10
Boring	5	0	5	12	17	10	10
Unreliable	-	-	-	-	-	7	7
Restrained	-	-	0	3	4	2	8
Racy	-	-	0	6	0	0	1
Familiar	5	3	25	5	3	-	-

Overall, many of those consulting the CEGB reported being reassured about the need for nuclear power (Table 9.3). Students are least likely to be reassured about waste, the Women's Group about financial cost, the local teachers, local school pupils, and polytechnic students about local impacts.

Visits to Sizewell "A" were most likely to reassure people about safety , financial cost, local impact and radioactive waste.

Impact on opinion

Table 9.4 shows that those attending the talks were the most likely to change their view of nuclear power from being uncertain to being in its favour. Those visiting the "A" station were the most likely to change from anti- to pro-nuclear; the readers of the Newsletter were the only group examined among the specific evaluative studies undertaken recording a change of view in an anti-nuclear direction. Overall, those with some degree of technical knowledge were least likely to change their opinion. The group of Young Wives visiting the power station exhibited the greatest shift of opinion from uncertain to pro-nuclear.

Assessment

Most people consulting CEGB information sources already have a pro-nuclear energy disposition. This is also borne out by the results of the public attitude survey. Where there was a change of attitude it was from uncertain to pro-nuclear energy and it was the talks that resulted in most movement from uncertain to pro-nuclear. The visits to the power station resulted in most change of attitude overall, and the Newsletter was the only source with a measured change from pro-nuclear to anti-nuclear attitudes. Students are least susceptible to changing their attitude upon receipt of the CEGB information; the less technically aware groups are most susceptible to changing their attitude.

There is therefore strong support for the statement made by Covello et al (1986) amongst others, that there is no such entity as the "public" in terms of risk communication. There are many publics, each with its particular interest, prior opinions and information needs. The logic following from this is that there is not a static, one-off form, style or mode of communication that will meet the needs or interests of the many publics. What follows is a series of suggestions and recommendations to enhance the quality of information in order to promote the educational and informational requirements for healthy participation in decisions on the siting of nuclear power stations.

Table 9.3

Reassurance Following Receipt of Information

	TALKS		POWER STATION VISIT			EXHIBITION		
Issue	Women's Institute	Teacher Student	Young Farmers	Young Wives	Poly-Technic Students	School Pupils	Youth Training	University Students
	%	%	%	%	%	%	%	%
Safety	57	40	87	89	76	57	65	71
Waste	38	20	74	63	62	52	42	35
Need	71	50	48	68	52	57	62	58
Cost	29	30	52	42	43	38	32	46
Local impact	38	0	57	53	19	24	38	29

Table 9.4

Attitude Change Immediately Following Receipt of Information

	TALKS		POWER STATION VISIT			NEWSLETTER	
Direction of attitude change	Women's Institute	Teacher Student	Young Farmers	Young Wives	Poly-technic Students	Local	Mailed
	%	%	%	%	%	%	%
towards pro	34	0	17	31	0	8	7
towards uncertain	5	0	0	0	10	8	5
towards anti	0	0	0	0	0	17	5

Recommendations

To provide a better information service for the public we have made the following recommendations:

* Enhanced organisational support should be provided for those designing and conducting the various forms of consultation;
* There should be more sensitive targeting of information to the many and various potential audiences;
* Greater reactivity is needed in responding to a changing menu of issues of public concern;
* There should be a more vigorous extension of the scope of consultative communications;
* The development of a CEGB house style would help integrate the public consultation effort.

Enhanced organisational support

At a general level, we have suggested that in-house liaison be established between responsible members of the CEGB Headquarters staff and those directly responsible for communicating with the public at particular local installations. Moreover the organization should maintain a high professional standard in presenting information.

The *Sizewell exhibition* provides a good example. It is demonstrably successful as an informative means of communication, and financial support should be increased to maintain and expand the exhibition to provide training for staff, and to make the expertise available to other establishments. Therefore, the CEGB should establish an exhibition unit in which staff could be retained and expertise built up. The unit should be made available to advise, collaborate and coordinate information activities both within the CEGB and also between other nuclear agencies. Interaction with professional bodies concerned with mounting exhibitions would be useful (e.g. The Society for the Interpretation of Britain 's Heritage). The CEGB should undertake to achieve a sufficiently high standard of excellence that the exhibition could for example be entered for national competitions, thereby attracting favourable publicity.

The *tours around Sizewell A* are also a very effective mode of communicating direct experience of a nuclear installation to the general public. Guides should be given refresher courses from time to time on specific energy-related topics, and also on methods of communicating information. When appropriate, consideration should be given to providing a brighter, more stylish uniform. Links should be established with staff in other installations with at least an annual meeting to enable them to share experiences. Liaison should be improved both within the particular establishments and between other nuclear related establishments. In addition, communication between Headquarters and the local station should be two-way.

The *Newsletter*, too, would be improved by better communication between the relevant CEGB personnel. A team should be given specific responsibility for its production. All CEGB personnel should be made aware of the aims of the Newsletter and be encouraged to contribute to it.

Targeting communications

It is obvious from the results of the detailed evaluations that there is no "average" member of the public. Readers of the Newsletter, visitors to the Sizewell "A" station, and casual visitors to the information offices in Leiston and Ipswich all vary in terms of the level of information they can cope with and also the topics that interest them. Greater attention should be paid before visits or talks to establish particular interests and, for example, to mount small temporary displays at the Sizewell Centre or information offices to meet these particular needs. Greater effort should be directed at providing information at different levels for the technologically unsophisticated as well as the technically aware.

Decisions should be made about who is the prime audience for the Newsletter. If it is to be aimed at local people, some concession needs to be made to the changes of emphasis in local issues over time, and the vocabulary used in the text should be modified to make it less technical. If the Newsletter is to be geared, in addition, to a scientifically sophisticated audience then special features or pull-out supplements may be needed to reflect their more specialist knowledge or needs.

Greater reactivity to changing information needs

Information about nuclear issues frequently reaches the general public through the local newspapers or television. Attention should be paid to this translation process and communications should be designed to minimise their transformation by the media.

Authorship of articles for the Newsletter should be encouraged from amongst experts in related disciplines and those from the environmental lobby. Letters from the general public should be included. The tone of the Newsletter should be livelier and more imaginative.

Active experience and involvement leads to greater recall, interest, enjoyment and learning. Both the exhibition and information offices as well as the talks service should be encouraged to have and/or develop pieces of equipment or models that members of the public can use.

Extension of scope of consultative communications

The most effective communications are those that involve direct experience. The power station open days should be regular events and greater effort should be spent on enlarging the present number of guided tours. The information offices are often used as a contact for school project workers. Closer liaison should be established with these schools.

There were some interesting gender differences in the assessment of the CEGB Sizewell Newsletter. Women were more likely to find it dull, unimaginative, impersonal, confusing and boring, while men more often rated it helpful, interesting, clear, factual and reliable. The women were also more likely to worry about information obtained from this source (23 per cent) compared with 11 per cent of men. Trustworthiness may be more appropriate in the long run.

We also concluded that it is important to target the differing interests of the various different sections of the public by producing information of different levels and styles. Again, marketing as well as educational approaches may be important here.

The industry should talk about accidents in an open and frank manner. If the staff do not know the answers, it is better to admit this rather than issuing bland reassurances. It is also important to make the information accessible, available and professional. Currently, CEGB consumer research consists of leaflets circulating among colleagues. But what appears unproblematic to an engineer may raise anxieties amongst the public. In a study we conducted evaluating the UKAEA's (UK Atomic Energy Authority) information stand at the Ideal Home Exhibition in London during 7th March to 1st April 1984, we found 22 per cent left the exhibit more concerned than before; only 11 per cent were less concerned and for 67 per cent there was no change.

The nuclear industry must also come to terms with the fact that the nuclear energy issue is part of a broader social and moral context. Shying away from controversial issues by declaring these as "no go" areas will only serve to increase the distance and alienation between the experts and the public whom they serve.

Acknowledgements

The research team conducting these evaluations comprised Joyce Henderson, Catriona McDermid, Kathy Rees, Helen White and the overall director of the study was Professor Terence Lee. Financial support for the investigation was provided by the Central Electricity Generating Board.

References

Brown, J. and White, H. (1987) Public understanding of radioactive and nuclear waste. *J. Soc. Rad. Protection.* Vol 7, pp 61-70.

Brown, J., Henderson, J. and Armstrong, H. (in press). Children's perception of nuclear power stations as revealed through their drawing. *J. Environmental Psychology.*

Covello, V., Winterfeldt, Von, D. and Slovic, P. (1986) Risk communication: a review of the literature. *Risk Abstracts.* Vol 3, pp 171-182.

Cvetkovitch, G., Vlek, C. and Earle T. (undated: 1987?). *Designing public hazard communication programs about large scale technologies.* (mimeo) Batelle Institute: Seattle.

Earle, T. and Cvetkovitch, G. (1987) Ethical issues in risk communication. *Science, Technology and Human Values.* Vol 12.

House of Commons, Environment Committee (1986) *First Report; Radioactive Waste, Vol 1.* (Rossi Report). HMSO: London.

Lagadec, P. (1985) Communications strategies in crisis situations. Paper presented to *Risk and Policy Analysis Under Conditions of Uncertainty*. International Institute for Applied Systems Analysis: Vienna. November 25-27.

Lee, T. (1986) Effective communication of information about chemical hazards. *Science of the Total Environment*. Vol 51, pp 149-183.

Ministry of Housing and Local Government (1969) *People and Planning*. Report of the Committee on Public Participation in Planning. HMSO: London.

Moscovici, S. and Hewstone, M. (1983) Social representations and social explanations: from the "naive" to the "amateur" scientist. In Hewstone, M. (ed). *Attribution Theory: Social and Functional Extensions*. Blackwell: Oxford. pp 98-125.

Royal Commission on Environmental Pollution (1976) *Nuclear Power and the Environment*. Sixth Report. (Flowers Report). HMSO: London.

Royal Society (1985) *Public Understanding of Science*. Report of an ad hoc group. Royal Society: London.

Ryder, N. (1982) *Science Television and the Adolescent; a Case Study and a Theoretical Model*. Independent Broadcasting Authority: London.

Slovic, P., Fischhoff, B. and Lichenstein, S. (1982) Why study risk perception? *Risk Analysis*. Vol 2, No 2, pp 83-93.

10 Evaluating the Effectiveness of Safety Measures

John Adams

Abstract

The road safety literature is replete with claims for the efficacy of a wide variety of safety measures, but none of these claims stands uncontested; advocates of engineering solutions are dismissive of the claims of the believers in behaviour modification, and vice versa, and some are critical of both. There are two main reasons for this lack of consensus about what "works". The data on which road safety research relies are terrible, and its objectives confused.

Fatality data are accurate, but the numbers of fatalities are usually too small and variable to yield conclusive results. Injury numbers are much larger but usually too inaccurate to yield conclusive results. Something is dangerous if it has the potential to cause harm; something is safe if such potential is absent. Where danger is present, but accurately assessed and prudently dealt with, this potential is not realised. Thus accident statistics, the conventional measuring rod of success in road accident research, are an unreliable and often misleading measure of danger or safety. Because of risk compensation, safety measures commonly lead to the displacement of accidents, and/or safety benefits being consumed as performance benefits.

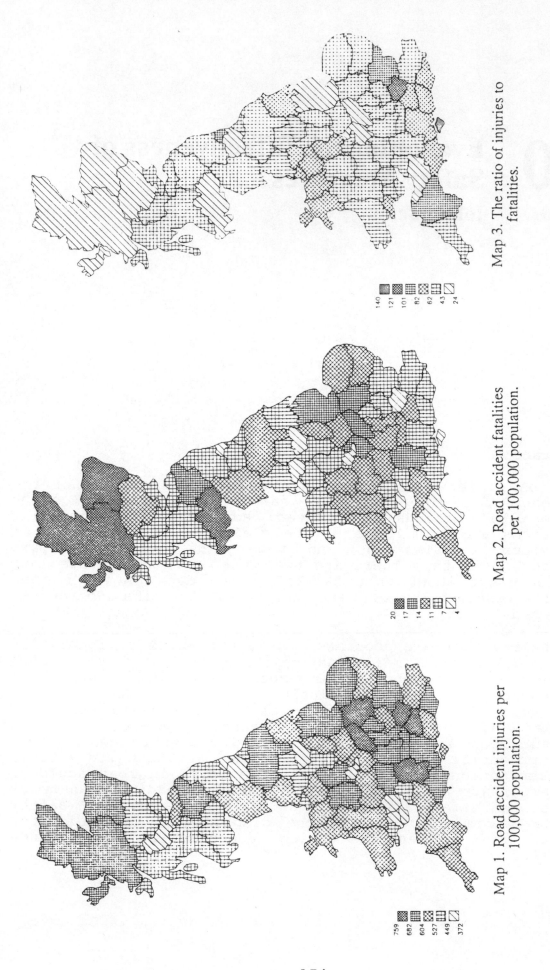

Map 1. Road accident injuries per 100,000 population.

Map 2. Road accident fatalities per 100,000 population.

Map 3. The ratio of injuries to fatalities.

Figure 10.1: Road accidents in Britain.

174

Introduction

Something is risky or dangerous if it has the potential to cause harm; guns, knives, nuclear reactors and fast traffic are examples. Something is safe if such potential is absent. Where danger is present, but accurately assessed and prudently dealt with, this potential is not realised. Thus accident statistics are an unreliable and often misleading measure of danger or safety.

There is at present great uncertainty amongst those seeking to promote road safety about what ought to be done. Frank Haight has been editor of *Accident Analysis and Prevention* for many years. There can be few safety researchers who have reviewed more work in this field. He observes:

> One sees time and again large sums of money spent (on road safety) in industrialised countries, the effect of which is so difficult to detect that further sums must be spent in highly sophisticated evaluation techniques if one is to obtain even a clue as to the effectiveness of the intervention (Haight 1985).

Ezra Hauer, another highly respected authority on the subject, comments: "when it comes to managing road safety we're in the dark ages. There's a lot of arm waving but very little knowledge of what works" (Hauer 1986).

1986 was *European Road Safety Year*. Throughout Europe special publicity campaigns were organised to heighten public awareness of the threat of road accidents. In Britain the number of people killed in road accidents increased from 5165 in 1985 to 5397 in 1986.

The road safety literature is replete with claims for the efficacy of a wide variety of safety measures: compulsory wearing of seat belts and crash helmets; lights-on legislation; speed and blood alcohol limits; vehicle safety regulations; accident blackspot treatment, public awareness campaigns and road safety training. These are but some of the measures for which substantial accident reductions have been claimed. But none of these claims stands uncontested; advocates of engineering solutions are dismissive of the claims of the believers in behaviour modification, and vice versa, and some are critical of both.

What "works"?

One reason why it is difficult to get agreement among safety experts about what works, is that they often disagree about what "works" means.

Consider the problem presented by British accident statistics for "A" roads in "built-up" (with speed limits of 64 kph or less) and "non built-up" areas (with speed limits in excess of 64 kph). For every kilometre travelled on an A road in a built-up area a motorist has a 42 per cent higher risk of being injured than he would if travelling in a non built-up area. Does this mean that the roads with lower speed limits are more dangerous for motorists? Not necessarily. The same source of statistics suggests that the risk of being *killed* is two and a half times higher on the non built-up roads (RAGB 1985, Table 26). There is a higher injury rate on the slower roads and a higher fatality rate on the faster roads (Maltby and Bennett 1986). The statistics suggest, not implausibly, that fast roads have fewer accidents, but that the ones that do occur are more severe.

This phenomenon has an interesting geographical pattern. London, with the highest population density in Britain, also has the highest recorded injury rate (759 per 100,000 population - Figure 10.1, Map 1). But, in company with most of the other English conurbations, London has one of the lowest recorded death rates (7.3 per 100,000 - Figure 10.1, Map 2). Map 3 shows the wide variation that existed in Britain in 1985 between injuries and fatalities. The injury:fatality ratio varies from 103:1 in London down to 23:1 in Dumfries and Galloway. The ratio for the Isle of Wight is 140:1, but this is based on a fatality figure which is small (5) and unstable.

So which class of road, or area, is safer? How many injuries equal one life? Is London the most dangerous part of the country for road users, or one of the safest? If safety measures were implemented which slowed traffic on a road with the result that the injury rate dropped but the fatality rate increased, could the measures be said to have "worked"?

Where numbers of accidents are small the accident statistics commonly display great variability - both temporally and geographically. Because the ratio of all injuries to fatalities is large, and because it is much easier to achieve results that are "statistically significant" if one uses large rather than small numbers, road accident statisticians have an understandable preference for injury data over fatality data, especially when they are dealing with roads or areas having only modest numbers of accidents. This preference can be expected to bias their conclusions about what "works". Safety measures such as straightening bends in roads, lengthening sight lines, improving cambers or raising the coefficient of friction of road surfaces could all have the effect of reducing numbers of accidents, but also of increasing speeds and the number of fatal accidents. In a small area or at the site of a treated accident blackspot the decrease in the number of injury accidents might be "significant" and the increase in fatalities "insignificant".

Increased speeds for motorists might also have the effect of increasing the burden of risk borne by non-motorists. Consider again the case of A roads. The *injury* rate for pedestrians per vehicle kilometre is 19 times higher in built-up areas than in non built-up areas; the *fatality* rate is only four times higher. But these are rates per *vehicle* kilometre. Because of the Department of Transport's long neglect of pedestrians, there are no comparable measures of exposure for pedestrians. If the volume of pedestrian traffic in built-up areas is more than four times that of non built-up areas, then the chances of a pedestrian being killed per kilometre walked, or per road crossed, would be higher in non built- up areas. For cyclists, where measures of exposure do exist, the injury rate in built-up areas is almost twice that of non built-up areas, while the fatality rate is less than one third (RAGB 1985, Table 26).

The relationship between deaths and injuries has also changed substantially over time. Between 1930 and 1985 the number of people killed annually on the roads in Britain decreased by 29 per cent (down from 7305 to 5165), while the number of people injured increased by 72 per cent (up from 185,000 to 318,000). There are a number of possible explanations of the differences over time and space in the ratio of deaths to injuries, but the first question to ask is "are the differences real?"

Dubious accident data

> The government are very keen on amassing statistics. They collect them, raise them to the nth power, take the cube root and prepare wonderful diagrams. But you must never forget that every one of these figures comes in the first instance from the village watchman who puts down what he damn pleases. (Sir Josiah Stamp 1880-1941, quoted in Nettler 1978).

A caveat to be borne in mind when scrutinising the relationship between death and injury rates, such as those discussed above, is that injuries are under-recorded- variably, sometimes very substantially.

Since 1930 there have been improvements in rescue and casualty services, and cars have become more crashworthy; so perhaps the increase over time in the ratio of injuries to fatalities is real. But cars have also become much more powerful and faster, and lorries have become much heavier with the result that the physical destructiveness of many accidents has increased. Further, in 1985 there were twice as many police in Britain as in 1930 (120,903 compared to 60,261 (HMIC Reports). So perhaps the change is simply the result of a larger fraction of injury accidents being recorded now than in 1930. It is also possible that at least part of the geographical differences in the injury:fatality ratios might be accounted for by a higher degree of under- reporting of minor injuries in more sparsely populated areas where the police are thinner on the ground.

The *"Severity Iceberg"* (Figure 10.2) represents an attempt to indicate the way in which uncertainty in the data increases as the severity of injury decreases. The fatality statistics are almost certainly the most accurate and reliable of the road accident statistics. Death on the road is treated very seriously; a Transport and Road Research Laboratory study which compared police and hospital statistics found that all fatalities recorded by the hospital were also recorded by the police (Hobbs et al 1979).

For injuries the situation is very much less satisfactory. The classification of injuries is done within a short time of the accident by medically unqualified police; it is generally not based on any evidence from a medical examination. The British Medical Association in evidence to the House of Commons Transport Committee has called the resulting numbers not only defective but positively misleading.

> The existing definitions on which records are based are misleading. Only one in four casualties classified as seriously injured are, in fact, seriously injured and many of those classified as slightly injured are, in fact seriously injured. The existing definition of "seriously injured" covers everything from a broken finger to total paralysis and to death occurring more than 30 days after the accident. Within these unsatisfactory definitions there is widespread under-reporting and mis-reporting of casualties and the distribution of these errors varies widely between different categories of road user. The information is very defective in the case of pedestrians and cyclists, who are at high risk of serious injury as a result of their lack of protection (British Medical Association 1983).

The British Medical Association went on to estimate that some 30 per cent of traffic accident casualties seen in hospital are not reported to police, and that at least 70 per cent of cyclist casualties go unrecorded. It is not known how much of the variability in the injury:fatality ratios described above is real, and how much is the result of variations in recording practice. There is evidence from the Transport and Road Research Laboratory study discussed above that the degree of under-reporting increases markedly as severity decreases. Towards the bottom of the Severity Iceberg under-reporting will approach 100 per cent; there will be a degree of severity which is sufficiently slight that neither the injured person nor the police will think it worth reporting.

The official definition of a slight injury is "an injury of a minor character such as a sprain, bruise or cut which is not judged to be severe, or slight shock requiring roadside attention" (RAGB 1985, p6). The definition of "slight" as "minor", "not severe" or "slight shock" leaves the interpretation highly subjective. The number of injuries recorded will vary from person to person, from time to time and from place to place. It is likely to be influenced by the priority that individual police officers and police forces place on road safety relative to other demands on their limited resources. It will also vary with the person power available to record and process the information.

Because the number of injuries increases as severity decreases a small move of the threshold up or down is likely to lead to a large change in the numbers officially injured. When large numbers of police are in pursuit of bombers or rippers, or embroiled in industrial disputes, the reduced numbers available for recording injuries, especially minor ones, is likely to lead to a raising of the threshold at which an injury is deemed worthy of recording - producing a statistical safety improvement.

The rectangles in the Severity Iceberg diagram represent officially recorded numbers of casualties. The superimpositions illustrate the magnitude of known errors: 75 percent of serious injuries wrongly classified (British Medical Association), 21 per cent under-recording of serious injuries, 34 per cent under-recording of slight injuries (Hobbs et al 1979). The source of the British Medical Association estimates (that only one in four injuries recorded as serious is actually serious, and that 70 per cent of cyclist injuries and 30 per cent of all injuries are not recorded), is not given in the Parliamentary report, but the estimates appear to be generously rounded versions of numbers found in the report by Hobbs et al (1979). One in four is close to the 26.7 per cent found by Hobbs et al. The under-reporting estimates are based on the application of police definitions to casualties seen at hospital but not recorded by the police; Hobbs et al (1979) put the figures for cyclist injuries unreported at 66 per cent, and all injuries unreported at 28 per cent.

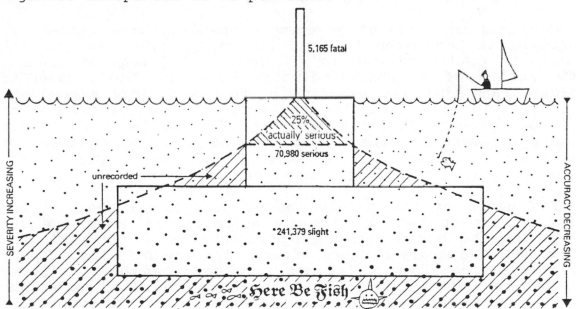

Figure 10.2: The "Severity Iceberg". The areas of the rectangles are proportional to the number of casualties recorded in Road Accidents in Great Britain 1985.

Beyond those known errors are all the injuries that are recorded by neither hospitals nor the police. The volume of the unrecorded bottom of the iceberg - injuries that are slight but nevertheless real - is likely to be large. The existing definitions of "injury" make the decision about whether or not to record an incident inescapably subjective, and the variable pressure on police resources renders the exercise of police discretion inevitably variable. What gets recorded is likely to be a mixture of what the policeman "damn pleases" and what circumstances permit. The deeper one goes below the statistical surface of Figure 10.2, the fishier the numbers become.

Using the data

When the stories told by injury data and fatality data lead to different conclusions, as they did for example in the seat belt debate (Adams 1985, pp 178-188, 1986 (appendix) and 1986b), one is confronted by the choice of whether to believe the large numbers or the accurate numbers. The Severity Iceberg provides reasons for preferring accuracy. Most studies on the safety effects of local scale measures, such as accident blackspot treatment, still rely on the largest and least reliable numbers - total injury accidents. For analyses of the nationwide effects of measures such as compulsory seat belts (Harvey and Durbin 1986) or drunken driving measures (Broughton and Stark 1986), statisticians working for Britain's Department of Transport still place most of their trust in the KSI series (killed and seriously injured). However, this is a series in which variations in the accurate fatality numbers are overwhelmed by uncertainties, both of definition and recording, in the much larger "seriously injured" category.

Measured in terms of government spending, road safety in Britain is dominated by road building. The cost of the national road programme is measured in billions of pounds. The method of economic analysis (known as COBA), used to demonstrate that the benefits of this programme exceed its costs, typically estimates the accident reduction benefits of road schemes at 15-20 per cent of total benefits. Thus the Government in effect claims to be spending hundreds of millions of pounds on safety, a sum which dwarfs the expenditure on any other road safety programme.

The basis of the safety benefit claims is shaky. The claims rest on two questionable assumptions: that one can estimate the accident reducing effects of a new road, and that one can convert these effects into cash. The problem of converting lives and limbs into cash has been explored elsewhere (Adams 1974). It will simply be noted here that the method employed by the Department of Transport is irredeemably arbitrary. Nevertheless, in March this year, admitting that it had no "firm empirical guidance" to support the action, the Department proposed that the values of both lives and slight injuries should be increased by 40 per cent and that the value of a serious injury should be increased by 63 per cent (Department of Transport 1987, p7).

Estimating the accident reducing effects of road schemes, while not presenting the metaphysical conundrums encountered in the attempt to attach cash values to life and limb, is also beset with difficulties. The Standing Advisory Committee on Trunk Road Assessment (SACTRA 1986) recently spoke of "an urgent need for better methods of predicting the changes in the number of accidents following urban road improvements" para 10, 25). The need would appear to be no less urgent for rural roads. Figure 10.3 shows the wide variation characteristically found in accident rates for short sections of road. The data displayed are injury rates, incorporating all the uncertainty in recording discussed above, but also incorporating the doubtless genuine random variation in accident rates. If one were to try to construct a similar graph using the more accurate fatality figures, most of the values would be zero; there was, on average, one fatality per 67 kilometres of road in Britain in 1985, and the survey embraced only 241 kilometres of road. Moreover, the roads on which this variation occurred all conformed to the design standards to which the Department of Transport builds new roads. Figure 10.3 is thus indicative of the uncertainty that must attach to estimates of the effect on accidents of building or "improving" roads to meet these standards.

Hauer and Persaud (1983) and Boyle and Wright (1984) have identified systematic biases in the assessment of the effects of road improvements on accidents. The sort of geographical variation in accident rates depicted in Figure 10.3 is, it would appear, invariably accompanied by temporal variation. In a succeeding time period many of the high points on the graph would come down and many of the low points would rise. This is known as the "regression-to-the-mean effect", and it can profoundly bias before-and-after estimates of the effectiveness of safety treatments.

To the extent that road improvement programmes seek out for treatment those parts of the road network with the worst accident records, they will be treating sites whose accident records could be expected to show improvement without treatment. Hauer and Persaud demonstrate that the magnitude of the potential bias of simple before-and-after comparisons is very large. Boyle and Wright have discovered a further, and probably related, complication. While the numbers of accidents at an accident "blackspot" commonly fall after the implementation of safety measures, they appear to go up in the surrounding network. They call the phenomenon "accident migration".

Undaunted by these difficulties, and seemingly oblivious to the competing claims of the advocates of other safety measures, the Department of Transport claims in its COBA manual:

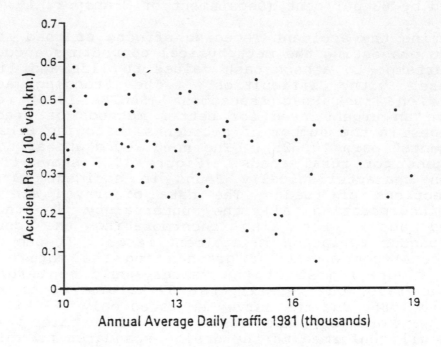

Figure 10.3:   Variations in accident rates on single lane
                rural roads (Maltby and Bennett 1986).

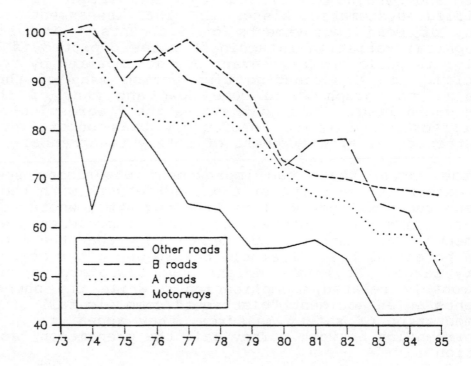

Figure 10.4:   Death rate indices by class of road over time.
                The index for 1973 = 100.   (RAGB 1983, 1985).

Most of the reduction in accident rates which has occurred over the years may be attributed to road improvements and the transfer of traffic to safer types of road. There is little evidence to show that this trend will apply to a given unimproved road. Current accident rates are therefore assumed in COBA9 to remain constant over time (para 2.4.2).

Figure 10.4 presents some relevant evidence. It shows that all types of road have enjoyed substantial reductions in death rates since 1973. Traffic has grown on all types of road, while on all these types with the exception of motorways, the number of deaths has fallen. Motorways have enjoyed the largest decrease in death rate per vehicle-kilometre since 1973, although if the year 1974 is used as the base year, they enjoy the smallest decrease. The graph is not projected back beyond 1973 because there was a revision of the traffic estimates from that year on. Estimates of traffic on A roads were reduced by 7 per cent and on "other roads" 24 percent (RAGB 1982, Table 3, and RAGB 1983, Table 2). "Corrections" of this magnitude to the denominator of the casualty rates serve as a reminder of yet another source of uncertainty in the data at the heart of debates about road safety.

Only a minute fraction of the 270,000 kilometres of "other roads" can have been improved since 1973, so some other explanation for their decreasing fatality rate must be found. Further reasons for doubting the Department of Transport's claims for the benefits of road building can be found in Adams (1985, pp 38-49, and 1987).

The assumptions embodied in COBA - that only road improvements will reduce casualties, and that casualty rates on unimproved roads will remain constant - plus the proposal to increase greatly the cash value of casualties, produce hundreds of millions of pounds worth of "safety benefits". Figures 10.2, 10.3 and 10.4 suggest that these benefits, and the road building that they serve to justify, have no firm basis.

Safety for whom?

Even if drivers are driving more dangerously as a result of seat belt wearing, it is already clear that casualty savings among car and van occupants far outweigh any increases in casualties among other road users (RAGB 1983, p16).

The conclusion that the casualty benefits to occupants outweighed the costs to other road users has been disputed elsewhere (Adams 1985, pp 178-188, 1986 (appendix), and 1986b, pp 217-218). Here I wish to examine the assumption that saving a number of car occupant casualties at the cost of causing a smaller number of pedestrian and cyclist casualties represents a road safety improvement. Whether it does or not depends, it would appear, on the perspective from which one views the change.

Buses and Heavy Goods Vehicles would appear to be very safe - for their drivers. In 1985, the last year for which statistics are available, there was one bus driver and 54 lorry drivers killed. These numbers might be compared with the equivalent statistics for cycling, apparently a very dangerous mode of travel - for cyclists. In 1985 there were more than five times as many cyclists killed, despite the fact that bicycles accounted for less than one fifth as many vehicle kilometres as buses and lorries. A bus or lorry driver can travel about two and a half times further than a car driver and about 27 times further than a cyclist for the same chance of being killed (see Figure 10.5).

However, when one considers the threat posed to other road users the situation looks very different. Cyclists rarely kill anyone other than themselves. But, for every bus or Heavy Goods Vehicle driver killed there were over 18 other fatal accidents involving buses or Heavy Goods Vehicles. A cyclist can travel about 16 times farther than a bus or lorry driver and about 3 times farther than a car driver for the same chance of being involved in an accident in which someone else is killed.

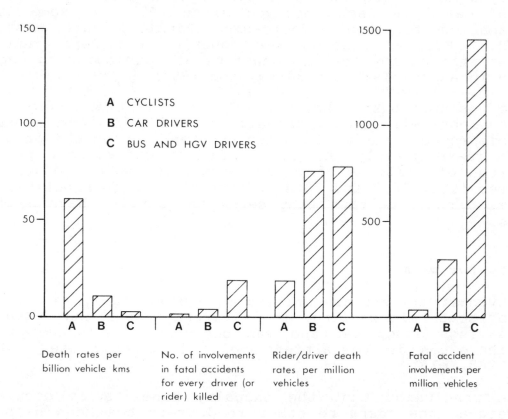

Figure 10.5:   Safety for whom? Different perspectives on road accident fatality statistics. (Sources: RAGB 1985, Transport Statistics Great Britain 1975-1985, and Friends of the Earth UK bicycle population estimate of 15 million).

If one makes allowance for the fact that buses and lorries travel considerably greater distances in a year than cars or bicycles the picture changes again. Because the average bus or lorry covers about two and a half times as many kilometres in a year, the average bus or lorry driver stands, over a year, about the same chance of being killed as the average car driver. The average cyclist who covers much less ground stands a much smaller risk of being killed.

Finally, if one considers fatal accident involvement rates per vehicle, the 1985 statistics show that the average bus or lorry is about 5 times more likely to kill someone than the average car, and about 69 times more likely to kill someone than the average bicycle.

What do we mean by safety?

This fundamental question is generally considered under three headings: the safety of roads, the safety of vehicles, and the safety of the behaviour of road users. On numerous occasions over the past twenty years I have had an opportunity to compare traffic in Britain with that in the United States and Canada. Under each of these headings I judge the traffic in Britain to be more dangerous.

On arriving in North America from Britain one is impressed by the large size of North American cars, and by the fact that they appear to cruise around in slow motion on wide roads, with wide shoulders and grass margins beyond. Pedestrian traffic in North America appears better behaved; pedestrians often wait at red lights even if there is no traffic coming, and there is usually more help for school children in the form of warning signs and crossing guards. Traffic in residential areas also seems better managed, with many all-way stop intersections and street layouts discouraging through traffic.

On returning to Britain one is impressed by the much smaller size of the average car and the fact that it offers less protection to its occupants in a crash. The roads are much narrower - most of them were built before the car was invented - and separation distances between oncoming vehicles are much smaller. Speed limits on motorways are much higher and enforcement is minimal - surveys suggest that over half the drivers on motorways exceed the speed limit. Car traffic seems quick and darting compared with the more stately progress of North American traffic. Pedestrian traffic is more anarchic, red lights being merely advisory for pedestrians, but not mandatory. And the density of traffic is much higher - although Britain has fewer cars per head of population than the United States, it has more than twice as many per mile of road.

"Subjectively", British traffic seems to me, and to many others I have questioned, to be more dangerous. But "statistically" the average North American is about twice as likely to be killed in a car accident as the average Briton.

Does this mean that "objectively" Britain is safer? Do I merely (mis)perceive it to be more dangerous?

Consider a second conflict between perception and accident statistics. Muswell Hill Road in North London is a busy road on which traffic routinely exceeds the 30 mph (48 kph) speed limit. My family lives on one side and my children go to school on the other. I consider it a dangerous road and, along with most other parents, forbid my children to cross it unaccompanied by an adult. Local residents have been pressing for many years for measures to slow the traffic down. We have had meetings with the official responsible for road safety in our area and he shows us, with the aid of his road accident map, that we do not have a problem. Statistically, Muswell Hill Road is a reasonably safe road. Again, do I merely (mis)perceive it to be dangerous?

There are many other examples of situations in which impressions of danger are confounded by accident statistics. Most people who are not conversant with accident statistics are surprised to learn that when road conditions are very bad (snow and ice) both the numbers of fatal accidents and the severity of accidents decrease markedly, or that when Sweden changed from driving on the left to driving on the right the number of road accident fatalities during the changeover month plummeted to 40 per cent of the normal level (Adams 1985, pp 43 and 45) . Most road engineers have anecdotes to tell about stretches of road for which they are responsible that local people consider dangerous, but which are "safe" - that is they have very ordinary accident records.

Risk Compensation

All people monitor their environments for signs of danger, and take avoiding action when such signs are detected; all motorists alive today, for example, display a tendency to slow down when they come to a sharp bend in the road. This idea has been elaborated in a theory of risk-taking behaviour known as "risk homeostasis".

The theory postulates that at any given time there will be a level of risk that an individual is prepared to tolerate, or even seek. There is a corollary to the theory: safety measures which attempt to reduce the potential of some thing, or activity, to cause harm, but which do not alter people's tolerated level of risk, will be nullified by behavioural reactions which re-establish the level of risk with which people were originally content. There is some statistical support for the theory. Since the beginning of this century, indices of death caused by accident or violence in most countries for which the data are available show no downward trend despite the volumes of safety legislation and regulation which they have passed, and despite the appointment of small armies of safety regulation enforcers (Figure 10.6). There appear to have been two main effects of all this regulatory activity:

186

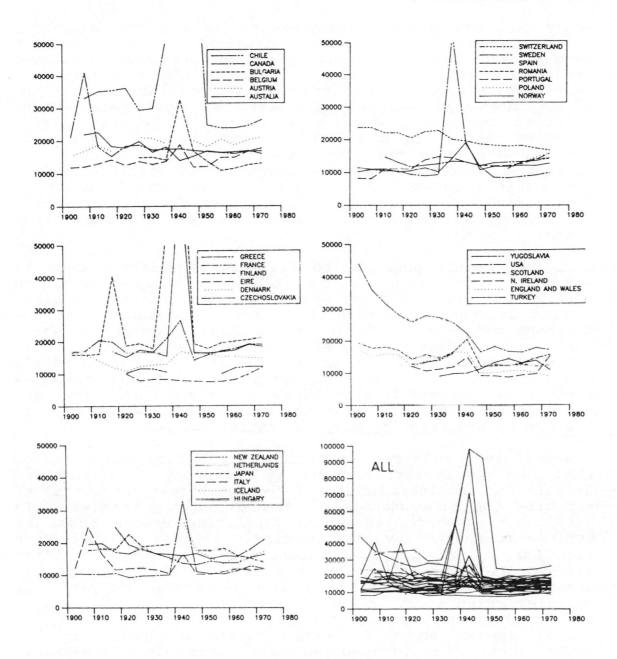

Figure 10.6: Indices of death by accident and violence (all causes including homicide and suicide) for 31 countries. The indices are standard mortality ratios derived with a factor of 10,000. England and Wales 1951-1975 serve as the basis for standardisation (Adams 1985, p142).

187

a redistribution of risk, rather than a reduction, and a tendency for potential safety benefits to be consumed as performance benefits.

Risk redistribution

Redistribution effects, sometimes called accident migration or displacement, are rarely considered in road accident research. The monitoring of road accident blackspot treatments provides an example. Most of the claims for the beneficial effects of such treatments simply assume that the effect does not exist. The work of Boyle and Wright referred to above and, more recently, Persaud (1987) suggests that it is an effect that must be taken seriously. How far accidents might migrate from treated sites is at present a matter for speculation. It is possible that a systematic programme of blackspot removal would result in lower levels of vigilance on the part of motorists, leading to a more diffuse pattern of accidents, but the same total number.

It is clearly possible to eradicate specific causes of accidents. Banning motorcycling would eliminate motorcycling as a cause of death. But for this to represent a true decrease in accidents it must be assumed that the dispossessed motorcyclists, Hell's Angels included, would turn to some other totally safe form of transport or totally innocuous recreation. It is unlikely that the banned Hell's Angels would sit at home drinking tea, but the range of other risky alternatives to which they might turn - from sky diving to glue sniffing - is so wide as to be beyond hope of capture by any existing body of statistics.

Some safety measures redistribute risk from one class of road user to another. There is currently a campaign in Britain for the introduction of "benign street furniture" to minimise the consequences of single vehicle crashes. In Birmingham, where pedestrian fatalities exceed those of vehicle occupants involved in single vehicle crashes by a wide margin, a policy has recently been adopted of siting all new lighting columns at the back of the footpath, in order to reduce the risk of injury to the occupants of vehicles which stray on to it (Proctor et al 1987). There are similar campaigns in the United States. A number of States appear about to pass legislation requiring the replacement of rigid roadside mail boxes with "breakaway" types which do less damage to errant cars (IIHS 1986).

But the added risk to pedestrians on the footpath will not necessarily be reflected in an increased number of accidents involving pedestrians. Equally an absence of accidents does not signify safety. The fact that there are many fewer children killed in road accidents in Britain today than there were 60 years ago does not mean that the roads are safer now. They are much more dangerous; if children played in the streets today with the same heedlessness to traffic that they exhibited 60 years ago there would be slaughter on a massive scale. The child fatality statistics indicate that children's behaviour has changed in response to the increased danger. Children have yielded territory to the car.

Safety versus performance

A second problem that frustrates the endeavours of those who seek to reduce accidents is the tendency for potential safety benefits to be consumed as performance benefits. If, for example, a vehicle is fitted with improved brakes, motorists tend not to drive in the same way as before and enjoy an additional safety margin. They tend to drive faster, or start braking later, or drive with less care and attention. The vehicle with the improved brakes or steering, or suspension, or tyres - becomes not a safer vehicle, but a higher performance vehicle.

In Germany risk compensation has been enshrined in the road traffic law; coaches fitted with seat belts have a permitted top speed of 100 kph, while those without are restricted to 80 kph. A recent report in Care on the Road (RoSPA March 1987) described the likely trade-off between safety and performance as follows:

> In Germany coaches with belts are allowed to travel faster than those without thus allowing drivers to cover more miles in the hours they are allowed.

But one person's performance gain can be another's safety loss. There are many more people killed by buses and coaches than are killed in them - in Britain about seven times as many (RAGB 1985, Tables 22 and 23).

It is not only motorists who trade safety for performance. Appleyard and Lintell (1972) have demonstrated that as the threat of traffic increases the frequency with which pedestrians cross a road decreases (Figure 10.7). The fact that a road has a low accident rate might mean not that it is safe, but that it is terrifyingly dangerous. It is not only road users who trade safety for performance, nor is the phenomenon of recent origin. An historical example is provided by the Davy Safety Lamp. This was an invention by Sir Humphry Davy which cooled the flame of a miner's lamp below the ignition point of methane. According to one account "the Davy Lamp saved thousands of lives and is one of the earliest examples of how pure science could help industry" (Albury and Schwartz 1982). Help industry it did, but the saving in life attributed to the lamp was entirely hypothetical. After the lamp was introduced there was an increase in the numbers of explosions, fatalities and tons of coal mined. The lamp encouraged mining in methane rich atmospheres previously considered unworkable.

Danger or riskiness cannot be measured directly, certainly not by accident statistics. But its presence can be detected by its influence on behaviour.

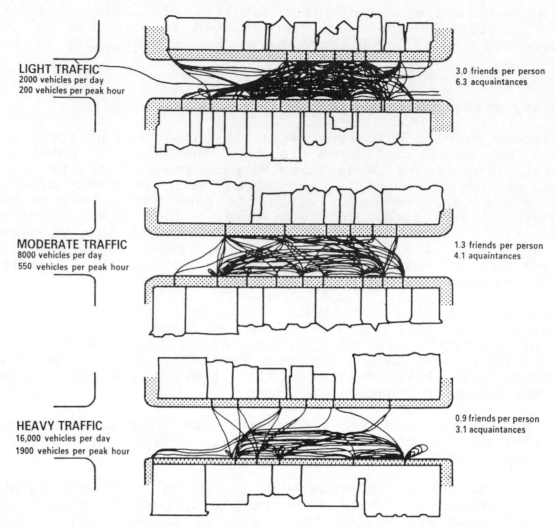

LIGHT TRAFFIC
2000 vehicles per day
200 vehicles per peak hour

3.0 friends per person
6.3 acquaintances

MODERATE TRAFFIC
8000 vehicles per day
550 vehicles per peak hour

1.3 friends per person
4.1 aquaintances

HEAVY TRAFFIC
16,000 vehicles per day
1900 vehicles per peak hour

0.9 friends per person
3.1 acquaintances

Figure 10.7:   The effect of traffic volume on cross-street
interaction. Streets were chosen to be as
similar as possible except for differences in
traffic. Lines connect dwellings where people
said they had friends or acquaintences
(Appleyard and Lintell 1972).

Conclusions

The management of road safety is in the dark ages for two
main reasons. The data on which it relies are terrible, and
its objectives are confused. These conclusions also apply
to many other hazards.

With the exception of studies based on fairly highly
aggregated fatality statistics, there is a gross disparity
between the sophistication of the statistical methods
commonly used in safety research, and the crudeness of the
casualty numbers that are manipulated by these methods. The
injury data are rendered unreliable by the looseness of the
definitions used, and by their dependence for collection on
the police, a group not qualified to make the medical

judgements required and who often have better things to do. There appears to be little prospect of this state of affairs improving.

But even if there were to be a dramatic improvement in the quality of the accident data a problem would remain. The frequently proclaimed objective of *safety* programmes is the reduction of *accidents* - hence the central role played by accident statistics in the safety literature. But accident statistics, even accurate ones, provide a hopeless measure of safety or danger; if risk compensation does take place, if people do routinely adjust their behaviour in response to increases or decreases in safety or danger; then to seek to reduce accidents by reducing danger is to chase a chimera.

So, if the statistics are suspect, and would not measure safety even if they were accurate, what should those seeking to promote road safety do? I conclude with four suggestions. They should:

* seek indirect measures of safety and danger which conform better with road users' perceptions; the Appleyard and Lintell approach, which combines observation of behaviour with questionnaire surveys provides a useful model;
* make explicit allowance for risk compensation, regression-to-mean, and displacement or migration effects in every prediction they venture of the consequences of a safety measure, and every attempt they make to evaluate the result;
* pay particular attention to the way in which the burden of road accident risk is shared, and question the presumption of most safety measures that in situations of potential conflict it is the most vulnerable road users who should defer to the least vulnerable, and
* not require communities to produce road accident martyrs before they take seriously their concerns about safety.

References

Adams, J.G.U. (1974) ...and how much for your grandmother? *Environment and Planning A*. Vol 6.

Adams, J.G.U. (1985) *Risk and Freedom: the record of road safety regulation*. Transport Publishing Projects: Cardiff.

Adams, J.G.U. (1986) Risk homeostatis and the purpose of safety regulation. Paper presented to the CEC Workshop on risky decision making in transport operations. TNO Institute for Perception: Soesterberg, The Netherlands.

Adams, J.G.U. (1986b) Discussion of the paper by Professors Harvey and Durbin. *Journal of the Royal Statistical Society A*. Vol 149, Part 3, pp 217-219.

Adams, J.G.U. (1987) Smeed's Law: some further thoughts. *Traffic Engineering and Control*. February, pp 70-73.

Albury, D. and Schwartz, J. (1982) *Partial Progress: the politics of science and technology*. Pluto Press.

Appleyard, D. and Lintell, M. (1972) The Environmental
    quality of city streets: the residents' viewpoint. *AIP
    Journal*. March, pp 84-101.
BMA (British Medical Association) (1983) Memorandum
    submitted by the Board of Science and Education, BMA, to
    the House of Commons Transport Committee, Second Special
    Report. *Road Safety: Inquiry not completed*. Appendix 37,
    No 275.
Boyle, A.J. and Wright, C.C. (1984) Accident "migration"
    after remedial treatment at accident blackspots. *Traffic
    Engineering and Control*. pp 260-266.
Broughton, J. and Stark, D.C. (1986) The effect of the 1983
    changes to the law relating to drink/driving. *TRRL Report
    RR 89*. Transport and Road Research Laboratory:
    Crowthorne, Berks.
COBA9 (1981) The British Department of Transport's cost
    benefit analysis manual. Assessment Policy and Methods
    Division, 2 Marsham St, London S.W.1. issued in 1981,
    subject to periodic partial revision.
DTp (Department of Transport) (1987) *Values for Journey
    Time Saving and Accident Preventions*. DTp: London.
Haight, F.A. (1985) The developmental stages of
    motorization: implications for safety. Pennsylvania
    Transportation Institute, Penn. State University:
    University Park, PA.
Harvey, A.C. and Durbin, J. (1986) The effect of seat belt
    legislation on British road casualties: a case study in
    structural time series modelling. *Journal of the Royal
    Statistical Society*. A. Vol 149, Part 3, pp 187-227.
Hauer, E. (1986) quoted in *Toronto Globe and Mail*. 12
    November.
Hauer, E. and Persaud, B. (1983) Common bias in before-and-
    after accident comparisons and its elimination.
    Transportation Research Record. 905, pp 164-174.
HMIC (Her Majesty's Inspector of Constabulary) Annual
    Reports for 1930 and 1985, HMSO.
Hobbs, C.A., Grattan, E. and Hobbs, J.A. (1979)
    Classification of injury by length of stay in hospital.
    TRRL Report LR871. Transport and Road Research Laboratory:
    Crowthorne, Berks.
IIHS (Insurance Institute for Highway Safety) (1986) *Status
    Report*. Vol 21, No 9.
Maltby, D. and Bennett, R.W.G. (1986) Variations in
    accident frequencies on rural single carriageway roads in
    England. Proceedings of Seminar P, Road Safety, PTRC
    summer annual meeting. pp 197-211.
Nettler, G. (1978) *Explaining Crime*. McGraw Hill: New York.
Persaud, B. (1987) "Migration" of accident risk after
    remedial blackspot treatment. *Traffic Engineering and
    Control*. January, pp 23-30.
Proctor, S., Greaves, D., Graham, S. and Dias, M. (1987)
    Accidents involving loss of control: identification and
    treatment of high risk sites. Paper presented to the
    Symposium on Crash Protection and Behavioural Aspects of
    Single-Vehicle Accidents, University of Birmingham,
    January 1987.

RAGB (1985) (Road Accidents Great Britain) Department of Transport, published annually, HMSO. SACTRA (1986) (Standing Advisory Committee on Trunk Road Assessment) *Urban Road Appraisal*. Department of Transport, HMSO: London.

RoSPA (1987) (Royal Society for the Prevention of Accidents) Care on the Road, published monthly: Birmingham.

11 Assessing Programme Effectiveness: a 1987 Report on Warning Systems in the USA

Eve Gruntfest

Abstract

Warning systems are gaining in popularity as flood hazard mitigation measures in the United States. The systems emphasize forecasting through stream and rain gauges. Thus far, in most instances the warning response has been neglected. Since most systems are relatively new, few have been tested in real events. This chapter discusses the results of a survey of 18 flood warning systems which have been established recently in the United States. Specifically, the problems, pleasant surprises, issues to consider, and areas for future research are presented.

Introduction

The focus on whether or not a programme is working requires much more thought than simply discussing what approaches may or may not work. We need to be forced to evaluate our own effectiveness as researchers, policy- makers, educators and journalists. To adequately address the question of programme effectiveness we must take a long hard look at our own work and that of our colleagues to see which of our intended goals are being achieved and which are not. Then occasionally we must have the courage to change gears and radically shift away from a programme that appeared so promising in theory.

This chapter discusses the effectiveness of warning system experience in the United States. The discussion is organized into two parts. First, I present the results of a recently completed project which surveys where we stand in

195

the US on warning systems. The other portion of the chapter highlights lessons from this survey with particular attention to problems, pleasant surprises and issues to consider.

Flood warning systems in the United States

Deaths from most natural hazards in the United States have declined over the past two decades, but loss of life from flooding has increased. Currently nearly 200 people die in the US each year from floods. Catastrophic flash floods and dam breaks, as opposed to slow rise floods, have proven most costly: for example, 237 lives in Rapid City in 1972 and 140 lives in Big Thompson Canyon in 1976.

One of the major changes in flash-flood loss reduction in the past decade is the number of communities which have adopted warning systems (United States Army Corps of Engineers 1981a, 1981b). According to a recent study conducted by the Hydrology Subcommittee of the Federal Interagency Advisory Committee on Water Data, out of the 20,000 flood-prone communities in the United States, approximately 1000 had local flood warning systems in operation as of August 1985. At that time only about 100 of these systems were automated, but recent developments in automated systems have increased their popularity. It is estimated that 500 automated systems will be in operation within this decade (HSFIACWD 1985).

It is important to note that a local flood warning and response system should be only one part of a comprehensive effort to mitigate the hazards of flooding. A warning and response system is effective primarily in reducing loss of life and providing limited protection to existing flood-prone property, but it does not necessarily promote significant long-term mitigation. The most cost-effective and significant mitigation opportunities occur either before development or before reconstruction after a flood and require a strong local floodplain management program.

Survey approach

The survey was prepared for the US Bureau of Reclamation as part of their investigation into the utility of early warning systems as a tool for reducing the threat to public safety posed by potential dam failure. The research described in the report consisted of a survey of 18 warning systems in the United States developed by communities or regions to provide protection against flash flooding, dam breaks, and some combination of flash floods and slow rise floods. A matrix for comparing the 18 systems has been prepared (Table 11.1, found at the end of this chapter). For this chapter, the matrix serves as the summary of each system. The reader is referred to the complete study for more detail. In the space allowed here attention is focused on the survey results.

Selection of warning systems for study was based on the researcher's experience with the extent of systems available, interviews with key researchers and agency officials and interaction at several workshops and conferences where warning systems were central themes, including: the symposium *What We Have Learned Since the Big Thompson Flood* (July 1986, Boulder, Colorado); the annual *Natural Hazards Workshop* (July 1987, Boulder); the annual Association of State Floodplain Managers meeting (June 1987, Seattle); the *Fifteenth Anniversary Commemoration* symposium of the Rapid City Flash Flood (June 1987, Rapid City, South Dakota); and the American Society of Civil Engineers convention (August 1987, Williamsburg, Virginia).

The systems examined are representative of the types of systems being adopted, ranging from voluntary systems such as in Lycoming, Pennsylvania, to state-of-the-art systems like that in Harris County, Texas, and from small, compact systems such as the Heppner, Oregon system to large, sophisticated, integrated systems like the Passaic River Basin arrangement. Systems that have been tested by flooding were preferred, but this could not always be the case since many of the systems are recent innovations. Most of the systems operate within the boundaries of individual states. Five systems either have remote gauges in separate states or they report to more than one state. In all, 18 states are represented in the survey.

Variables assessed

The following information was gathered on each of the systems surveyed: background information including the impetus for implementing the early warning system, the basin size, and the population at risk; details on establishment of the system including date of implementation, initial cost, and funding sources; components of the system including details of the flood detection, decision making, and message dissemination and evacuation portions of the system; maintenance responsibility and cost; a discussion of any flooding that has occurred since implementation; general comments about the system including pleasant surprises and unanticipated problems that have developed; and, a key individual involved with the system who can be contacted for further information.

Every effort was made to make the information as compatible as possible for comparison. However, each system is designed for a particular problem or series of problems, and systems are not always readily comparable. It is much easier to describe all the components of a simple system, the people involved, the expenses and the expected effectiveness. When several states and millions of people are involved, much less detail is possible in a brief narrative. The officials involved all have their own terminology and each system is somewhat idiosyncratic.

Issues

Although the economics of flood warnings systems are crucial there is *no consistent measure* of how much money an effective warning system should cost; nor is there a rule for what is acceptable per capita expense for a warning system. Costs of the surveyed systems range from US$500 to US$4,000,000. When compared with costs for rebuilding a dam even the most expensive warning system can seem relatively cheap. Nevertheless, costs for some of the systems seem excessive when related to the population at risk. There appear to be no criteria for determining which communities are most at risk based on where warning systems have been implemented.

Maintenance receives inadequate emphasis. In addition to periodic maintenance required to keep the gauges clean and functioning, most interviewees mentioned unanticipated costs due to equipment failure or damage or personnel time requirements in excess of what was originally expected. Maintenance costs will probably increase as these systems age. Despite the large cost required to maintain some of these systems (up to US$75,000 annually for the Passaic River system), in many cases there were no accurate estimates of annual maintenance requirements. Accurate maintenance costs seem particularly important for small communities with limited budgets.

In reviewing the case studies, it is apparent that there is a wide range of *local community commitment* to and involvement in the systems. Those that are most effective are ones in which officials have put a lot of energy into informing and involving the public. The volunteer system in Lycoming County was viewed as successful because of the high degree of local community involvement: a performance indicator more commonly used in assessing aid projects in developing countries. The key individual for that system felt that there was generally little local commitment to a system resulting from federal initiatives. Because local communities do not view such initiatives as their systems, they are reluctant to provide the necessary maintenance required to keep the systems operational. A case in point is the Heppner system. Because of political changes which have resulted in a lack of local commitment, responsibility for the Heppner system has temporarily reverted to the US Army Corps of Engineers. In the original plans Morrow County was to assume responsibility after installation.

There is *excessive reliance on technical aspects* and an underemphasis on response capability. The warning systems have been designed with the objective of reducing loss of life and property damage. However, few of the systems pay much attention to getting the message to the population at risk. In most cases the systems can be more aptly termed "flood detection systems" since no element of response is included.

On an annual basis Boulder distributes public education brochures and conducts drills which include public officials and floodplain residents, but this is the exception rather than the rule. Santee Cooper has also paid a great deal of attention to the responses aspect of flood warning. In the Pikes Peak case as well as elsewhere the key individuals recognise the importance of response capability but consider it less of a priority to the community than developing the data base on the stream basins. In some instances funding has been approved by agencies only for the forecasting and detection components rather than for the response component.

There are several vendors for the technical upstream prediction aspects of warning systems; however, no companies specialize in how a community or region can best incorporate the information into public preparedness. If the goal of warning systems is to save lives and reduce property losses there needs to be greater attention paid to warning dissemination and public awareness.

There is a tendency to *over-rely on warning systems*. Warnings are only part of a comprehensive flood loss reduction programme. Some communities find flood warning systems to be an inexpensive alternative to politically unpalatable, long term solutions which call for restricting floodplain land uses and enforcing existing regulations. It has been said that development of a warning system is an indication of failure to adequately manage floodplain land use. For many communities there seems to be the sense that if funds are allocated for a warning system, especially the initial outlay for the prediction components, then no funds need to be set aside for developing an adequate response component or for the ongoing maintenance expenses.

One concern frequently raised was the *need for redundancy* in all aspects of the systems because various mechanical parts have proven unreliable. For example, batteries have needed replacement more often than expected. Unanticipated damage to equipment by the weather, wildlife, and vandalism has been frequent.

One of the most surprising findings of this survey was the *wide spectrum of performance standards*. While the Bureau of Reclamation sought some guidance of what the prevailing view of federal agencies and communities has been for warning systems, the clearest message is that each system has different objectives. In some instances the system presents information in a manner which requires practically no training to be understood, while for others the individuals need to be highly trained to understand the system components. Some systems surveyed included highly formalized procedural plans for notifying public agencies and individuals with delineated responsibilities by name, while others seemed completely unstructured with informal protocol for making decisions. The wide range of objectives and approaches further complicates comparative assessments.

Pleasant surprises

Many of the systems are installed in basins where the available hydrologic record is relatively incomplete. This means that the warning systems can provide an important data collection source, and the models must be regularly recalibrated to account for the new data. Assessments should not ignore such potential side benefits. Systems such as those for Lena Gulch and the Pikes Peak Region initially are calibrated regionally; it takes several years and/or storm events for local refinement of the systems. Some of the surveyed systems, such as the Santa Ana system, are designed more for data collection than for direct public warning potential; while officials in other communities, such as those in Maricopa Country, who implemented the system for flood warning have discovered the main use for the system has been data collection.

A second important positive result in an area not normally considered by evaluations, was that many of those involved in establishing and operating the systems, particularly those dealing with the Chesapeake and Ohio Canal National Historical Park, the Santee Cooper Project and the Mount Airy system, have been pleased with the degree of interagency cooperation that has been demonstrated.

Finally, in light of the reduced budgets for large construction projects and the greater appreciation of the liability of dam owners, early warning systems offer an alternative to large structural modification projects which have become difficult to fund and are frequently politically controversial. In three of the case studies, the Blue Ridge Dam, the Heppner system, and the Santee Cooper Project, implementation of an early warning system was chosen as the most cost effective solution to the flood hazard in these areas.

Issues to consider

Drainage basins do not respect political boundaries, thus interjurisdictional decision-making is important. Six of the case studies dealt with systems which involved more than one state. These include the Blue Ridge Dam, the Chesapeake and Ohio Canal National Historical Park, the Passiac River, the Mount Airy, the Mount St. Helens, and the IFLOWS systems. Regional districts or entities manage the systems in Maricopa County, Ventura County, Boulder, Lena Gulch, the Pikes Peak region, and Harris County. The interjurisdictional aspects of some of these systems will be of particular interest to the Bureau of Reclamation in establishing dam break systems. Research on this trend toward multi-jurisdictional agencies has been observed in the floodplain management literature, most recently in the work by Platt (1987).

Many of the systems surveyed require cooperation among several federal agencies. While the Bureau sought a clear and simple description of the policies established by the other federal agencies involved in warning, particularly the Federal Emergency Management Agency and the Corps of Engineers, these agencies are in a policy formulation stage similar to the Bureau of Reclamation. Although warning systems are of increasing popularity, the roles of the various agencies are still being worked out as is the nature of cooperative agreements between the agencies. The policy is developing on many fronts including the National Research Council's evaluation of dam safety (National Research Council 1983, 1985), the Hydrology Subcommittee of the Federal Interagency Advisory Committee on Water Data which completed its report two years ago, and the American Society of Civil Engineers' Task Committee on Spillway Design Flood Selection whose assignment was to suggest standards for the hydrologic safety design of dams. Their final report should be published in 1988.

In our contact with the experts around the nation, different opinions existed as to the future approaches to flash flood warning systems. Several officials of the National Weather Service expressed a belief that integrated, interjurisdictional systems are the way of the future. It was predicted that in the not too distant future the Front Range of Colorado would consist of one integrated system rather than a collection of regional systems. On the other hand, others think that in the past decade the emphasis has shifted away from large, integrated, regional approaches to local flash-flood mitigation (Cahail 1987). Cahail viewed IFLOWS as a beneficial experiment which has greatly increased the awareness of people in the area, but he expects future flash flood mitigation efforts to occur in localized regions or special districts (Cahail, p 90).

An important question raised by the Blue Ridge Dam warning system is that of how much protection is reasonable? What present criteria should be applied to older dams and what protection level should be provided by them? Is it cost-effective to require older dams to handle the probable maximum flood (PMF)?

Areas for future research

More detailed case studies are needed. As stated earlier this report shows the breadth of systems in existence in the United States as of 1987. However, the current study was designed as a survey rather than an analytical comparison. Selecting a few systems for more detailed comparison using a predetermined survey form including site visits could evaluate the systems from several viewpoints identifying areas of strength, contradiction and/or contention.

Federal agency policies regarding warning systems require clarification. Several agencies are involved as dam owners. This survey indicates involvement by some obvious federal actors (for example the Corps of Engineers) and some less obvious ones (for example the National Park Service). The next study could explore the explicit policies of other agencies which own or manage dams including the agricultural and the energy agencies.

Clearer delineation of the public and private sector responsibilities and ranges of choice is needed. Private dam owners and private consultants are taking leadership roles in safety and forecasting. More communities are finding it necessary to hire private meteorologic consulting firms to help with forecasting obligations and to reduce municipal liability. Since only five percent of the dams in the country are federally owned, private ditch companies and many individuals play a major role in dam safety efforts. What precisely are the actions being taken by the private sector?

Concluding thoughts

This study indicates that flood warning systems are gaining in popularity. Warning systems are seen as a promising means of responding to increased vulnerability to flood losses. The record is too short for a precise appraisal of how successful these systems are. Limited experience, evolving relationships between federal and local agencies, and the possibility that many years will elapse between flood events which test the systems, complicate the Bureau of Reclamation's decisions on policy directions. While we can be only cautiously optimistic at this stage, flood warning systems should be pursued as one component of the Bureau's goal of reducing the threat to public safety posed by potential dam failures.

New areas for the development of performance criteria are those of interagency and intergovernment cooperation, and community involvement. The most optimistic interviewees were associated with warning systems which are interjurisdictional and which integrate various levels of government. Community involvement appears to be essential if the systems are to achieve the goals of reducing loss of lives and property from flooding.

A definitive recommendation regarding the adoption of warning systems to deal with the flood threat is premature. Many of the systems have been installed so recently that their records are short and it is difficult to assess long range prospects for success. However, as more communities adopt warning systems, the future will provide additional experiences on which to base a more precise appraisal. Thus far the record on risk communication is a weak link in the chain that emphasises forecasting and technological fixing.

The Bureau of Reclamation posed some interesting questions:

* How should the experience with warning systems be evaluated when considering applications to very rare events?

* How are other federal agencies dealing with the flood hazard? and
* How does warning system effectiveness compare for slow rise floods, flash floods and dam breaks?

Increased attention is being paid to cross hazard studies, and the interagency attention and unprecedented cooperation is promising. In the next few years the important questions posed by the Bureau of Reclamation will be widely discussed and perhaps resolved.

References

Cahail, S. (1987) *An Examination of the Development and Utilization of Automated Flood Warning Systems*. Masters Thesis submitted to the University of Massachusetts Department of Geology and Geography, Amherst.

Gruntfest, E. (1988) *Flash Flood/Dam Failure Warning System Survey*. US Bureau of Reclamation: Denver.

HSFIACWD (Hydrology Subcommittee of the Federal Interagency Advisory Committee on Water Data) (1985) *Guidelines on Local Flood Warning and Response Systems*. United States Geological Survey, Office of Water Data Coordination: Reston VA.

Platt, R. (Ed) (1987) *Regional Management of Metropolitan Floodplains*. The University of Colorado, Institute of Behavioral Science, Program on Environment and Behavior: Boulder (Monograph 45).

National Research Council (1985) *Safety of Dams: Flood and Earthquake Criteria*. National Academy Press: Washington DC.

National Research Council (1985) *Safety of Existing Dams: Evaluation and Improvement*. National Academy Press: Washington DC.

US Army Corps of Engineers (1981a) *Community Handbook on Flood Warning Preparedness Programs*. Research Report 81-R06.

US Army Corps of Engineers (1981b) *Effectiveness of Flood Warning and Preparedness Alternatives*. Research Report 81-R08.

Table 11.1
Summary of systems examined.

LOCATION	FLOOD TYPE	POPULATION AT RISK	BASIN SIZE	INITIAL COST	IMPLEMENTATION	FLOODING SINCE IMPLEMENTATION
Passaic River System, NJ	Slow Rise Flash	The system monitors a highly industrialized, densely populated area. The 1980 census reported a population of 2,000,000.	935 mi^2	$700,000	1987	None
Mount Airy, NC	Flash Slow Rise	The population at risk totals 2,000 in industrial, commercial, and residential properties located in the 100 year flood plain.	60 mi^2	$60,000	1986	Flooding occurred 2/27/87. During the flood 134 people were successfully evacuated, and no major damage was sustained.
Heppner, OR	Flash	Several hundred residents of the small town of Heppner are at risk.	50.8 mi^2	Not Available	1985	None
Lycoming County, PA	Slow Rise	The population of Lycoming County, 118,416 in the 1980 census, is at risk.	1,200 mi^2	$500	1976	The system has been activated to some degree about 50 times. Early warning in 3/79 reduced damages by $750,000.
Santee Cooper, SC	Dam Break	There are 697 residences in the flood inundation area, which is 90% swamp land.	Not Available	$1.5 million	1986	None
Gatlinburg, TN	Flash	The resident at-risk population is several hundred. The tourist population can add 6,000 to the population at risk.	41.6 mi^2	$104,000	1987	None
Harris County, TX	Flash	The population of Harris County, which includes the city of Houston, exceeds 2,700,000.	1,740 mi^2	$300,000 to date	1982	Flooding associated with Hurricane Alicia occurred in 1982. The system worked well.
Mount St. Helens, WA	Dam Break Flash	There are approximately 10,000 residences and 40,000 people at risk who are served by the warning system.	1,230 mi^2	Not Available	1980	Mud flows in early 1980's were successfully detected.
IFLOWS	Slow Rise	The IFLOWS system includes 150 counties in seven states: Virginia, West Virginia, Kentucky, Tennessee, North Carolina, Pennsylvania, New York.	N/A Per Community	Approx. $50,000 Per Community Community	1981	Yes

LOCATION	FLOOD TYPE	POPULATION AT RISK	BASIN SIZE	INITIAL COST	IMPLEMENTATION	FLOODING SINCE IMPLEMENTATION
Maricopa County, AZ	Flash	The population of Maricopa County, which includes the city of Phoenix, totals approximately 1,000,000.	9,000 mi^2	$25-50,000	1981	None
Santa Ana, CA	Flash Dam Break	The population of Orange County, which includes the city of Los Angeles, totals approximately 5,000,000.	2,450 mi^2	Not Available	1975	None
Ventura County, CA	Flash	The majority of Ventura County is a rapidly urbanizing area with a population at risk of 150,000-200,000.	2,046 mi^2	$36,000	1979	Flooding occurred 3/1/83. There was some damage to utilities and farms, but no lives were lost.
Boulder, CO	Flash	The flood hazard area consists of residential, commercial and government property and affects approximately 25,000 people.	400 mi^2	$150,000	1978	None
Lena Gulch, CO	Flash	Lena Gulch is a small urban watershed. Approximately 2,400 people either live or work in the floodplain.	13.8 mi^2	$100,000	1985	A 5-10 year flood occurred 6/8/87. Lead time provided by the warning system allowed the evacuation without injury of two mobile home parks.
Pikes Peak Region, CO	Flash	Approximately 10,000 residents in five communities are at risk. In addition there are 580 non-residential structures in the floodplain, including commercial establishments which attract a large tourist population.	580 mi^2	$200,000	1987	None
Blue Ridge Dam, GA	Dam Break	There are 350 residences at risk. These residences are located in two small towns, one in Georgia and one in Tennessee, and the rural areas around these towns.	232 mi^2	$1.1 million	1984	None
Emerson, IO	Flash	Approximately 300 people in the small town of Emerson are at risk.	43 mi^2	$30,000	1985	In recent flooding the hand held receivers that alert the emergency personnel did not work.
C and O Canal National Historical Park, MD	Flash Slow Rise	The population at risk consists of visitors to the Park islands, run by the National Park Service.	13,000 mi^2	$25,000	1986	A quick rise in 7/87 resulted in the successful closure of a portion of the Park.

Section Summary IV
Issues in Assessing the Success of Risk Communication

There is no doubt that evaluating the success of risk communication is fraught with difficulties. But this may or may not mean that risk communication itself is highly inefficient: in many cases we simply do not know. Indeed, what is both surprising and disturbing is that so little is known about the success or failure of risk communication, even measured simply in terms of response. This is especially surprising when we consider the high levels of government and private investment in attempting to give the public messages about the risks that they face, and in trying to persuade them to change their attitudes or behaviour. The absence of information on effectiveness has serious implications for both the risk communicators and the researchers.

Four key issues are apparent in the area of evaluating the success of risk communication and response. The first issue concerns the *definitions* used in the evaluation, and the second the *operationalisation* of those definitions in terms of the approaches used, the research design and the data that are collected. Both are crucial to the validity and use of the research results. Third, is the *complexity of the factors* affecting the success of risk communication, however success is defined, and how this affects the research process. Unless these many factors are separated and unravelled, our understanding will not progress. Fourth, there is the problematic *link* between the evaluative investigation and the policy effects of those results, including their interpretation. Unless this link is sound, the research will not be of lasting value.

Definitions: what do we mean by "success"?

It is clear from the chapters in this section that the specification of terms and definitions when evaluating risk communication is absolutely central to the value of the research. Clear definitions enable the establishment of objectives without which evaluation is virtually impossible. The problem is that different people have different definitions, objectives and understanding.

Thus in Parker and Neal's evaluation of flood warning system effectiveness, it is clear that their respondents had different definitions of "flood". The nature of a "warning" is such that one person's useful warning may lack the specificity or appropriateness essential to another: the "success" or "effectiveness" of the "warning" may thus be evaluated quite differently by the different respondents. In conventional terms this makes the control of the survey methodology problematic. However, it may be that consumer satisfaction with the warning system is an appropriate performance measure, in which case the vagueness surrounding the concepts of "warning" and "success" become much less important.

Even clearer is that the official definitions of "safety" and "accident" fundamentally affect the collection and the very nature of road "safety" statistics, and profoundly affect the results of research based on these data. Adams views the road "safety" statistics as hopeless, precisely because the only data that are unambiguous - those on fatalities - are too sparse to allow meaningful analysis. While the data that are plentiful (and therefore most used) employ a definition of "serious injury" that makes the use of the data to evaluate road safety improvements in any rigorous manner nearly impossible.

However, it is not just that different groups have different definitions, or that the definitions do not represent what is needed in policy terms. There is also a problem of technical terms inhibiting the research process when that process itself involves "customer" surveys of the recipients of risk communications. For example, most risk communication research finds great difficulty in defining the level of risks, and in using concepts such as the probability of an event and presenting such concepts in language that respondents can understand. This frequently results from a failure to appreciate that risk is as much a social as a scientific construct.

More attention needs to be given to the definitions of risk and related terms used in research. This is inevitably an important initial stage in any relatively new research area, and the youthful risk communication research field is no exception. Until this stage is more developed, the assessment of risk communication success is likely to remain incoherent.

Operationalising the research: methodological and data problems

If adequately defining risk communication terms is problematic, then the task of transforming these terms into data and results is even more daunting.

Performance indicators

First, we need "performance indicators" against which to measure the success of risk communication. There are a number of alternative approaches, and it is not always clear which is appropriate. Both Parker and Neal, and Wilkins, stress the value of looking at risk communication failures rather than attempting to define success *per se*. However, Adams suggests that a key flaw in official evaluations of road safety is that "safety" is operationalised by antithesis: as an absence of accidents.

The whole objective of those promoting road safety measures today appears not to promote *safety* as such, but to focus on those cases where roads are not safe by one particular definition: where there are accidents. Where the risks are so great that there are few accidents, or where pedestrian behaviour has been so modified that road traffic takes complete precedence, then roads are defined as "safe". This hypothesis receives support from Tompkins (1987). In his review of the US Aviation safety reporting system he observes that:

> ... some of the most dangerous airports are the safest. It is well known ... that O'Hare (Chicago) is a zoo; consequently only the best pilots are sent in and out of the airport ... And they .... know to be alert ...

The definition of safety by antithesis - as accidents avoided or risks transferred - has profound implications for subsequent policy and the distribution of the burden of avoiding risks: in Adams' case transferring risks from road users to cyclists and pedestrians. Similarly, if safety is defined as the absence of accidents, and successful risk communication as the absence of failures, it means that accident migration is almost automatically ignored, risk compensation is under-played, and success is minimally defined. Thus, the use of performance indicators derived from defining success by looking at failures can have major drawbacks. Definitions of safety, and success in risk communication, should go beyond death and injury statistics and be related to the satisfaction of those affected.

Measures of consumer satisfaction, such as the linguistic variables mentioned in Chapter 1 and employed by Parker and Neal may be more appropriate. Adams therefore stresses the importance of measuring risk perception rather than accidents. In the same way, Gardiner (Chapter 15) indicates that it is not just the reduction of flooding that is important, but that reduction of the fear of flooding is also significant. Here we are confronted with a number of issues, and by the fact that individuals will not all react in the same manner. Yet risk communication systems tend to assume a homogeneous collection of "customers" for which standard messages and signals are produced. As we have seen in Sections II and III, there are both theoretical and empirical objections to this assumption. A fundamental question is whether we aim to reduce fear of hazards or reduce the hazards themselves: where do we stand when faced by a risk that is increasing, but for which fear might be reduced by "successful" communication or propaganda? Do we attempt to communicate the reality of risks that people face or are we merely concerned to reassure and pacify?

Finally, it is most important that the performance indicators are not limited to those criteria which are easy to measure. For example, issues of ethics and values appear to be central to risk acceptability and may be the driving force behind many risk communication programmes, yet they are rarely considered in assessments. Kasperson and Palmlund (1987) discuss these and other assessment criteria (Table IV.1), many of which are typically ignored in evaluations even though they may be critical to programme success. Again we are led back to our definition of "success".

Methodological problems

A second key group of difficulties in evaluating risk communication research are the methodological problems concerning "control" of the "experiment". There are many strands to this issue, centring on the fact that our "laboratory" is the irregulated real world. For example, evaluating official or formal risk communication success is liable to be virtually impossible if there is a widespread informal risk communication process occurring in parallel. The farmers interviewed by Parker and Neal, and many of the recipients of the warnings systems surveyed by Gruntfest and by Winchester, received many different cues about floods. The official warning is but one part of a total environmental information system, and to separate out this official or formal component for analysis and evaluation is not easy (Penning-Rowsell and Handmer 1986).

Thus we need to specify explicitly what we are attempting to measure. This would include placing boundaries on the evaluation in terms of how far the social, political and other contexts form part of the analysis. (Context is discussed in Section III).

A related problem concerns the evaluation of individual elements of a multi-media risk communication process. Brown reviews a number of media used to communicate risk and other information about nuclear power. While this multi-media approach is useful, in that it is possible to compare the different results and gain some insight into relative efficiency, it is also inherently problematic in terms of developing a rigorous research framework. The respondents who were exposed to different combinations of information

Table lV.1

Criteria for evaluating risk communication programmes from
Kasperson and Palmlund (1987).

Needs appraisal
   what do the risk bearers need to know and how best to meet
   this?
Risk complexity and social pluralism
   make complex phenomena understandable.
Risk in context
   comparison with relevant risks, benefits, regulatory
   standards; and information on what can be done about it.
Management prospectus
   risk managers should provide information on how they see
   the facts, legal status, decision-making process and
   likely results.
Timeliness
   risk communication should occur early on, but should not
   be premature.
Iterative interaction
   generally multiple or continuous two-way flow of
   information is necessary.
Empowerment
   the approach should empower those at risk to act for their
   own protection.
Credibility
   risk communication should build confidence in the
   information source as reliable and accurate.
Ethical sensitivity
   many issues including: avoidance of paternalism;
   conflicts of interest in the communicators; rights of risk
   bearers; avoiding the creation of undue worry and fear.
Resiliency
   the programme should expect surprises and failures, and
   plan accordingly.

sources will have had different experiences, and this may
have affected their opinions. The least likely group to
change their minds about nuclear energy as a result of the
CEGB risk communication material were the students, who
presumably had access to other information sources.
However, one could hypothesise that those who were exposed
to only the most apparently "successful" medium (the
exhibition and site visit) might subsequently become more
uncertain in their views if their exposure to other
information sources grew to match the students' experience.
The apparent success of the "successful" media, therefore,
might be only temporary. But this cannot be detected in a
"one-off" questionnaire survey.

The same methodological problems arise when evaluating
just one part of a risk communication process (Penning-

Rowsell and Handmer 1986). The risk communication and response process involves a complex interconnected system with many parts, and deficiencies in any one part will almost certainly degrade the whole system (Foster 1980). Yet, it is impracticable in research terms to evaluate the whole system at once, and parts are usually taken for investigation. Thus Parker and Neal evaluated the efficiency of warning delivery, in terms of response and consumer satisfaction, but any lack of success here cannot necessarily be ascribed to that dissemination or delivery process. It might be that faults are occurring elsewhere in the chain of communication before the message gets to the deliverer, but this is difficult to identify in a restricted research process. In essence within an interconnected system the evaluation of one part alone cannot necessarily provide insights into the effectiveness of that part; a link in a chain may be effective in its own right but have its performance degraded by "faults" elsewhere in the system.

Data collection

Having attended to both approach and methodology, the collection of data to evaluate the success or effectiveness of risk communication also provides many problems. The very nature of "success" or "effectiveness" is often unclear, and adaptation of the data to produce meaningful performance indicators is not easy. Thus road accident safety can be measured in, among other ways, injuries per kilometre, deaths per year, or public perception of risk.

However, each indicator will give different results. Flood losses reduced by warnings can include just tangible losses or can be widened to include intangibles. The perception of risk communication performance can be taken as the critical variable, or some determination of the objective "reality" of the process. Gruntfest uses cost per person in the warning target area as one variable, but that ignores the accuracy of the warning and the extent of the response. Parker and Neal stress the value of using a range of criteria - which is certainly a desirable approach - but this increases the complexity and expense of evaluation research. Hence it may reduce its accuracy, by lengthening questionnaires, or reduce its impact by confusing the policy makers.

All this suggests that the results of evaluative research concerning risk communication must be the subject of careful scrutiny and nothing should be taken at face value.

Unravelling the many factors affecting risk communication success

All research points in one way or another to the link between risk or hazard experience and the effectiveness of risk communication: people understand risk messages better in situations that they have previously experienced than when they have no such experience. Experience provides the necessary context for comprehension (Section II). However, this does not help much in attempting to communicate risks beyond the experience of a particular target population.

Nevertheless, substitutes for experience may help, as can references to analogous circumstances, but many examples cited elsewhere in this volume - particularly by Scanlon - show that this is not always successful. What does appear successful is making the risk message as personalised as possible; in part this explains the success of the exhibitions and talks concerning the Sizewell nuclear power station, and the relative lack of success of the impersonal Newsletter.

We can also see that people's prior knowledge affects their comprehension of risk information - Brown's students versus her Young Wives - which reinforces a point emphasised throughout the volume: that target populations are not homogeneous. (Of course, Brown is describing a programme designed to convince people to accept the risks associated with nuclear power.) In this respect, it is clear that adequately targeted risk information is more likely to have the desired effect in raising consciousness: risk communication which speaks directly to those to be warned, with specific messages for those in different situations, is more likely to be both understood and to elicit a response. The problems that this poses for the communicators are formidable, although modern technology can perhaps be deployed to transmit essentially the same message in different ways to different audiences.

As emphasised by Kasperson and Palmlund (1987), and by Gardiner in Chapter 15, institutional credibility is of vital importance to effective risk communication. Therefore not only are targeted messages more effective, but honest ones also appear more efficient in the long run; economy with the truth tends to catch organisations out in the end. It is inevitable, however, that there are vested interests; the road construction lobby in Britain is among the organisations that are most concerned to promote road safety. The CEGB engineers, communicating details about the safety of nuclear power, have an interest in building nuclear power stations.

Institutions affect risk communication in other ways, by their implicit or explicit policies either not to communicate risks or to be open with the public. Thus it would not be appropriate to criticise the individual Seven-Trent Water Authority engineers in the Avon division for the ineffectiveness of their flood warning systems: the individuals are working in a policy environment that does not recognise that such communication is necessary.

The link to policy

How should the analysis of risk communication effectiveness influence the policies of the agencies concerned?

A key conclusion from analysing effectiveness is the importance of risk communicators knowing what the public wants and/or what they need to know for their own safety. This knowledge should be in terms of: first, the information to be communicated; secondly, the policies of the risk managing agencies and the need for the communicators to meet those needs as far as possible. Feedback of information between the agencies and the public should inform the policies of risk managing agencies - such as electricity utilities, water authorities or road building organisations. The policies of these risk communication organisations are presumably designed to satisfy public needs and manage risk. But people may have expectations that are not achievable or may have pre-existing attitudes to the agencies concerned that preclude effective communication.

There are many opportunities for the link between evaluative research and policy change to be broken, and for risk communication to become a mere one-way public relations exercise. What, for example, would the CEGB do if their risk communication programme showed that the public was universally hostile to nuclear power and became more hostile as more information was communicated. Would they change their policy on nuclear power (and thus change the risks) or change their means of risk communication? One suspects the latter. If this is the case, it highlights the power and controlability dimensions which are central to the third definition of risk in Chapter 1. The reaction of the road safety officers in north London on being told that a road was perceived as very dangerous was to refute this by saying that according to their data it was quite safe. Thus, if risks are ineffectively communicated does this mean that the recipient of the information is stupid, or the management of the risk is incorrect? Is it the communication that is wrong, or the risk that the public faces incorrectly recorded?

This reveals a major problem with risk management; which is that communications about risk often cannot flow smoothly from those bearing the risk to those with official responsibility for its management. The frequent failure by the bureaucracy and industry to recognise the validity and importance of the views of the affected public generally indicates misunderstanding of the political and social nature of risk.

The implications for risk communication research

The weight of evidence suggests that evaluation of risk communication is more accurately undertaken by adopting an anthropological approach whereby the researchers experience the risks and the risk communication process, rather than relying on post-event surveys. In addition, a pre-requisite for both successful communication and valid evaluation is clear definitions and specification of objectives.

However, given the difficulties of research into risk communication effectiveness, there is a real danger that this research is used merely to justify the interest and policies of the risk managing agency. This must be avoided, because for risk communications to become mere public relations is irresponsible and dangerous. Information on risks can be communicated successfully, but only if certain risk-specific conditions are met. These conditions need to be further researched.

In this respect it must be recognised that there may be some important but uncomfortable messages from this type of evaluative research, if it is to be done with sufficient objectivity and rigour to be seen as valid. Communication of risk may come to be seen as carrying obligations if the public views the risk as unacceptable. If agencies do not respond to these obligations, questions arise as to why they communicated the risks in the first place and their potential liability if disasters occur. However, for the results to be incontrovertible, more evaluative research should be undertaken, because methodologies are still very crude, and much greater attention should be given to "quality control" within the research process.

References

Foster, H.D. (1980) *Disaster planning* (The preservation of life and property). Springer series on Environmental Management.

Kasperson, R.F. and Palmlund, I. (1987) Evaluating risk communication. CENTED, Clark University, Worcester and University of Stockholm. (Unpublished manuscript).

Penning-Rowsell, E.C. and Handmer, J.W. (1986) *Evaluating Flood Warning Effectiveness: the Conceptual, methodological and Practical Research Problems*. Centre for Resource and Environmental Studies, Australian National University: Canberra. (Working paper 1986/6).

Tompkins, R.K. (1987) On risk communication as inter-organisational control: the case of the aviation safety reporting system. Paper at *Colloquy on Natural and Technological Hazards*. University of Colorado: Boulder.

SECTION V
PROGRAMME DESIGN AND IMPLEMENTATION

12 Designing Public Education Programmes: a Current Perspective

Lynne Filderman

Abstract

Several societal trends are creating an enhanced environment for the provision of information on natural hazards. These are: the growth of the information society; increased reliance on, and availability of, high technology information systems; increased concern for public health and safety; and increased vulnerability to natural hazards.

To illustrate these trends and to provide insights into the design of programmes to raise hazard awareness, natural hazard projects from three organisations will be described: Children's Television Workshop; a national support programme for the American Red Cross; and a project to assist planners for the Organisation of American States.

In a world where an increasing amount of information competes for an individual's attention, it is the responsibility of the information providers to get the messages to the risk bearers. To help achieve this, the paper concludes with a series of detailed recommendations. These include the need to have a variety of perspectives within project teams, understanding what works with the specific target audiences, and increasing the amount of personal interaction in public education programmes.

Introduction

Natural hazards will always be part of the human experience. While the forces of the earth and its atmosphere can be majestic and a source of fascination, they can also be destructive and unyielding. Our technological society is undergoing a transformation and, thus, in many ways our vulnerability to natural hazards is increasing as is the need for natural hazard information. There are several trends which are creating a unique opportunity to provide this information. These trends are: the growth of the "information society"; a greater reliance on high technology and information systems; an increased concern for health and safety; and an increased vulnerability to natural hazards (see Chapter I).

This chapter briefly reviews these four trends, particularly as they are setting the conditions for greater interest and support for natural hazard education programmes as well as providing clues on how to design natural hazard information. To illustrate the convergence of the trends, the natural hazard education projects of the following three organisations are described: the Children's Television Workshop (CTW) in the United States; the American National Red Cross (ARC); and Organisation of American States (OAS) (see end Note).

The development process of these projects merits recounting since much can be learned about a range of factors: the alternatives to conventional public information programmes; the lessons from other areas which produce information that can be applied to hazard awareness programmes and warnings; the appropriate information for different target audiences; and how to assess programme success.

Societal trends

The growth of the *information society* is based on the revolutionary expansion of avenues for sending and receiving all types of information suited to every need. This is manifest in many ways including the widespread personal use of computer data-bases, word processors and desk-top publishing systems, and in the growth of television stations and specialist publications. This suggests that people seek natural hazard information when they need it, and that the information needs to compete with the vast amount of multi-media entertainment and advertising material. The design of future risk communication programmes should involve greater collaboration between all relevant parties.

The second trend concerns our *increased reliance on high technology systems* in all aspects of our lives. A continuous supply of energy is needed to run our modern systems, especially the artificial environments of modern buildings. These technologies give us many advantages, but also result in negative effects such as hazardous wastes, and infrastructure and environmental deterioration. In addition, this reliance is increasing our vulnerability to natural hazards in two ways. First, the failure of a centralised system, such as electric power, will affect an increasing number of people; and secondly, we are vulnerable to the loss of environmental information especially during emergencies, when we may not even receive critical warnings from the technology on which we have come to rely.

This indicates that environmental information should come from a range of sources, and that people need to be able to "read" the environmental indicators of, for example, dangerous weather.

The question "what is the acceptable level of risk?" encapsulates the third trend: our *growing interest in health and safety*. Underlying the trend is an explicit recognition of the trade-offs involving costs, risks and benefits which are central to risk related decisions. This is illustrated by changes in behaviour and attitudes to reduce risk such as smoking, the health food and fitness industries, and the proliferation of consumer and environmental protection laws. It has been demonstrated that some awareness campaigns have resulted in people taking appropriate actions when faced with disaster. Thus, under the right conditions advertising and the media can play major roles in encouraging appropriate behaviour.

The fourth trend, *changing and increasing vulnerability to natural hazards*, follows from the other trends. Exposure to hazards increases just by virtue of the growing population, its continuing concentration in urban areas, and the location of expanding cities in high hazard areas. Through the interconnectedness of the information society and the interdependency of energy, transport and communication systems, more people are likely to feel the effects of a disaster in another area. Also, the media may become a less reliable source of warnings as centralised programming and control becomes more common, and local content falls.

The convergence of these four trends: a unique opportunity for natural hazards education

These four trends point towards the growing need for natural hazard awareness and educational programmes. With a heightened concern for health and safety and a greater vulnerability to natural hazards, there are also opportunities to provide this important information. Natural hazard education can use the same techniques and principles underlying the information society, i.e. tailor information to meet specific individual, community and organisational needs in ways that can successfully "compete" with other information. Support for each of the projects described below came about during the past few years in recognition of the following facts. There is a need for tailored information. Alternatives to traditional educational or information programmes are needed. National/international organisations have access to resources to develop this information that are not available to many local communities and individuals.

Children's Television Workshop's Natural Hazard Project

The Children's Television Workshop (CTW) produces "Sesame Street", "3-2-1 Contact", and "Square One TV". Sesame Street is now entering its 19th television season and is seen in over 70 countries. 3-2-1 Contact, in its 6th season, is a science and technology show for 8 to 12 year olds. Square One TV, entering its second season, shows 8 to 12 year olds how mathematics fits into everyday life. For those who are not familiar with Sesame Street, this television programme for pre-school children was originally developed to reach minority children by using the power of television to deliver educational messages in an entertaining way.

The process CTW uses to develop its programmes, the CTW model of formative research, involves the collaboration of many people representing three areas - researchers, producers and educators. Extensive background work is done to determine the appropriate messages and mediums in order to reach a defined target audience. This mode is what has made CTW a successful production house and the largest independent producer of children's television programming in the world. One of the reasons CTW's productions work is that they specifically design their programmes and materials using formats that "work" with children and tailor the content, language and concepts so that they are age-appropriate.

The Community Education Services (CES) division has been involved in community outreach since CTW's inception in 1969. CES uses the appeal of Sesame Street as a catalyst for communities to address important safety issues. As a result of their successful Sesame Street Fire Safety Project, CES is developing materials to reach children and families covering a range of natural hazards - hurricanes, earthquakes, floods, severe thunderstorms and tornadoes. The project is funded by the Federal Emergency Management Agency with additional support from the National Weather Service and the American Red Cross.

The Natural Hazard Project presents an alternative to conventional natural hazard education programmes in that it is using Sesame Street as a catalyst to get families to think about natural hazard issues. Lessons learned from CTW's 19 years of experience and the formative research model have been applied to CTW's Natural Hazard Project and have guided its development. The extensive research activities, including field testing prototypes with the target audience, played a critical role in producing and refining materials that would meet the information needs of children and their families.

Project development

Tailoring information to meet the specific target audience's needs is a fundamental aspect of CTW's productions. The Natural Hazard Project is the first CTW Project to reach parents, pre-schoolers and older children. The formative research for the Natural Hazard Project included an extensive literature search, an informal investigation with children and adults around the country, a two-day seminar and a series of discussions with natural hazard researchers, practitioners and child development specialists. An essential ingredient in this process is the ongoing collaboration between specialists in these three areas - children, natural hazards and the media.

What was learned during the research and development stages demonstrated the challenge: to motivate children and families to learn about natural hazards when this is not a salient issue to many, and when there are major gaps in the levels of information held. In applying CTW's understanding of children and the media to the natural hazard area, the overall goals became: to motivate families to prepare ahead of time; to build on the characteristics and information needs of the target audience: to use the appropriate methods and media to convey this information; and to find ways to reinforce the information.

A synthesis of all of these elements led to the identification of what approach to take. This was not just developing a list of technically correct information and disseminating it. It was an attempt to build on pre-existing notions and fill the gaps. The *Big Bird Get Ready*™ Series of family kits are being developed, one for each natural hazard. Several issues appear constant no matter which hazard is being considered:

* Most children can cope with change, if they are prepared for it.
* Children's responses depend on those of the adults around them.
* People can learn to be prepared for natural hazards.
* Most people receive their natural hazard information from the media.
* Just after a natural hazard occurs, people's interest is temporarily heightened. This is the *teachable moment*.
* There are different regional, family and cultural contexts around the country for natural hazards.
* Information designed for children (and adults) should progress from the simple and familiar to the more complex.
* The official National Weather Service cautionary terms "Watch" and "Warning" should be taught and reinforced.

The first kit, *Big Bird Get Ready*™ for hurricanes, includes a 16 page booklet for the entire family (with essential information in Spanish), a recording of the "Hurricane Blues", a song for younger children, and a question and answer game called "Hurricane Force" which teaches hurricane

223

safety, facts and science (Figure 12.1). The kit provides basic facts about hurricanes, tips about what to do long before, during and after a hurricane, and suggestions for putting together a family safety plan.

Information in the family kit reflects the concepts found in the four societal trends outlined above. It is tailored to the target audience's needs and interests in a way that will appeal to them. For example, the song provides a powerful way to motivate younger children; the game is designed to take advantage of the 8 to 12 year old's curiosity about the world and a desire to be the "information bearer" to the family; and the booklet provides guidance and identifies activities for parents to use as they discuss hazards with their younger and older children. Information in the booklet also reinforces the importance of listening to the media around a natural hazards event, and having a portable radio in case there is no electrical power. It provides facts about the world around us with which many are not familiar. It offers ways to learn skills to cope with the loss of infrastructure systems, like electricity, and emphasises the importance of planning and preparing ahead of time to stay safe.

In addition to the family kits, a "Presenter's Package" is being developed. It will provide a videotape and guidelines for those who are involved in community safety to get the most effective use of the materials. It will offer an opportunity for personal interaction and community participation, which is a necessary component of these educational efforts.

As implementation is just beginning, it is too early to tell how successful the package will be. Here are some suggestions for criteria by which to assess the success of this programme. First, it needs to be assessed qualitatively, not quantitatively. One of the greatest values in CTW's project is that Sesame Street can be a catalyst to get people interested and involved who have been uninterested or unmotivated. The success of this project will be determined by the community coalitions that develop and the level of awareness that grows. This can bring about the heightening of community awareness and growth of coalitions of many individuals and groups in a new way. One way to monitor this kind of activity is through press and media attention.

A second measure will be the kind of demand there is for the *Big Bird Get Ready*^{TM} materials. A quantitative measure of demand is the number of copies of family kits and numbers of presenter's packages ultimately requested. Another way to gauge interest is by the range of groups and organisations that want to bring this information into their community. Finally, one of the most difficult things to measure, but a major goal and key to the success of the *Big Bird Get Ready*^{TM} Series, is how far families will be motivated to plan and prepare long before a hazard occurs.

Figure 12.1:   The BIG BIRD Get Ready™ hurricane kit for
                families is the first in a series produced
                by the Children's Television Workshop.
                (Copyright 1987 CTW.)

Figure 12.2:   A page from the hurricane booklet showing
                the essential items for a family safety
                kit. (Copyright 1987 CTW.)

225

The American Red Cross Disaster Community Education Programme

The American Red Cross (ARC) was chartered by the United States Congress in 1905 "to mitigate suffering caused by pestilence, famine, fire, floods and other great national calamities, and to devise and carry on measures for preventing the same".   Historically, this volunteer organisation has been involved in providing disaster, and health and safety services.   There are 2,700 Red Cross chapters across the United States and they are active in most communities, providing a range of services to meet the needs of their communities.   National Headquarters (NHQ) supports chapter activities by providing standards, guidance and materials.

In 1985, the Disaster Community Education Project (DCE) was established at National Headquarters to begin developing a comprehensive approach to increase public awareness and preparedness before disasters and to provide disaster education resources for chapters to use in their communities.   The more common approach to disaster preparedness in the Red Cross has meant preparing chapters to respond to the public's need in time of disaster. Disaster information from NHQ has generally taken the form of media-based information dissemination.   However, a number of chapters have now developed their own programmes, materials and activities in disaster community education.

The Disaster Community Education Project is developing as an alternative to traditional natural hazard public information activities.   NHQ is currently exploring new ways of developing materials and information to further the community-based educational activities of local Red Cross chapters.

The initial challenge of the Disaster Community Education project was to identify an appropriate role for NHQ in this area and to develop new products without competing with those chapters which had already established themselves as providers of disaster public education in their communities. An additional challenge is to establish this educational area as an integral part of Disaster Services.

As a result, the Red Cross Disaster Community Education Project's goals are currently designed to assist chapters by:

* Supporting existing chapter activities
* Facilitating networking among chapters
* Developing supporting or supplementary materials for public education, training or general information
* Designing a comprehensive national strategy to supplement chapter programmes.

In order to create an approach to support and supplement chapter activities, the first step was to identify as many chapters as possible with existing disaster public education and awareness programmes and explore how each chapter developed and implemented them. This would provide the DCE staff with baseline information on the degree of chapter involvement in this area, the range of chapter involvement to meet community needs, and potential areas for NHQ involvement. To this end *Chapter Activities in Disaster Community Education: A Resource Guide* (American Red Cross 1986) was produced. This Resource Guide documents 65 chapter educational activities in over 40 chapters.

The *Resource Guide* serves two valuable purposes for the Red Cross. First, it gives NHQ a better understanding of how to supplement chapters currently involved in this area and how to support chapters who are not involved in disaster community education activities. Second, after discovering the wide array of strategies and opportunities chapters created with their individual programmes, NHQ felt it important to share this "background" information with all Red Cross chapters.

The *Resource Guide* demonstrates that there are dozens of different strategies chapters have used to meet specific community disaster education needs. It is a compilation of chapter experiences and strategies grouped according to similar approaches taken by other chapters. Aspects of programme development include: how chapters work with the community; how chapters finance these activities; and how chapters promote and publicise activities. The overall framework for development and implementation is outlined. This outline is based on an aggregation of the array of strategies used by chapters.

To date, there have been several successful outcomes resulting from the *Resource Guide*. Several chapters consistently receive requests from other chapters for their materials, and some have indicated that the *Resource Guide* has given them new ideas for programme development. In addition, another division at NHQ has used the *Guide* as the basis for developing a similar guide documenting international service programmes, and another used it as a model for producing a guide on chapter programmes for the homeless. Ultimately, success will be the full institution-alisation of disaster community education, and providing disaster public education will be as integral a part of the American Red Cross as is providing disaster relief.

Currently, other activities are taking shape. CTW and ARC have entered into an agreement whereby CTW is customising its "Presenter's Package" to meet the unique needs of the Red Cross. Several new initiatives are in the development stage to further NHQ's role in supporting and supplementing the activities of chapters in Disaster Community Education.

As concern for health and safety increase, the Red Cross will continue to be an institution providing community service in these areas. Since their historical role in providing disaster services will continue, it is natural for the Red Cross to play a larger role in public education and awareness activities, possibly as an "information broker" of important "public service" information.

The natural hazard pilot project of the Organisation of American States

The Organisation of American States (OAS) is a regional governmental organisation with 32 member states from South, Central and North America and the Caribbean. Established in 1890, it is the oldest regional organisation of nations in the world. The Department of Regional Development (DRD) of the Economic and Social Secretariat of OAS provides technical assistance in integrated development planning. In 1983, OAS/DRD began work on the Natural Hazard Risk Assessment and Disaster Mitigation Pilot Project in Latin America and the Caribbean, with the support of the United States Agency for International Development and its Office of Foreign Disaster Assistance. The project is designed to assist planners in incorporating natural hazard risk assessment and mitigation measures into the integrated development planning process and in emergency management planning.

As part of this project, a primer on natural hazard management and integrated developing planning is being written. It is for use in large scale development planning and studies by a variety of professionals ranging from physical planners and economists, agricultural specialists, water resource and soils engineers to ecologists and administrators. The objective of the document is to provide guidance on natural hazard management, including the selection of assessment and mitigation measures for specific hazards. The emphasis is on prevention by considering natural hazards issues early in the development process. A summary of the primer's organisation and design reveals the importance of tailoring information for a target audience that is completely different from those of the two projects previously described in this chapter.

As the primer is being produced, it is designed to meet the information needs of a target audience with extensive professional experience, yet limited experience with natural hazards. OAS/DRD previously documented its integrated regional development planning process in a 1984 publication which lays out its 20 year old technical approach (Organisation of American States 1984). The current work is designed to replace the traditional lack of a disaster prevention focus in development planning which is character- ised as "responding once a disaster occurs". By incorporating natural hazards issues early in a development study, measures to reduce vulnerability can be identified and incorporated during the initial planning stages.

In editing the extensive number of papers to make up the four modules in the primer, the information needs of the development planner are a primary consideration. As in any field of endeavour, integrating information to fit into an already established profession can encounter problems. As with designing materials for other target audiences, such potential problems as information overload and questionable relevance are being treated by the primer's format, modularisation and layout. Another problem often encountered in providing technical information is its complexity. This is addressed by providing basic information on natural hazards, information technologies and techniques for assessing and mitigating hazards. Further, it explicitly integrates this information into the development planning process along with the key questions, important decisions and specific guidance for planners.

OAS/DRD's primer is being developed at a time of increasing vulnerability to natural hazards, but it is also a time of growing availability of new information and new technologies to understand and monitor the environment. This project reveals that there is a great need to show professional groups and organisations the applications of, and to provide guidance on, the use of state-of-the-art techniques and technologies. It also shows that natural hazard mitigation information needs to be incorporated into professional areas that can actually influence decisions affecting hazard vulnerability.

Conclusion

There are many pieces of information and components that comprise natural hazards education. In an information society there are increasing opportunities and needs for this information. When designing natural hazards education programmes, the following things should be considered, no matter who the target audience is:

* Concern for natural hazards is often not a high priority. Thus, it must be promoted and "marketed" to achieve success.
* Information needs, interests, problems and characteristics of the target audience should serve as the baseline for developing information.
* People do not want to work hard to get important planning and safety information. Information of interest on other subjects is readily available. Therefore, people will certainly not work hard to get information that is not a high priority, even if it is important to their well-being.
* Personal interactions and community involvement can strengthen public education programmes and make them successful.
* Successful natural hazard education programmes should establish long-term goals and continually build on them.
* Information needs to be presented to a wide audience and reinforced through a variety of media.
* National and international organisations can often make a substantial contribution to meet local information needs when the needs of the target audience are

considered, and suggestions, guidelines and standards on
how to make it work locally are provided.

We are rapidly entering the revolutionary new age of
information. Technological developments are transforming
the way we create, disseminate and receive all forms and
types of information. This will result in the production of
much greater quantities of information. Such quantities
will need to be suited to individual needs and interests in
order to avoid information overload. At the same time, our
reliance on high-technology systems and concern for reducing
risks to health and well-being point to a future where there
is a more deliberate consideration to minimise natural
hazard impacts and losses. Specially developed information
programmes will play a key role in showing individuals the
risks they face and how to mitigate them.

Future educational programmes will draw upon some of the
approaches that are currently being used to design multi-
media public education programmes. Essentially, some of the
lessons learned from designing natural hazard education
programmes show how important it is to involve several
perspectives on the project team, to understand what works
with the target audience, and to provide strategies for
individuals and communities to have more personal
interactions around natural hazard issues. Also,
determining the most important messages and how to present
them need careful consideration. With so many components
and pieces of safety information comprising natural hazard
education, sending unintended messages and too much
information are occupational hazards of the field. Finally,
individuals need to be motivated to do what they might
otherwise not do. Since natural hazard information needs to
"compete" with all other information, the responsibility
rests with the information producers to get it to the
information consumers in a way that will make a difference.

Note

The author serves as a consultant on each of these projects.
Anne Marie Santoro and Evelyn P. Davis of Children's
Television Workshop, David Bernstein and Dan Prewitt of
American Red Cross, and Stephen O. Bender of the Organisation of American States, provided many helpful suggestions
and comments on this paper. However, the views expressed in
this paper are those of the author and do not reflect those
of any organisation.

References

American Red Cross (1986) *Chapter Activities in Disaster
    Community Education: A Resource Guide* (ARC 4331).
    Emergency and Community Services, Research Development and
    Marketing: Washington DC.

Organisation of American States (OAS) (1984) *Integrated Regional Development Planning: Guidelines and Case Studies from OAS Experience.* OAS Department of Regional Development and Secretariat for Economic and Social Studies: Washington DC.

13 People and Warnings: So Hard to Convince

Joseph Scanlon

Abstract

There appear to be five reasons why risk communication often fails: the hazard is not identified; the warning comes too late; the warning system fails for technical reasons; it is not clear what should be done; or there is human failure.

The results from 31 case studies, undertaken by Carleton University's Emergency Communications Unit, are used to show that the fifth reason is the most important. People often ignore signs and warnings of danger, especially those of infrequent natural hazards. In contrast, regular experience with a particular hazard generally leads to more effective response and may result in the development of a "disaster subculture". However, this too has limitations. Suggestions are made to help ensure effective response. This is much more likely to occur if the warnings are based on a sound programme of public education.

Introduction

A man walked into the office of the Evergreen Mobile Home Park in Edmonton, Alberta, on the afternoon of July 31, 1987, and announced that "a tornado has hit the south part of the city. It's headed this way". Those present laughed. One told him, "we don't have tornadoes in Edmonton".

That attempt at risk communication - the process of telling people of a danger and convincing them it is real -

233

failed at Evergreen that afternoon. The tornado tore the trailer park apart. A number of people died, and scores were injured.

Risk communication tends to work effectively where there are continual threats and occasional impacts. It is not difficult to get people to take cover in "tornado alley" in the United States where tornadoes threaten or strike every year. In Topeka, Kansas:

> There is not only an elaborate pattern for sensitising the community to a particular kind of danger; equally as important, there is a widespread knowledge about the appropriate course of action to follow when certain cues are present ... Topeka is psychologically and socially prepared for tornadoes (Stallings 1956, p 18).

The best public awareness tool is direct or indirect experience with a flood, although it sometimes has its limitations, as outlined below. But where disasters are rare events, as in Edmonton, it is difficult to get people to take precautions. Most prefer to believe such things will not happen to them, and because disasters are rare events, for the most part this attitude is correct.

Definitions, and types of risk communication

The definition of risk that I prefer is set out by Burns and Hazen (1987, p 1): "the likelihood of an undesired event multiplied by the consequences of its occurrence". In other words, it is how likely something is to happen, times how bad it will be if it does.

A "risk" is therefore different from a "hazard". A river presents a hazard to those living near it because it may flood. An earthquake presents a hazard to those who live in an earthquake-prone zone. The ocean presents a hazard to those along its shores because of the possibility of high tides or storm surges. Risk, however, applies to the actual rather than the potential threat. If adequate floodways have been built (as in Winnipeg, Manitoba), flood levels which in the past would have been catastrophic may no longer present a danger. If buildings have been reinforced against earthquakes, structural collapse is far less likely. If sea walls or dikes have been built (or a flood barrier put in place) unusually high tides or storm surges may not pose the same threat. The hazards still exist; the risks involved have changed.

Risk assessment - the evaluation of risk - must take into account not the potential danger (the hazard) but the actual danger (the risk). Protective action, such as the construction of a levee, may reduce the risk but may still not prevent disaster. And it may increase rather than decrease the difficulty of risk communication:

> People may think there is no longer a flood problem due to the presence of flood protection works in the community...(Mileti 1982).

Given these definitions of risk, risk communication can take place in two ways. First, it can be an attempt to warn of an immediate threat; and, secondly, it can be an effort to sensitise people to a potential threat (i.e. to a hazard). In short, it may involve either immediate warnings or long term education .

To some extent these two modes of risk communication present the same problems, and to some extent they are in conflict. The basic requirements for both are identical:

(i)   the risk must be identified
(ii)   a warning message must be sent out;
(iii) that message must reach those who need to know;
(iv)   they must believe it; and
(v)   they must act on it.

The dilemma is that action on one element, say mitigation, may reduce the need for the other, warning. And an effective warning system may suggest there is no need for mitigation. In this respect Gruntfest questions elsewhere in this volume whether warning systems may be creating a false sense of security.

Five reasons why risk communication fails

There appear to be five reasons why risk communication - whether aimed at the short term or long term - often fails:

(i)   the hazard is not identified;
(ii)   the warning comes too late;
(iii) the warning system fails for technical reasons;
(iv)   it is not clear what should be done;
(v)   there is human failure.

These are discussed in turn below, but the evidence suggests that the first three problems, while they sound important, occur infrequently and may not be that important.

It was a *failure to recognise the danger* from the munitions ships in Halifax harbour, for example, which led to Canada's worst disaster - the Halifax explosion. After a collision on December 3, 1917 a French munitions ship, the Mont Blanc, exploded and devastated the Halifax-Dartmouth area. There were 1,963 dead, about 9,000 injured, and 199 blinded (Bird 1969, p 186). The dangers from Thalidomide and other drugs provide further examples of inadequate hazard recognition.

It was the *lack of adequate warning time* which took the Empress of Ireland to the bottom of the St. Lawrence river on May 28, 1914, with greater passenger loss than from the sinking of the Titanic (Croall 1978, p 144). The Empress of

Ireland sank in 14 minutes. Even if time is short, however, a warning can be effective. In "tornado alley" it takes only seconds for people hearing a warning siren to take cover. They know the threat, and they know what to do. That does not mean there are never time problems. So far only the Chinese have successfully predicted earthquakes. When the big one comes in California, or in British Columbia, it will probably come without warning.

It was *technical problems* which blocked warnings when tornadoes hit the Canadian cities of Woodstock and Barrie, Ontario. Both times the electrical power system failed prior to impact. The phones went down too, so that the weather office could not issue the warning to the local radio station or the police.

The fourth problem, the so-called *"stay or go"* issue, is not so much a reason why warnings fail as a reason why successful warning response is difficult . If there is a leak of radioactive gas from a nearby plant, the best response is to stay indoors, with windows closed, and wait for the gas to pass. The same approach may work best in a forest fire. During the 1967 fire in Tasmania (Wettenhall 1975), and in the 1984 Mount Macedon fires in Victoria, Australia, some people evacuated their houses and then died in their cars; their homes remained unscathed. The dilemma is how one decides whether to stay or go? How do those with the necessary information and experience transfer it to those who must make the decision? A choice also arises when there is an earthquake prediction. If evacuations are ordered for low probability forecasts, then those affected may gradually lose faith in the forecasting and stop responding: the reaction known as the "crying wolf" syndrome. Yet there is always the terrible possibility that this time it is for real.

But the fifth reason why risk communication fails - *human error* - is the most common. Individuals or agencies often act in a way which, in retrospect, was obviously inadequate. They fail to recognise an obvious hazard. They fail to react to obvious warning signs. They fail to act when warnings are passed on, or they fail to work with each other. In Chapter 8 Parker and Neal cite a whole series of examples where flood warnings failed because of human failure.

History provides glaring examples of warning signs ignored. The captain of the Titanic, Edward J. Smith, had a track record that should have frightened his company and (if they had known of it) every passenger on board. On 21 June 1911, Smith's ship, the Olympic, cut the stern off a tug, the Hallenback, in New York harbour; on 20 September, 1911, Smith's ship - again the Olympic - was in collision with a Royal Navy cruiser near Southampton; an inquiry held Smith and the Olympic responsible; Smith was nevertheless then still made captain of the Titanic (Lord 1986, p 39).

The ECRU investigation programme

Since 1970, the Emergency Communications Research Unit (ECRU) at Carleton University in Ottawa, Canada, has studied 31 events (Table 13.1). These studies identified, first, three occasions when events happened too fast for a warning. The nursing home fire took 21 lives but started at 3a.m. and developed so quickly that the building was an inferno in four minutes (Scanlon et al 1977). The air crash in Gander, which took 256 lives, happened so quickly that the crew could not even alert the passengers (Scanlon 1987). The earthquake, the first to hit New Brunswick in 60 years, derived from a previously unnoticed fault and there were no preliminary tremors (Scanlon et al 1982).

Our research has found one event where the warning came too late: this was the fishing disaster off the west coast of Vancouver Island where the storm warning came so late that some ships were committed to remain in the north Pacific (Scanlon et al 1988). We have also studied several events where there were technical problems: the two tornadoes (mentioned earlier), where power failure knocked the radio stations off the air; and again the fishing disaster where, as in the 1987 "hurricane" in England, technical problems damaged the ability of meteorologists to make a proper forecast.

We have also found a number of cases where there were options: for example in the forest fires in New Brunswick. Although people were told they should evacuate their houses they were not forced to do so and many stayed to protect their property.

In all but one of the remainder of the studies – 19 of 31 – the warnings either worked, or broke down because of people failures. And even in the events involving technical failures there were human failures as well. When the storm warning was finally issued during the fishing disaster it was not broadcast by the key Coast Guard station. Some who died could never have heard the warning.

Human error

In some of our case studies people have failed to recognise obvious warning signs. For example in North Bay, Canada, a building reeked from the smell of natural gas for three hours but just one person left that building. When the building blew up eight people died and 23 were seriously injured (Scanlon and Taylor 1975). Quotes from survivors (Scanlon and Taylor 1975) include:

> "When we smelled the gas, we opened some windows to get some fresh air"
> "When we first smelled the gas it wasn't that strong but it kept getting stronger and made my stomach feel sick"

Table 13.1

Events studied by the Emergency Communication Unit at
Carleton University

---

five toxic incidents, two involving road accidents, three
  involving train derailments;
two snow emergencies;
three major building fires - one in an apartment, one in a
  nursing home, one in a 600 bed hospital;
two air crashes;
five tornadoes;
two floods;
one ice jam (which threatened an area with flooding);
five forest fires (four in the same province on the same
  day);
one cyclone;
one mudslide;
one building explosion (natural gas);
one earthquake;
one fishing disaster;
one windstorm.

"I went to the workmen and said, 'Hey, this place is
filled with gas.' ... They said ... 'It's not that bad.
There is a little odour but it's not that bad.'"

Only one person left the building because of the odour. He
had taken his wife to visit a doctor in the building. When
he smelt the gas he told her to stay while he stepped
outside. She was killed and he survived.

  In Port Alice, British Columbia, there were so many signs
of a mudslide that the mayor was even on the telephone
discussing the possibility when the slide hit. Yet no one
was warned (Scanlon et al 1976). In Terrace, British
Columbia, the warning signs - heavy rain, unusually warm
temperatures, melting snow - were apparent for days before
flash floods knocked out the gas line, the rail lines, and
the highways. Yet none of the emergency agencies had
prepared for the oncoming disaster (Scanlon 1980). In
Sydney, Nova Scotia, in 1974, the local weather person knew
there was a storm coming, but because he was not a qualified
meteorologist he was not allowed to issue forecasts. The
link to the nearest weather office (Halifax) had broken down
because of the storm so no warning was issued (Scanlon and
Jefferson 1974).

  In three other cases studied by the ECRU, a warning of
some kind was issued but there were problems. In San Diego,
California - in a mid-air aircraft collision - both pilots
involved were warned, but they failed to see each other
until impact (Scanlon and Prawzick 1985). In Nickabeau,
Quebec, a tornado warning was passed through the province's
official information system, but this is a system which does

not reach the tiny radio station which serves Nickabeau. A warning for the Edmonton tornado was given on the radio, but many did not react. Although it was technically possible to do so, no-one put the warning onto the cablevision network. One of those who did react was the news director of the largest radio station. While listening to his own station he heard the advice to take cover and this he did. The tornado hit his home.

In several other cases, there were breakdowns of various kinds in the warning process. In Petawawa, following a train derailment, a major military base was considering evacuation because of confusion over wind direction (Scanlon et al 1988). During a snow emergency in Prince Edward County some agencies acted, but others ignored the same warning information (Scanlon and Taylor 1977). In the lead up to Cyclone Tracy in Darwin, Australia, most people - including officials - failed to take any precautions despite precise and accurate information that the storm was en route (Scanlon 1979). During an ice jam at Princeton, British Columbia, the warning process was confused: people were told by one agency there was a possible danger; and simultaneously by another that there was immediate danger (Scanlon and Prawzick 1987).

Risk perception, "disaster sub-culture" and human response

Are these many findings unusual? It is clear that they are not. Researchers in all parts of the western world have found a remarkable capacity to ignore threats. In California, people interviewed about local hazards mentioned all sorts of things before earthquakes; indeed only 2.4 per cent mentioned earthquakes at all. Problems such as crime, cost of living, taxes, unemployment, smog and pollution, transportation, crowding, education and bussing all came to people's minds before they thought of earthquake danger. In England, people living in the floodplain of the Lower Severn River seem unaware of the dangers involved: only some 9 per cent of those citing disadvantages mentioned flooding, whereas 21 per cent mentioned poor provisions of buses and the community services (Parker and Penning-Rowsell 1982, p 222).

The concept of a disaster culture was first outlined by Harry Moore and others in 1964. In only a few places, such as Topeka, has this disaster subculture developed to the point where people prepare for a threat in effective ways. And even then there is danger that the people will assume they are ready for all levels of threat, by assuming that they know from experience what will happen in the future. But disasters are rare events, and therefore it is inherently unlikely that what has already been experienced is a guide to what could happen.

This matches what happened in Cambridge, Ontario, when the city engineer was told about flood danger. Cambridge gets minor floods every year, so he ignored the warning.

239

Thus we have the incredible situation around noon on Friday. A city is about to be inundated. The Chief Engineer, who has received warnings, tells no one (because he thinks it will be like the flood they have every year). The mayor and the chief administrator do not realise it. The police do not learn of the possible flood until it has started. (Leach 1975, p 62).

We need to question why there are so many human problems. One very simple answer is that people do not want to think about risk (see Chapter 2). It is easier not to.

Programs designed to prepare people for uncertain disaster must compete with immediate and pressing human concerns. This unequal competition is inherently unfavourable to communications and activities oriented to the uncertain future rather than the present (Fritz 1961, p 662).

Mary Douglas, has put the same idea in a broader context:

Most common everyday dangers tend to be ignored. On the other end of the scale of probabilities, the most infrequent, low-probability dangers also tend to be played down. Putting these tendencies together, the individual seems to be able to cast off his perceptions of highly probable risks so that his immediate world seems to be safer than it is, as he also casts off his interest in low probability events, distant dangers also fade (Douglas 1985, p 30).

The result, as Sandman noted, is that it is difficult to get a message through:

Learning depends on motivation and risk is no exception. It is very difficult to explain risk to persons who don't want to know (Sandman 1986).

When people know they need to know, things may be different. A Dutch farmer was isolated with his family on his farmhouse roof during the catastrophic floods of 1953. A helicopter flew up, a cable was lowered to the roof, and the family invited to come aboard and be evacuated away from the surging waters and bitter wind. The farmer said "no, he did not want to leave". But he fastened the cable to a tree so the helicopter could not fly away. Just in case he changed his mind (Williams n.d., p 6).

What does it take to overcome these human problems?

A Canadian scholar, Tyhurst (1957), suggested more than 30 years ago that there were three criteria for effective warnings. The Carleton research discussed in outline above suggests a fourth.

First, people must be told precisely what the problem is, and, secondly, they must be told precisely what they can do about it. There is no point in saying a danger exists or telling people that they ought to take precautions without being specific. A warning such as "flood" is next to meaningless. Each individual has their own definition of what that means. Third, effective risk communications must be reinforced. Many people - hearing a warning - will want to check it out. If that check leads to contradictory information, they are unlikely to take action. Finally - and this is most important - warnings work best when they do not just come out of the blue, but are based on public education. A sound pre-danger knowledge base about possible threats, and about what to do, significantly affects response. Where the warning time is short this is essential.

> Extensive public education might lessen the tendency to ignore or neutralise a warning message. Flood-prone communities should conduct emergency drills, train officials in the kind of situations which may arise prior to, during, or after a flash flood; distribute brochures to the population-at-risk; hold public discussions among officials and residents regarding the flood hazard and require realty companies to disclose that property lies in the floodplain before it is sold (Gruntfest 1977, p 26).

This explains almost precisely why the warnings worked so well in Mississauga, Ontario, when the police evacuated more than 200,000 people after a train derailment led to five dangerous chemicals - caustic soda, styrene, toluene, propane and chlorine - leaking from overturned tanker cars (Scanlon and Padgham 1980). The police told the people of the dangers (gas and an explosion), they told people precisely what to do (take your car and go to a relative or friend), and the same message was repeated both over the police loud hailers and over the media. Police had taken similar actions in previous incidents.

The police followed exactly the criteria that Tyhurst (1957) and others since him have recommended:

> A warning message, to be an effective one, must inform the recipients specifically and unambiguously that they are in danger and what the danger is. They must be informed specifically and unambiguously what they can do to avoid or reduce the danger and how long they have to take such actions. Warnings must either transmit all this information to them at the time of danger or they must present a signal which brings into play that pre-existing information which is specifically and unambiguously appropriate (Williams n.d., p 5).

Some would argue that effective warnings exist only when those being warned have experience. Certainly experience helps. In fact, the receptivity to risk communication may be highest shortly after experiencing an event. Researchers from Sesame Street have found that when an incident occurs, there is a "teachable moment"; an opportunity for education not found at other times. People affected by the event want to know more and their concentration is temporarily heightened. (See Section II and Chapter 12).

Most researchers observe that there is no substitute for experience of flooding. Those who have experienced flooding are more likely to respond effectively than those who have not - the more events experienced the more appropriate actions were likely to be in subsequent floods.

Experience is not the only effective teacher. Research by Carleton University suggests that good planning - planning which involves public education - is also effective. The ideal combination would, of course, be experience plus education. The Carleton research also found that good planning results from good leadership. In Corner Brook, Newfoundland, where firefighters ignored the toxic spill, the eventual response was extremely well managed because the mayor had insisted that there was a plan. The same was true for the train derailment in Medicine Hat: the mayor's leadership had led to good planning. Others may take the lead. In Mississauga the drive for planning had come from the Chief of the Peel Regional Police Force. In Gander, Newfoundland, the driving forces were the manager of the airport (for overall planning) and the Royal Canadian Mounted Police (for site planning).

Conclusions

If risk communications are to be really effective, they must be constantly re-emphasised and monitored. That means regular updating of plans and regular exercises. It also means checks on public awareness with the use of surveys such as undertaken by those running the AIDS campaign in the United Kingdom (Chapter 14).

Effectiveness can also be increased if risk communication is made more meaningful. Do not, for example, talk about a 100 year flood. Talk about 22 per cent - a one in four - chance that there will be a major flood while the person lives in that home (Slovic et al 1982). Effectiveness can also be increased if the message is made interesting. Lynn Filderman's work with the US television character "Big Bird", and the "get ready, get set, go" theme of the hurricane education campaign, indicates how messages can be simplified and made acceptable (Chapter 12).

Finally, messages can be plugged into mainstream education. There is no reason why children in school learning about their society should not learn about environmental dangers. After all they take part in fire drills: why not other kinds of crisis education, too?

None of this, of course, obviates the need for the basic strategy mentioned above. First, there must be careful hazard evaluation so hazards are identified and accurate information about them and the risk they create made available . Secondly, that information must be sent to all those concerned: those who can take mitigation action; those who can be protected by such action; those responsible for emergency response; and those who may need to be warned. Thirdly, the effectiveness of those messages must then be driven home not just by planning, but by regular exercises and simulations and by timely (perhaps seasonal) messages to the media. One way to ensure that the media is involved is to ask them to start by developing their own emergency plans: have they, for example, got their own back-up power?

The key, of course, is effective official and public education and that is the same whether short-term warning or long-term planning is needed. Officials will not spend money on mitigation unless they believe the threat. The need to convince is the same. "People are reluctant to accept and act on warnings of those dangers they do not directly perceive as immediate and personal" (Fritz and Williams 1957, p 43).

But even given all this, two major problems remain. Even if experts are convinced that their problem is important and life-threatening - as it may well be - how do they convince others to heed their message when there are so many potential life-threatening dangers around - the chance of an accident, the chance of smoke-related cancer etc. "No one person can know more than a fraction of the dangers that abound ... yet even if we did it would still be necessary for us to agree on a ranking of order" (Douglas and Wildavsky 1982, p 50). And, how do we convince officials that a warning system does not obviate the need for defensive action of other kinds, and convince the public that defensive action does not entirely eliminate the risk?

References

Bignell, V. Peters, G. and Pym, C. (1977) *Catastrophic Failures*. The Open University Press: Stony Stratford.

Bird, M.J. (1967) *The Town that Died*. McGraw-Hill: Toronto.

Burns, C.C. and Hazen, M.T. (1987) Risk analysis and contingency planning in risk management. *World Conference on Chemical Accidents*. July 7-10: Rome.

Croall, J. (1978) *Fourteen Minutes*. Sphere Books: London.

Douglas, M. (1985) *Risk Acceptability According to the Social Sciences*. Russell Sage Foundation: New York.

Douglas, M. and Wildavsky, A. (1982) How can we know the risks we face? Why risk selection is a social process. *Risk Analysis*. Vol 2, No 2, pp 49-51.

Fritz, C. (1961) Disaster. in Merton, R.K. and Nisbet, R.A. (eds) *Contemporary Social Problems*. Harcourt, Brace & World Inc.: New York.

Fritz, C. and Williams, H.B. (1957) The human being in disasters: a research perspective. *Annals of the American Academy of Political Science*. January, pp 42-51.

Gruntfest, E.C. (1977) *What people did during the Big Thompson Flood.* Institute of Behavioural Science, University of Colorado: Boulder. (Working Paper No. 32).

Hewitt, K. and Burton I. (1971) *The Hazardousness of a Place.* University of Toronto Press: Toronto.

Leach, W.W.(1975) *Royal Commission Inquiry into Grand River Flood 1974.* Queen's Printer: Toronto.

Lord, W. (1986) *The Night Lives of New York.* William Morrow and Co.: New York.

Mileti, D. (1980) Human adjustment to the risk of environmental extremes. *Sociology and Social Research.* Vol 64, (April), pp 327-347.

Moore, H.E. with Bates, F., Altson, J.P., Fuller, M.M., Layman, M.V., Mischer, D.L. and White, M.M. (1964) *And the Winds Blew.* The Hogg Foundation for Mental Health: Austin.

Parker, D.J. and Penning-Rowsell, E.C. (1982) Flood risk in the urban environment. in Herbert, D.T. and Johnston, R.J. (eds) *Geography and the Urban Environment.* John Wiley & Sons: London.pp 201-229.

Sandman, P. (1986) *Explaining Environmental Risk.* Office of Toxic Substances, U.S. Environmental Protection Agency: Washington, D.C.

Scanlon, J. (1979) Day one on Darwin: once again the vital role of communications. in Reid, J.I. (ed.) *Planning for People in Natural Disasters.* James Cook University of North Queensland: Townsville. pp 134-155.

Scanlon, J. (1979) It's the real thing: the continuing problem of recognition and response to genuine signs of danger. *Emergency Planning Conference:* Arnprior, Ontario. January 29-31.

Scanlon, J. (1980) The media and the 1978 terrace floods: an initial test of an hypothesis. *Disaster and the Mass Media.* Proceedings of the Committee on Disasters and the Mass Media, US National Academy of Sciences. pp 254-263.

Scanlon, J. (1987) *The Gander Air Crash.* Emergency Preparedness Canada: Ottawa.

Scanlon, J. with Jefferson, J. (1974) *The Sydney Big Storm Report.* Emergency Planning Canada: Ottawa.

Scanlon, J. and Taylor, B. (1975) *The Warning Smell of Gas.* Emergency Planning Canada: Ottawa.

Scanlon, J. and Taylor, B. (1977) *Two Tales of a Snowstorm.* Emergency Communications Research Unit (ECRU), Carleton University: Ottawa.

Scanlon, J. and Padgham, M. (1980) *The Peel Regional Police Force and the Mississauga evacuation.* Canadian Police College: Ottawa.

Scanlon, J. and Prawzick, A. (1985) *Too Late to Return: Fishermen and Weather Warnings on Canada's West Coast.* Prepared for Atmospheric Environment Service: Ottawa.

Scanlon, J. and Prawzick, A. (1987) *The Princeton Ice Jams of 1983: The Need for an EOC.* Emergency Preparedness Canada: Ottawa.

Scanlon J. and Prawzick, A. (1988) *The San Diego Air Crash.* Emergency Preparedness Canada: Ottawa.

Scanlon, J., Jefferson, J. and Sproat, D. (1976) *The Port Alice Slide.* Emergency Planning Canada: Ottawa.

Scanlon, J., Harapiak D. and Tario, M.L. (1977) *The Goulds Fire: Emergency Communications in Newfoundland*. Emergency Planning Canada: Ottawa.

Scanlon, J., Dixon, K. and McClellan, S. (1982) *The Miramichi Earthquakes: the Media Respond to an Invisible Emergency*. ECRU, Carleton University: Ottawa.

Scanlon, J., Prawzick, A. and Farrell, A. (1984) Challenges to the DRC (Disaster Research Center) model on toxic spill response. Presented at American Sociology Association: San Antonio, Texas. Aug 27-31

Scanlon, J., Prawzick, A., Osborne, G., Medcalf, L. and Cole, S. (in press 1988) *The Petawawa Train Derailment*. Emergency Preparedness Canada: Ottawa.

Slovic, P., Fischoff, B. and Lichtenstein, S. (1982) Why study risk perception? *Risk Analysis*. Vol 2, No 2, pp 83-93.

Stallings, R. (1956) *Description and Analysis of the Warning Systems in the Topeka, Kansas Tornado of June 8 1956*. (DRC Research Paper No. 8), Disaster Research Center, University of Ohio: Columbus.

Tyhurst, J.S. (1957) Psychological and social aspects of civilian disaster. *Canadian Medical Association Journal*. March 1, pp 385-393.

Wettenhall, R.L. (1975) *Bushfire Disaster*. Angus and Robertson: Sydney.

Williams, H.B. (n.d.) Human factors in warning and response systems. Unpublished paper from the library of The Disaster Research Centre, University of Delaware.

14 The UK AIDS Public Education Campaign

Roger Tyrrell

Abstract

This chapter describes the aims and objectives of the British Government's public education campaign on AIDS and the progress made so far. The campaign uses a step-by-step approach and all forms of mass communication media to disseminate basic messages about AIDS and HIV infection, and to persuade people to modify their sexual and other behaviour so as to protect themselves and society in general.

The four elements of the Government's overall strategy for dealing with the AIDS epidemic are: public health measures; research; the development of services for people with AIDS and HIV infection; and the public education effort itself. An important fifth element of the Government's strategy is its commitment to the international effort to combat AIDS under the auspices of the World Health Organisation's Special Programme.

The chapter also discusses the development of the national AIDS "Helpline" and the outcome of some evaluative research into the effectiveness of the first year of the campaign. Finally, the possible future direction of the campaign, which has now become the operational responsibility of the newly constituted Health Education Authority, is discussed.

Introduction

This chapter describes a major risk communication programme of truly national and international significance, in discussing what has been done in the United Kingdom to educate the public about AIDS and HIV infection. The Public Education Campaign has sought, by a step-by-step approach, to convey to the public the basic facts about AIDS and HIV, and to persuade people to act on this information and modify their behaviour accordingly, so as to protect themselves and society in general from this alarming new risk. AIDS (Acquired Immune Deficiency Syndrome) is caused by the Human Immunodeficiency Virus (HIV). This virus attacks the body's immune system weakening it so that normally minor infections become potentially fatal.

Officials, generally, have volunteered to work in the AIDS Unit of the UK Department of Health and Social Security. The hours and pressure of work are very great. One reason for this is that AIDS is a sensitive political subject and public and parliamentary interest is unrelenting.

AIDS is distinguished from other medical conditions, not simply because of its gravity but also because it involves issues of morality as well as personal behaviour. The sociological and psychological aspects of AIDS and HIV infection range far and wide. It is important to consider what it means to be infected with HIV. At the present time it may be difficult for those infected to get a mortgage and insurance, and they may well find employment problematic. All this despite the fact that people infected with the virus are perfectly safe in that they present no risk to the people with whom they might be working.

The chance of finding a cure to eliminate the virus from the body, at least in the foreseeable future, is very uncertain, so this is a long term problem. The difficulties involved in sustaining campaigns of this kind and maintaining public awareness of the risk of infection are formidable.

Aids in the United Kingdom

In the UK there were 1227 recorded cases of AIDS up to the end of December 1987, and 697 of these people have died (Table 14.1). If you get AIDS you die. It might take a longer or a shorter time but nonetheless you die.

Table 14.1

UK AIDS cases by patient characteristics:
cumulative totals up to end of December 1987

	Males	Females	Total	Deaths
Homo/Bisexual	1,032	-	1,032	577
Intravenous Drug Abuser (IVDA)	14	5	19	11
Homosexual & IVDA	19	-	19	8
Haemophilia	69	1	70	54
Recipient of Blood:				
- abroad	9	7	16	10
- UK	6	2	8	7
Heterosexual:				
- possibly infected abroad	24	11	35	14
- UK (no evidence of being infected abroad)	3	6	9	7
Child of HIV Positive Mother	5	8	13	6
Other/undetermined	5	1	6	3
TOTALS	1,186	41	1,227	697

Source: AIDS Unit (1988)

In terms of HIV infection we know of just over 8000 cases, but we only know about these because they are people who have come forward to be tested (Table 14.2). We have little idea of the true number of people that may be infected and who are unaware of the fact. Estimates of the number vary between 30,000 and 50,000, based on the results of testing of blood donations. We know of the main transmission routes and have disseminated advice about these and importantly about the way the virus is *not* transmitted. The government is funding research and is contributing to the international effort to find a cure and vaccine. We are not dealing here simply with a medical problem but also, potentially, a social one. The government fully recognises this and the Secretary of State for Health and Social Security has been able to convince his cabinet colleagues of the urgency of the problem.

Table 14.2

HIV antibody positive reports by patient characteristics:
cumulative totals up to end of December 1987
for England, Wales and Northern Ireland

	Males	Females	Unknown	Total
Homo/Bisexual	3,641	-	-	3,641
Intravenous Drug Abuser (IVDA)	815	437	26	1,278
Homosexual & IVDA	52	-	-	52
Haemophilia	1,082	3	1	1,086
Recipient of Blood	35	29	-	64
Heterosexual: - Contact of above groups	5	57	1	63
- Contact of other groups*	113	75	-	188
- No information	61	54	4	119
Child of HIV Positive Mother**	29	29	29	87
Several Risks	8	-	-	8
No information	1,213	95	122	1,430
TOTALS	7,054	779	183	8,016

Note: These figures relate to England, Wales, Scotland and Northern Ireland.

*   Includes persons without other identified risks from countries where heterosexual transmission is believed to play an important role

** The presence of antibodies in a baby's blood is not an accurate guide to infection

Source: AIDS Unit (1988)

Because the AIDS disease is both a health and social issue there are not too many parts of government that do not get affected by it in one way or another. We know, of course, that AIDS could have a huge impact on National Health Service spending in years to come. But many other government departments are also concerned with the AIDS issue. For example, the Department of Education and Science is involved in communicating with young people; the Ministry of Defence is involved in terms of educational initiatives for members of the Armed Forces; the Foreign and Commonwealth Office concerns itself with the international dimension; and the Home Office with prisons and immigration.

Therefore the government machinery that has been established to deal with AIDS has needed to be quite complex. First, to provide expert advice to ministers and officials involved in making policy, the Chief Medical Officer chairs an expert advisory group. Secondly, there is an interdepartmental group which consists of officials. This group pools information and ideas on educational initiatives affecting the various parts of government. Thirdly, there is also a Coordinating Group on AIDS Public Education which is the Committee I am most concerned with. The Group provides a forum in which to consider the future direction of the AIDS campaign. Finally, there is a working group considering the impact of AIDS on the National Health Service.

United Kingdom government strategy on AIDS

The government's strategy for tackling AIDS has five key strands. The first is concerned with public health measures such as screening of blood and blood products, measures to gauge the prevalence of the disease and to monitor the spread of infection.

The second element in the government's strategy is research. The government is funding research into AIDS both nationally and internationally. This includes research into treatment and care as well as the search for a vaccine and a cure. Research is also underway into the social and economic consequences of the disease.

The third strand of the government's strategy is to develop services for people with AIDS and HIV infection both within the National Health Service and outside.

The fourth strand, and the one that I am most concerned with, is public education. We have no vaccine against infection and neither do we have a cure. In the absence of either we must do all we can to slow down the spread of infection, and public education is the main weapon in our armoury, at least for the foreseeable future.

In terms of risk communication there is a highly problematic moral dimension to AIDS and HIV infection. However, the government decided early on in its AIDS work that it would not embark on a moralising campaign but would concentrate on health education. The government was thereby able to carry influential groups in society with it in this respect, including the main churches. The decision was based on a view that it is for others - teachers, parents and the churches - to provide the moral dimension to health education messages.

The fifth strand of government strategy is the international dimension. The government fully supports the international effort to combat the spread of infection and contributes to the World Health Organisation's Special Programme on AIDS and to the international research effort. Less formally, there is a continuing dialogue with health professionals and health educators abroad. In January 1988, a Summit of Ministers of Health was held, co-hosted by the UK Government and the World Health Organisation, which considered programmes for AIDS prevention - a unique gathering.

The AIDS public education campaign

The campaign has sought both to inform the public about action they can take to protect themselves and to give them certain basic facts about AIDS and HIV. As such the campaign has also sought to counter sensational and inaccurate press reporting about AIDS, which may have given rise to public alarm and the growth of myths and misconceptions about transmission routes. Lack of understanding also threatened the tolerant and compassionate attitude the government wishes to encourage towards AIDS sufferers and those infected with HIV.

In this respect, it must be remembered that two years ago AIDS was a bar-room joke. It is not a bar-room joke any longer and this is a measure of the way the campaign has succeeded both in informing and changing attitudes. The campaign deliberately sought first to inform and then to influence both attitudes and behaviour in order to reduce the risk of infection.

Campaign phasing

The campaign began in March 1986 in a very "low key" way with advertisements in the national press. These were really quite dry, just lists of facts, and they continued through the early part of 1986. The government also established a system of taped telephone messages and the Health Education Council (HEC), as it was known then, published a leaflet called *AIDS - What Everybody Needs to Know* giving factual information.

However, by November 1986 it became quite clear from correspondence and the reaction from evaluative research that the public not only wanted more information, but were prepared to accept a much more hard-hitting approach. As a result there was a distinct change of gear in late 1986, when the government set aside 20 million pounds sterling for a one-year intensive mass media campaign. The previous six to eight months of "low key" campaigning had cost some 2.5 million pounds.

The intensive campaign utilised all forms of mass communication media. There were advertisements on television and in the cinema, full page hard-hitting material in the press, and advertisements in youth magazines (Figure 14.1). Some of these were quite ingenious and employed novel techniques such as having mirror inserts in magazine pages to show what a typical person carrying the virus might look like. The campaign also involved the delivery to all households in the UK of the leaflet *Don't Die of Ignorance*.

We also significantly enhanced our telephone "Helpline" link as a three tier system. The first tier consisted of taped messages; the second was for people who wanted to talk to somebody and get detailed information; and the third tier was for people who were worried that they might have been infected, or were close to someone who might have been infected, and who wanted to discuss their problems at some length. The Helpline now employs advisors able to talk about the drug-related risks of infection and advisors drawn from minority ethnic communities. As awareness and knowledge levels increased we began to concentrate resources on the third tier - now known as the National AIDS Helpline - giving free telephone advice 24 hours a day, supplemented by an ordering service for literature.

Diversity and problems

Alongside the official campaign, voluntary organisations such as the Terrence Higgins Trust and Body Positive have been active in providing help and advice, particularly to those at most risk. Also, the broadcasting authorities have cooperated in a novel way. They gave free air time to AIDS advertising and scheduled an AIDS week at the end of February 1987 which provided a conclusion to the first intensive phase of our campaign: some 19 hours of programmes about AIDS were screened.

However, with any campaign of mass education there are always gaps that need to be plugged. We needed, for example, to reach people with reading and learning difficulties and the sensorily disabled. We funded an audio cassette for the blind and a sophisticated video with sign language for the deaf. The Adult Literacy and Basic Skills Unit has also agreed to help us prepare a taped message on AIDS for those with poor reading and learning skills. Other specific AIDS educational initiatives included the provision of educational material aimed at the workplace and at staff and inmates in prisons.

We also needed to ensure that ethnic communities received information about AIDS in ways sensitive to their needs. There are two aspects to this. First, there is the need to

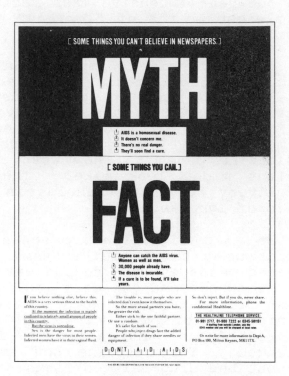

Figure 14.1: Newspaper and magazine advertisements.

disseminate information that people can understand if their first language is not English. Secondly, and perhaps more important, there is the need to ensure that the campaign took account of cultural and religious sensitivities regarding AIDS and sexual behaviour. If you transmit messages that alienate groups of people and hurt their sensitivities then nothing will be achieved. We felt that one way, perhaps the best way, into the problem would be to involve the communities themselves.

To this end we arranged a meeting with the ethnic press attended by Tony Newton, the Minister of State for Health. The response was magnificent and the press representatives were four deep around the table. Much of the concern was because people from these communities were worried that they might be made scapegoats. Black people were certainly very worried that AIDS might be labelled a "black disease" in the same way that it had earlier been labelled a "gay disease". It was first necessary to convince them that we were very much on their side, and to try to get their support in the campaign. We have now therefore set up a dial-and-listen service for the Asian and Chinese communities in the first instance, to provide them with basic information about AIDS. As I mentioned above we have also recruited ethnic advisors for the National AIDS Helpline. We now need detailed research into ethnic attitudes to AIDS and sexual behaviour and this is under consideration by the Health Education Authority.

Campaign evaluation

In the first year of the campaign three elements of evaluative research have been established. One was into people's attitudes to condoms. Attitudes to condoms tend to fall into four categories. The first group used condoms long before the AIDS question emerged and all we needed to do was to reinforce that behaviour. The second group became known as "attitudinal acceptors": they know there are risks, they know the risks are personal to them, but they will not actually change their behaviour accordingly. The third group are risk deflectors. They know that there are risks, they appreciate what they are, but believe that the risks apply only to others. The fourth group represent those in society who find difficulty in accepting or understanding either the risk of infection or ways of protecting themselves.

The second and third elements of evaluative research concerned the campaign itself. There were "dip-stick" surveys to gauge levels of knowledge at key points in the campaign. However, the most important research consists of a longitudinal tracking study. Four waves of in-depth interviews, conducted throughout the first year of the campaign by independent market researchers, were designed to measure awareness of advertising, levels of knowledge and attitudes to AIDS.

The research showed that the campaign was accompanied by the raising of public awareness of AIDS and HIV infection and increasing knowledge about the ways in which HIV infection is spread. Importantly, the research also indicated widespread public approval for the government's action in mounting the campaign. Key facts emerging from the research were that almost three-quarters of the adults interviewed had read or looked right through the household leaflet. Nearly nine out of ten of adults interviewed knew that AIDS could be spread by heterosexual activity and more than eight out of ten knew that using a condom could reduce the risk of infection. Three-quarters knew infection was spread by sharing injecting equipment. These figures represent significant advances over the course of a year. The results of this research were published in full by the Department of Health and Social Security (1987), and the data emerging from the study have been made available to researchers and health educators both inside and outside the UK. They indicate that, in terms of raising awareness, the AIDS campaign has probably been the most successful social persuasion campaign ever mounted in Britain.

However, such evaluation is not straightforward. It is difficult to unscramble the effects of the official campaign from the effect of work being done by other agencies. Nevertheless, it is clear that the government's campaign acted as a catalyst. Much media exposure would probably not have been given if the government had not acted as it did. The campaign has therefore provided a helpful stimulus as well as being intrinsically effective. We now need to move on from information-giving, to the much more difficult task of ensuring that people act on what they have been told.

Current and future AIDS campaign activities

At the beginning of the campaign there was considerable criticism from those who felt that it should address only those at particular risk. The government decided, however, to opt in the first instance for a campaign addressed to the general public.

However, now that this is done, the campaign will begin to address particular groups in an attempt to dissuade them from risky behaviour. The latest stage of the campaign thus focuses on the risks from drug takers sharing needles and injecting equipment. Such risk communication material needs to be explicit and hard-hitting if it is to be persuasive (Figure 14.2).

Later stages of the campaign will be developed by the newly constituted Health Education Authority (HEA). The Authority, together with its sister agencies in Scotland, Wales and Northern Ireland, will bring AIDS into the mainstream of health education and will encourage local as well as national activity. A coordinating group forms the link between the HEA and other government departments to

**NOW YOU KNOW WHAT
A TYPICAL AIDS
CARRIER LOOKS LIKE.**

If you're thinking "I'm not gay, so I can't get AIDS", think again. Up until now, AIDS has been confined mainly to small groups of people, but it's spreading all the time.

Men and women can and do pass the virus to each other during sex, if one of them is infected.

If a man carries the virus, it's in his sperm. If a woman carries it, it's in her vaginal fluid.

So in the future, the more sexual partners you have, the greater your chance of catching it.

And if you ever have sex with someone you're not completely sure about, use a condom. (Or make your partner use one.)

A condom can keep both sexes free from infection.

You might find it hard to accept that AIDS could affect your life. But, the more you turn your head away, the more danger you're in.

For more information and advice, telephone 01-XXX XXXX.

△ DON'T AID AIDS

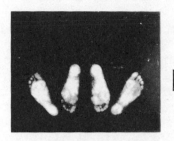

NOW IT CAN CAUSE DEATH AS WELL AS LIFE.

Next time you have sex, think about what you could be starting. AIDS is incurable and it kills.

Up until now, it's been confined mainly to small groups of people. But it's spreading all the time.

The virus can be passed on between a man and a woman during ordinary sex, if one of them is infected.

In an infected man, it's in his sperm. In an infected woman, it's in her vaginal fluid.

So in the future, the more people you have sex with, the greater your chances of catching the virus.

To reduce the risk, sleep with as few people as possible. And if you do have sex with someone you're not completely sure about, always use a condom. (Or make your partner use one.)

Any contraceptive can prevent a new life from starting. But only a condom can prevent your death.

For more advice and information, ring 01-XXX XXXX.

△ DON'T AID AIDS

DON'T INJECT AIDS

Imagine somebody who knows a bit about drugs. Somebody who's smoked, swallowed and snorted most things. But so far, they've never used a needle.

If they do, though, the first needle they use will probably be somebody else's.

At that moment, they'll be in serious danger of catching AIDS.

And sharing a needle or other equipment with someone who carries the AIDS virus is the easiest way to get infected. Now does this somebody sound a bit like you? If it does, don't inject. And never share.

For more information and advice, telephone 01-XXX XXXX.

△ DON'T AID AIDS

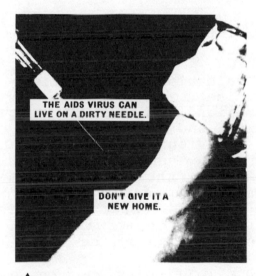

THE AIDS VIRUS CAN LIVE ON A DIRTY NEEDLE.

DON'T GIVE IT A NEW HOME.

AIDS is incurable and it kills. And sharing a needle or equipment with an infected person is the easiest way to put the virus straight in your bloodstream.

If you're thinking of injecting drugs for the first time, don't. If you can't give up injecting, never share.

For more information and advice telephone 01-XXX XXXX.

△ DON'T AID AIDS

Figure 14.2: Recent anti-drugs and anti-AIDS advertisements

ensure the necessary continuity and effectiveness of AIDS educational initiatives.

AIDS education for schoolchildren

The Department of Education and Science has undertaken a number of initiatives, including publishing leaflets to help teachers answer children's questions about AIDS.

A teaching package has been developed. Launched in December 1987, it includes a 25 minute video giving factual information. The video is in modular form and includes an explicit condom animatic sequence as we know that many adults as well as teenagers are unsure about the correct way to use a condom. The decision on whether or not to show the whole video or particular modules to children will rest with school governors. However, the results of piloting are very encouraging in demonstrating governor's willingness to cooperate.

Other activities have included the revision of leaflets for people travelling abroad and the issue of guidance to professions whose activities involved skinpiercing - such as tatooists and acupuncturists.

Future initiatives

As has been indicated the Health Education Authority will continue to develop the campaign, including its mass media element.

Evaluation will continue but will need to become more precise in its measurement of the extent to which the campaign succeeds in persuading people to modify their sexual and other behaviour. So far there is little evidence of behaviour modification, with the notable exception of the "gay" community. Research during the first year of the campaign showed that homosexuals had made significant changes in sexual behaviour, but we have little or no information about bisexuals or the more covert "gays". Research into sexual behaviour generally is therefore under consideration by the Health Education Authority.

One difficulty we have needed to address is to convince people of the urgency of the AIDS threat in the absence of strong evidence of heterosexual spread in the UK. This has made it difficult to persuade people to personalise the messages we are disseminating. But these difficulties should not be taken as an argument for curtailing the campaign. The essence of prevention is not to wait until an epidemic assumes cataclysmic proportions before taking action: prevention is the watchword of the British government's campaign against AIDS and HIV infection, as it must be for the global struggle against the disease.

References

AIDS Unit (1988) *AIDS: the UK response*. Department of
    Health and Social Security: London.
Department of Health and Social Security (1987)   *AIDS –
    monitoring response to the public education campaign
    February 1986 – February 1987*. HMSO: London

15 "Promoting" a Risk Reduction Project: Experience in Thames Water

John Gardiner

We can never survey our own sentiments and motives, we can never form any judgement concerning them; unless we remove ourselves, as it were, from our own natural station, and endeavour to view them as at a certain distance from us. (Adam Smith 1759)

Abstract

Although project management in flood alleviation is still the province of the civil engineer, who can be expected to provide solutions to technical problems, the promotion of an environmentally sensitive risk reduction scheme in the public domain requires wider skills and sensibilities. Merely to brief the public on the professionals' final design is today likely to provoke the public response that this prevention (however good it actually may be) may be no better than the original risk they face, and that the associated environmental damage is unacceptable.

In the end, efficient implementation of a risk reduction project will depend on just two factors: the public's perception of risk and the credibility of the project promoter. Both are critically influenced by the quality of the value judgements made over resource utilisation; especially in the project's conceptual phase, based on the scope and level of risk as perceived by the professionals and their correct understanding of public concerns. Finally, the protocol of formal consultation with local authorities must be considered, to ensure the integrity of public consultation and thereby the promoter's credibility.

Introduction: uncertainties in risk reduction and risk management

A marriage of sociology and psychology into the family of engineering interests brings scope for all-round enlightenment. The engineer's training brings convictions generally focusing on tangible considerations such as contracts, yield stress, factors of safety and measurement of quantities: "unforeseen circumstances" may be welcomed as a challenge to ingenuity (or a claim on the contract), but statistics are worrying - how far can we rely on 95 per cent confidence limits?

The idea that an engineer is a risk manager is as foreign as it is uncomfortable to many in the profession, and yet risk permeates the engineer's work as it does the stockbroker's. Big gains mean big risks in most fields of endeavour. Once the technical aspects of a project are understood, today's engineer must embark on a voyage across a sea of uncertainty and intangibles in order to implement a flood alleviation scheme. Unforeseen circumstances become the norm, not the unusual: technical problems are replaced by people problems. The need for technical training and experience is suddenly matched by the need for interpersonal and group control skills, and an awareness of practical psychology.

A complex risk reduction policy, plan or scheme needs active promotion at all stages. Yet the skills to promote a preferred solution have rarely been part of the engineer's preparatory training: the business is one of risk management. To plan both the technical assessment and the promotion campaign, the "promoter" must have knowledge of the public's perceptions at the earliest stage possible. The initial consultation package should address the subject from the viewpoint of the audience rather than attempt a full technical exposition. Understanding the public's perception therefore influences not only the scope, scale and direction but the entire promotional strategy of the project.

This promotion process can be greatly assisted by modern communication methods: the idea of a video to lift the burden of endless public repetition of the project concept, and perhaps lend the credibility of the visual documentary, is appealing. But what should it show, and what should it say? The involved process of making such a video for the Maidenhead Flood Study is outlined, together with an assessment of its contribution to the public consultation campaign. But first let us look at the problems inherent in this risk communication process.

Problems the engineer faces in risk communication

The environmental awakening which coincided with the period of high inflation in the mid-1970s changed public attitudes dramatically. Not only were river management and flood alleviation schemes increasingly questioned on environmental grounds, but economic efficiency and value for money also became key public issues as water rate bills soared. The strength of both the economic and environmental cases is, of course, entirely dependent on assessments of risk (frequency and magnitude, or threat and susceptibility respectively). Risk assessment is therefore also the major technical factor in the efficient implementation of any flood risk reduction scheme. But they are also the governing factors in the successful and cost-effective promotion of schemes, especially where a determined, proactive stance has been adopted.

Accurately (and comprehendably) defining the risk

"I'm not very used to Public Speaking, but to show willing I'll fight any man in the house". Buster Keaton's words parody the engineer's dilemma when first faced with public consultation. The wish is to serve the customers rather than fight them, but how should the campaign be planned? Clearly, the flood threat must be defined, with its implications and options for alleviation (with their implications). Jargon must not be used, but should the public be addressed from the engineer's point of view, or from the public's point of view? What is the public viewpoint? Who is the "public"?

Perhaps the most significant problem facing today's engineer as project manager in the Thames catchment is the lack of recent flooding on a regionally significant scale. A recent massive public consultation exercise in the Lower Colne valley, while confirming overwhelming support for reduction in flood risk, also drew some comments querying the need for such work in the light of the dearth of flood events in recent years. However, the renewed incidence of flooding in October 1987, although relatively minor, drew critical references about Thames Water (the responsible authority) from individuals and the press.

Preparing environmentally sensitive flood alleviation schemes is therefore most appropriate while not under political pressure to act precipitously, although there is a grave danger that the scheme will then be perceived as unnecessary owing to the lack of a flood risk. Even if such a scheme cannot be implemented (despite the most excellent of marketing campaigns) until the "teachable moment" of a major flood, it should be ready and waiting for this moment to arrive in order to take rapid advantage of the opportunity.

It must be acknowledged, however, that the ideal situation - if only in economic terms - would be for the flood to follow immediately on completion of the scheme. Recognition of this situation stimulates the project manager to promote the project actively in the public eye. If necessary, simulation techniques such as modelling and video can be used to persuade the public, without causing the confusion, distress and other intangible damage wrought by an actual flood event.

Perceptions of standards: "natural" and "induced" hazards

There is clearly a world of difference in the public's perception between acceptable risk from "natural" hazards and acceptable risk from hazards induced by technology. While a policy of protection against a major river flood with an annual occurrence probability of 1 in 100 is held to be reasonable, such odds (albeit for simple, rather than compound risk) would not be tolerated for the safety of a dam or reservoir providing essential water resources, let alone a nuclear power plant. Nor is it merely the scale of damage which is always at stake here: although the potential damage from major river flooding of Thameside towns would be at least equivalent to that from the rupture of a sizeable dam, the latter will conventionally invoke a higher protection standard. The other obvious influence of "who pays" for the protection is at present common to both reservoirs and flood protection, so far as the public is concerned, yet the standards the public appears to demand differ significantly.

While intuitively this difference can be appreciated, there is an irony here. The real difference is between taking the risk into the community in the case of a reservoir, and taking the community to the risk in the case of river flooding. We are not, after all, obliged to build and live in the natural floodplain. The fact that individuals do, the argument continues, implies acceptance of the natural risk, and yet the more we build the more the scale of damage from that risk increases - as is currently being investigated quantitatively in the Maidenhead Study by Thames Water.

Is this distinction useful, or merely a curiosity? It is suggested that it is not merely useful, but essential for the project promoter to understand the consequences of the distinction - especially if the projects to be promoted are a mix of different types. Clearly, scheme costs and the assessed risk of loss of amenity and disturbance caused by a scheme will be tolerated to differing degrees according to the perceived scale of the "Do Nothing" risk. The Thames Barrier was held to be so vital to London that no potential damage assessment was carried out. The damages were held to be so high, despite elaborate warning procedures, as to warrant building the Barrier whatever the cost. Yet even the 1 in 1000 (0.1 per cent) flood protection standard for London claimed from the year 2001 may prove to be conservative. It is interesting to speculate how the acceptable degree of protection and cost of works relates to public experience and perception of risk.

Grasping the consequences: "doing nothing" is risky

There are two major components of risk, which call for equal ranking in the determination of project success:

(i)   The "Do Nothing" hazard (i.e. damage from flooding)
(ii)   The "Do Something" hazard (environmental damage caused
       by the risk reduction project itself).

The first component is relatively easy to grasp, and traditionally it was the only thing necessary to grasp. Hydrology will provide a flow/frequency relationship. River modelling will derive the area and depth versus frequency relationship, and the Middlesex Polytechnic FHRC databank, or site property survey, will produce the depth/damage curve, from which damage/frequency and eventually the project's present economic value can be calculated.

Prior to the mid-1970s, it was quite possible to implement flood schemes using rough calculations of benefit and risk. Professional standing, together with a lack of public interest in environmental and even economic considerations, facilitated in good faith many schemes which would not be tolerated today. It is now understood that the situation is much more complex, and that the real risks are still not being properly assessed. For example, while the intricacies of indirect and intangible flood damage are not for this chapter, many will argue that intangibles such as ill-health, loss of irreplaceable memorabilia and fear of event recurrence should be the real issues in flood alleviation. The significance of this fact is brought to the fore later in this chapter.

The second component, the "do something" hazard, is amorphous and largely subjective, ranging perhaps from pre-scheme planning blight through to the noise, smell, dust and general disruption of construction, and to permanent loss of habitat and amenity.   It is not easy to grasp professionally, but all too easy to grasp emotionally for the potential NIMBY (Not In My Backyard) customer, and an even more fruitful field for argument and disagreement than the scheme economics.

Whether from genuine concern or a desire to be controversial, reluctant customers can therefore assail all too easily the need, the standard and the risks involved in a risk reduction scheme. The engineer must be ready technically and conversationally with all the answers - couched so as to win the questioners over rather than alienate them. This is despite the fact that the customer can manipulate public meetings by asking simple questions with complex answers, complex questions with difficult answers and outrageously provocative questions with no answers. An example of each type of question follows: "How do you calculate the benefits?" "In the event of the scheme proceeding with a standard less than 1% (or 1 in 100 annual chance of flooding) how in detail will the water authority attempt to ensure that no further development of floodplain land takes place?" "When will you resume the annual river maintenance programme which used to be carried out, making such a capital scheme an unnecessary waste of money?"

Project "promotion"

For all these reasons, engineers today are understandably unclear about how best to "promote" their schemes. Undoubtedly, the simplest line is taken by those who continue to believe they alone know best, and who have no hesitation in programming the project to present what they regard as an environmentally sensitive scheme to the customer, immediately prior to implementation. The risk they run is clearly that "execution of the scheme" may not describe what they had intended – and their own *Dies Irae* might follow. Environmental sensitivity is meaningless unless the customers have been involved to complement the professional view with their own perception.

Undoubtedly, the cautious engineer could discover, albeit subjectively, every conceivable environmental impact (adverse or beneficial, direct or indirect, long or short term, reversible or irreversible, strategic or local) starting with the eleven disciplines covered in the Colne study (Gardiner *et al* 1987) or the seventeen in the Datchet, Wraysbury, Staines and Chertsey Study (Figure 15.1). For the fullest comparative analysis the impacts would be registered for all available engineering options, for a range of levels of flood protection. However, this engineer's *Dies Irae* might occur once time and money budgets had been exhausted, perhaps half-way through such a mammoth undertaking.

The key question is how to carry out a sufficiently thorough engineering, economic and environmental appraisal for successful promotion and public acceptance, within a reasonable budget. These areas of concern, related to the project's phases through the appraisal, design and construction functions are shown in Figure 15.2.

An initial concept phase should define the subsequent morphology of the entire project by scanning all the disciplines involved for sensitivity, and resourcing the project programme accordingly (Gardiner and Evans 1987). This concept phase should also programme the external consultation required, in particular whether the project warrants the early exposure which may flag problem areas of local authority or public concern.

It should be noted that overall project promotion includes two distinct phases, consultation and promotion, but the word "promoter" is applied here to describe the person responsible for the overall promotion activity.

Presentation video

Following the initial concept phase, the use of video to explain the flood risk reduction project in the process of public consultation is an attractive proposition on many counts. First, it provides consistency and a permanent record of what was said to the public. Second, at a public

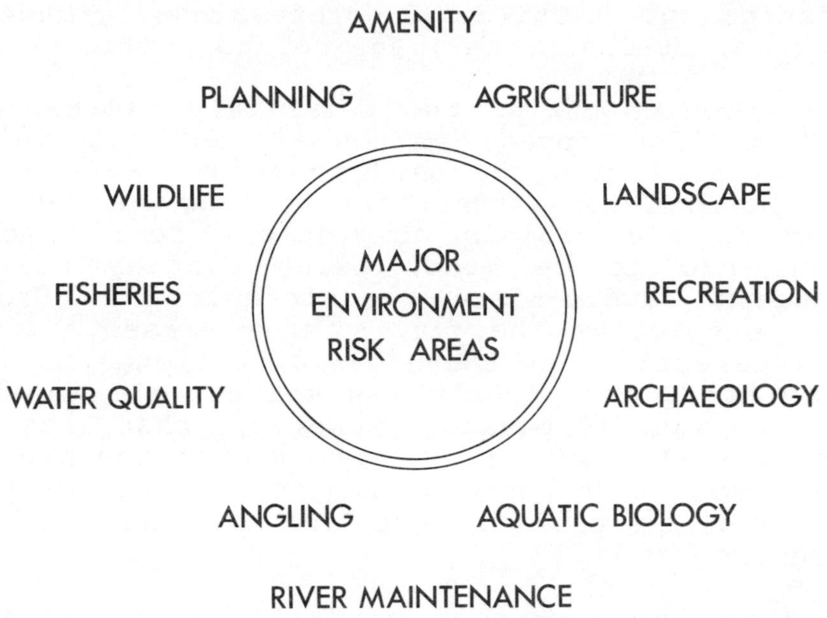

AMENITY
PLANNING
AGRICULTURE
WILDLIFE
LANDSCAPE
MAJOR
ENVIRONMENT
RISK AREAS
FISHERIES
RECREATION
WATER QUALITY
ARCHAEOLOGY
ANGLING
AQUATIC BIOLOGY
RIVER MAINTENANCE

Figure 15.1: Major environmental risk areas considered in recent flood alleviation studies by Thames Water.

ENGINEERING
/ECONOMICS
ENVIRONMENT
DETAILED DESIGN
PROJECT
APPRAISAL
DEVELOPMENT
TECHNICAL
ASSESSMENT
PROMOTION
CONSTRUCTION
PROJECT FRAMEWORK

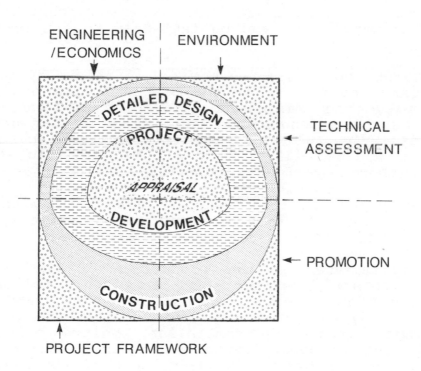

Figure 15.2: Diagram of project development functions.

meeting it allows the promoter to remain fresh for the subsequent question and answer period - repeating the same story verbally at more than three consecutive meetings can be most fatiguing. Third, a professionally-made video presents a good, businesslike image to the public.

The reasons behind making the relatively expensive video for the 30 million pounds Maidenhead Project were thus concerned primarily with the need to impart a large amount of information in a consistent, interesting and descriptive way. Prior to the video's completion, four traditional presentations had to be made, using display boards but without modern audio-visual assistance. From the presenter's perspective the first three presentations were moderately interesting, as there was a challenge to give the full, 3 year story efficiently and effectively in about 40 minutes. It was fortunate, however, that the fourth presentation was the last without the video: the prospect of a further 20 such marathons was grim to say the least - even the video began to pall by the end of the full public consultation programme.

However, there are numerous pitfalls, both professional and technical. The video script must be professionally written. Checking it can be extraordinarily difficult, and ensuring that the shooting sequence matches the technical aspects of the script requires a level of constant promoter attention which is rarely possible. Adam Smith's words find context in this activity: the promoter's inevitable sentiments and motives are likely to be faithfully recorded by the scriptwriter - and be invisible to the promoter for what they are: bias.

The script should also be checked therefore by someone who is at least indifferent to the project being promoted. As an example, the Maidenhead video script concluded the passage on the second (West Bank) flood relief option with the words, "The full story of this option's disadvantages only time would tell". This was a clear signal of bias which, although perfectly true and included in all good faith, is known to have damaged the credibility of the video and the promoter for several members of the public audiences. Such a firm *promotional* stance was inappropriate in what was billed as a *consultation* exercise.

As a first step in the production of the video, the professional script writer spent some hours talking to the team members and visiting the sites. Her draft was then worked over by team members, senior management and the in-house video production specialist, before being finally agreed. The producer and director then worked with the script writer to produce a shooting sequence to match the script and, having obtained agreement from the project manager, set about obtaining the required film footage.

The promoter was persuaded, because of the weight of information which could not be directly supported visually (without distraction), that narration should be on-camera, i.e. using a "talking head" narrator. Editing the result was a long business, and it was found that the "talking head" decision had an unexpected implication. The voice, even when used as a voice-over to an illustrative shot, was recorded on site with background noise of a level and type impossible to reproduce in the editing room if a script change was required. Very few changes could therefore be made at this editing stage, to what effectively became the final product. The talking head may indeed have been appropriate, but it was found irritating by many who subsequently commented on the finished product. It also reduced the value of the footage as library material, as well as limiting the possibility of changes to the first cut.

Risk reduction and economic appraisals

Intangible damage and promotion

The risk communicator faces a dynamic situation: today's public may well be very concerned about the risk of environmental damage caused by a scheme at least equivalent to concern about the risk of damage caused by flooding.

Past reliance on estimates of a scheme's tangible benefits to exceed both scheme costs and perception of environmental damage, is no longer adequate. Intangible damages of the "Do Something" option are unlikely ever to be acceptably compared with the tangible damage of the "Do Nothing" option, because of the absence of an agreed numeraire. Their equivalence with the intangible damages of the "Do Nothing" option may be subjectively balanced by a measure of environmental enhancement, as a cost to the scheme. This leaves tangible benefits to be compared with basic and balancing costs, and a far simpler philosophy to be offered for public comprehension in the consultation phase. Thus, whereas project promotion has concentrated on tangible flood damage in the past, it is now clearly appropriate to concentrate, qualitatively if not quantitatively, on intangible and environmental flood damage, and the definition of the risk of such damage in the "Do Nothing" scenario should have a higher profile in future promotional activities (Table 15.1).

If the overall intangible damages and benefits of "Do Nothing" and "Do Something" can be perceived as potentially equivalent, the tangible benefits of flood alleviation can be directly measured against the costs. The focus of attention then moves to the cost of equivalence, in terms of environmental protection and enhancement to be afforded by the scheme. This is in many ways a more logical approach, and perhaps more attractive philosophically and easier to understand for the public in the consultation phase.

Keeping it simple, may, perhaps, be the key to successful project promotion. Clearly, the process of public consultation cannot hope to go into all the available

Table 15.1

Balancing tangible and intangible risks.

Value-base	Time	Intangible Effects, Flood Event (A)	Intangible Effects, Short-Term (B)	Scheme Event Long-Term (C)	Environmental Enhancement (D)
	Pre/Post Event	Ill-health, stress, anxiety, frustration over environmental losses (floodplain property development)	Concern over environmental risk/ damage	Concern over residual env. loss	
Anthropocentric	Event	Loss of invaluables /memorabilia Landscape degradation Amenity loss	Landscape degradation Loss of {amenity {recreation Dust, noise, smell		Landscape improvement (medium-long term) Amenity} extended Recreation
	Event	Loss of flora, fauna	Loss of habitat, fauna		Conservation, reinstatement, increased diversity and enrichment of habitat and fauna
Biocentric	Pre/Post Event	Loss of habitat in floodplain property development		Change in habitat type, possible residual loss Recovery of habitat and fauna	Floodplain/ upland/urban habitat conserved by catchment management planning: flow control and floodplain zoning

270

detail. The public relies on the professional to summarise the technical work in words that laypeople can understand, and can be very suspicious that the truth (perhaps), but not the whole truth is being told. At the same time, gross simplification may be seen as professional arrogance or, at best, patronising.

Benefit/cost and economic perceptions

In this respect the professional can be uncomfortably aware of the gross simplification in the derived benefit/cost ratio summarising, for the public, the economics of major flood alleviation projects. Intangible benefits are often excluded, and only "allowed" to a total of 20 per cent of direct benefits as a maximum by the Ministry of Agriculture, Fisheries and Food for grant-aided schemes. Tangible benefits are based on a complex translation of catchment hydrology into floodplain levels which are linked with property surveys, and estimation of indirect damages such as traffic disruption. The hydrology may have to be extrapolated for rare events, and interpolated for those events between threshold of flooding and 1 in 50 year return periods which can heavily influence net present value calculations.

To put forward a single figure as the ratio for benefit/cost is therefore clearly inadequate to describe the economic worthwhileness of a scheme. To add to the uncertainty, should the design maximum flow occur in, say, the fifth year after completion of the scheme, it is likely that the payback period of the scheme will be recognised as five years: a good investment in anyone's estimation, but inherently unpredictable at the time the investment is made.

It is perhaps difficult for the public, and sponsors, to understand a statement which says that there is a range of probability of benefit/cost ratios between, say 0.9 and 1.2 as lower and upper 95 per cent confidence limits of the hydrologically-derived, optimum-economic standard of protection. The customer, especially, can rightly claim to being blinded with jargon. It may be more appropriate to talk in terms of likely pay-back periods, even assigning a probability (expressed as a "percentage chance") of the period varying between, say, 40 and 100 years for a 70 year scheme. It is suggested that the public would feel better informed if told that there was an 80 per cent chance of a 40 year payback period for a scheme, for example, even if the scheme yielded a benefit/cost ratio of unity at a 1 in 70 year standard.

Project choice

To illustrate the problems inherent in oversimplification, and "truth", the preferred option for flood alleviation in the 40 million pounds sterling Maidenhead, Windsor and Eton scheme involves construction of a second channel, similar in capacity to the Thames, over several kilometres of farmland. Initially, it was promoted as a channel some 40m wide and over 4m deep, with river-augmented flow at all times other than very low flow in the River Thames (to protect navigation and abstraction).

Public feedback stressed concern over loss of local amenity: it was feared that such a channel would attract anglers and picnickers to the area, and encourage the gravel exploitation that had been fiercely resisted by the residents for many years. Although it was hoped that existing low groundwater levels could be increased by the new channel, Thames Water's staff confirmed that introduction of river water into relatively high quality groundwater would limit the considerable ecological potential of the new channel.

It was then suggested that the channel could have a diverse morphology, including stretches about 200m wide and up to 2m deep, with streams meandering through and no normal river flow augmentation. This would provide good quality, diverse habitats without attracting anglers or picnickers. It would also remove only overburden, leaving the commercially useful gravel in place and thereby preserving the status quo in terms of mineral abstraction.

The strategic change seemed to the promoter to offer advantages to the worried residents. However, their reaction was that Thames Water had moved the goalposts in an attempt to confuse the issue. This was entirely unexpected by the promoters who were genuinely responding to the public's concern. Hindsight showed what a sociologist might have forecast - enthusiasm for responding to public concern did not allow for gift-wrapping the package. A sensitised public perception needed a more caring and careful approach in suggesting possible alternatives to the identified risk areas.

While giving the public an opportunity to feel constructively involved with a project, it is all too easy to blunt their commitment with inappropriate questions - simple ones are all that is needed for encouragement. A recent Department of Transport pamphlet canvassing public opinion on a proposed underpass put forward the preferred option, disposing of two rejected alternatives in five lines of explanation, and asked just two questions. These were: did the Customer support the need for improvement, and did he/she support the DTP's proposals?

In the excitement of developing a major project, it is all too easy to lose sight of the objectives of the exercise. Flood alleviation is only required to protect people and property from flooding, but not only must the cost of the work and environmental damage be the minimum consistent with what is required, but every opportunity should be taken to facilitate enhancement of the customers' environment. The customer will be the final arbiter over the degree of success achieved, and the Authority's credibility for the next project will change accordingly. This influence has been strongly felt in every major study so far, when adverse public comment reflected the Authority's perceived inadequacy, in terms of environmental sensitivity, on previous work in the locality (involving rivers, water supply or sewerage). When the public is given no choice, there is no chance to identify positively with the project. Even those projects built solely on land owned by the Authority, which may have no need of public approval, can shape the customer's perception of the Authority to its detriment. Whereas a little extra effort can realise an opportunity to gain public approval and a better image.

Constraints: local authority consultation and protocol

Water Authorities enjoy a General Development Order facility for in-channel works, but need land use planning approval for new channels. Close liaison and consultation with local authorities is an obvious requirement for the latter: it is no less appropriate for the former, if only because the results of the scheme are likely to influence land-use planning and the local environment.

The complication arises when turning to public consultation, which must follow a well-established sequence from Regional Land Drainage Committee technical approval to formal consultation with local authorities, followed by Parish Councils, local societies and the general public. This protocol is a very necessary constraint on the process of public consultation. It ensures that elected members and community leaders have full opportunity to familiarise themselves with proposals and safeguard their credibility with their constituents, who may well want to discuss the implications with them as soon as the proposals are made public.

This public approval route implies promotion of a preferred risk reduction option, albeit hedged with alternatives and their disadvantages. Indeed, it has been established above that resources in land drainage are unlikely to permit all options, with their various levels of protection and environmental impacts to be promoted after the style of recent motorway projects.

But promoting only the professionals' best practical environmental option leads inevitably to unevenness between the three types of public reaction - positive, neutral and negative. Little is likely to be heard from the first two categories, compared with the chorus of dissent over the perceived threat from the third, unless the Authority makes an appeal for support (which could be misinterpreted as insecurity).

Constraints: credibility - the key issue

It is no exaggeration to say that efficient implementation of flood alleviation projects depends on the degree of credibility in the promoter(s). It matters not whether the question concerns professional colleagues, local authority members or the general public - if they do not believe what is being said, it would be better left unsaid and the project postponed or abandoned.

This truth has serious implications for risk management:

(i)   Major projects, likely to involve Public Inquiries, must be *professionally secure* - this can mean involving nationally recognised experts to check areas of uncertainty.

(ii) The process of project development should be carefully planned and subject to *critical quality control* directed towards the perceived uncertainty areas involved.

(iii) A genuine *desire for integrity with the public is not enough*. First, it may prove difficult to be totally open with the project's customer advisory group when protocol (over making new information public via formal channels) has to be maintained. Secondly, using environmental impact to guide development of the project should cause change, sometimes strategic change, in the thinking. Unless this change is most carefully handled, the public or their representatives may become confused and believe they are being manipulated in some way. If this happens, the goal of visibly integrating public opinion in the project and thereby gaining credibility may be totally reversed.

(iv) Every project will, in some way, influence or change the opinions of members of the public. *Credibility* painstakingly built up over many months on a single project can be easily destroyed by a single thoughtless action - possibly by a different group within the same Authority.

The image of the Authority should be jealously guarded, which must imply strong co-ordination or control of planned customer contact. Unless this is the case, the Authority's credibility is at the mercy of enthusiastic professionals of every discipline other than marketing psychology, or even sociology, which might provide guidance through the minefield of public consultation.

While some customers may respond better to the enthusiasm and "professional integrity" approach than to an orchestrated campaign reeking of corporate identity, there is little doubt that most will feel more secure if the project obviously has the fullest corporate backing and is carefully directed to their needs and concerns.

Video feedback

The benefits of a planned, corporate approach were discovered by building the initial round of Maidenhead public consultation on the professionally-made video discussed above.

Undoubtedly, the audiences were impressed with the depth and range of technical consideration given to the project. Unfortunately, the bias toward the identified best practical environmental option annoyed those who did not support this option, while failing to draw much support from those who did (who apparently assumed it was not required). Simple presentation of all the options and their implications, without bias, would have removed the particularly adverse reaction and probably drawn a more representative range of positive, neutral and negative comments from the audiences.

Specifically requested comments on the merits of the video brought a range of reactions:

> "Gets message over well - good base for technical argument".
> "Use more graphics and less of the talking head".
> "Too long: experts rather serious and unfriendly".
> "Too slick: turned off by slightly patronising narrative".
> "Good: Newsreel footage, local residents could have featured more prominently; obvious environmental sensitivity".
> "Excellent start, but momentum and impact lost with talking head".
> "All too complicated - unrelated to customers perceptions".
> "This was Thames Water's view, not the public's".
> "Budget figures were global, not related to family budget".
> "Public figures were good, but technical details boring".
> "Didn't mind talking head, but facts were not sold to public".
> "More personalised, social impact details wanted - graphical descriptions with human implications rather than options with effect just on archaeology and wildlife".

These comments show that much of the video material was well received but for some the message was too complex, too biased, too patronising or too dominated by the narrator. Clearly, we need more pre-launch circumspection and market research on potential audience reaction, to tailor this exciting new risk communication medium to our customers' needs.

Conclusions

In marketing, there is a dictum that all the advertising in the world won't sell a rotten product more than once. The public no longer appears to attribute quality and professional integrity to public authorities (or anyone else?) unless and until it is demonstrated that they are indeed applicable to a particular product and a particular promoter.

At the same time, the reverse is also true: however good the product, unless it is customer-oriented and carefully advertised, it is unlikely to sell. Today's project manager rapidly develops multifunctional knowledge of the business and recognises the truth of the statement made by Clark's Chairman Peter Pritchard; "Our most successful managers are people who spend most of their time attending to the customers".

There has been a transition in Thames Water's attitude, dictated by changing customer perceptions of value for money and environmental quality. We have moved from bare notification of intent to do works, to a position of caring enough to include customer perceptions as a baseline study, to match the professional engineering and environmental resources surveys, and complete the framework of reference for the project team. The expertise of sociologists and psychologists specialising in this field is clearly needed to advise on the scope, scale, direction and detail of the promotional investment required.

The dialogue with the customer in the feasibility analysis phase is essentially to confirm the strategic approach of the study - for example, on which major option to concentrate future work. But a wealth of detailed information will also usually come from the public at this stage, which will help in the design phase. Such cooperation is encouraged by a consultative rather than merely an informative approach - and visual aids such as videos must be made with that central attitude firmly established.

Once successful dialogue has established the definition of the preferred scheme, it is felt that a gearchange into more active promotion of the scheme is warranted. While the need to "keep it simple" still applies, the message must be that the preferred scheme is the product of professional best practice influenced by public knowledge and opinion, and that future consultation will be more focused in order to progress the detailed site survey, design and implementation.

References

Gardiner, J.L. and Evans, E.P. (1987) Project development in flood alleviation. Presented to the MAFF *River and Coastal Engineering Conference*. Ministry of Agriculture, Fisheries and Food: Loughborough.

Gardiner, J.L., Dearsley, A.F. and Woolnough, J. (1987) The appraisal of environmentally sensitive options for flood alleviation using mathematical modelling. *IWEM Journal*. Vol 1, No 2, pp 171-84.

Smith, A. (1759) *The Theory of Moral Sentiments*. (1st edition) A. Millar: London and Edinburgh.

16 Improving Public Response to Hazards through Enhanced Perception of Risks and Remedies

Tom Saarinen

Abstract

Risk communication can lead to substantial improvements in public response to hazards. Although there is little support from the hazards literature for a direct relationship between awareness and behaviour, personal experience is an exception, and many studies have methodological errors.

These issues are explored in a literature review and by two case studies: one of a landslide hazard warning in Kodiak, Alaska, and the other warnings of the Mt St Helens volcanic eruption. In Kodiak the communication led to anxiety and hostility. In the Mount St Helens region results were mixed, but the warning was effective in saving lives and property. People have difficulty grasping the significance of predicted rare events and relating them to their own location and circumstances. Efforts must be made to establish the credibility of the risk, to communicate the warning message in a form in which it can be understood, and the consequences of the forecast events need to be made tangible. Information on what to do to reduce the risk is also needed. Achieving this requires knowledge of the hazard, the people involved and the location at risk.

Introduction

Substantial improvements in the public response to hazards can be expected if accurate risk information and appropriate response procedures are communicated in a comprehensible, credible, and timely fashion to the people most affected.

279

To provide such communications requires an accurate knowledge of the particular hazard, the people involved, and the place. Some means of confirmation of the information is also important.

I will attempt to support these assertions by means of personal case study experience in Kodiak, Alaska and at Mount St Helens in the state of Washington, USA. In both cases an effort was made to communicate scientific information on a natural hazard to the public. In the Kodiak case the communications were not well received. On the contrary they generated anxiety, suspicion and hostility. At Mount St Helens the results were mixed. Where communicated effectively the information became very important in saving lives and lowering the risk of damages. However, certain gaps in the communication processes led to negative consequences. Detailed reports of the case studies are found in Saarinen and McPherson (1981) and Saarinen and Sell (1985).

My opening assertion, about the communication of risk information leading to improvements of public response, seems to fly in the face of much evidence about the relationships between perceptions and behaviour as well as research findings regarding human rationality . So, some background comments on these topics are necessary.

Much past research on natural and human-made hazards has focused on people's perceptions of the risk. The term "perception" as used in this research is roughly equivalent to awareness or knowledge of the hazards. The term would thus include attitudes, ideas or feelings as well as the individual's understanding of the character and relevance of the hazards for self and/or community. Often the people's perceptions are compared with objective measures of the hazards in order to determine what sort of information might be provided to enhance public hazard perception.

Public perception of risk is studied because there is an assumption that people's perceptions determine, or are important influences on, their behaviour. If awareness of a hazard is increased it is assumed that there is a greater likelihood of adoption of appropriate mitigation measures. Because this is widely believed, and yet there is much scepticism that more information by itself will lead to appropriate adjustments, I examined the relationship between perception and behaviour in a previous paper (Saarinen 1982).

Perception and behaviour

There is very little support from the hazard literature for a direct relationship between awareness and behaviour. This parallels some of the findings in the debate on this issue in psychology and sociology. The failure to find a strong link between attitudes and behaviour is often the result of methodological errors. Very general measures of attitude are related to specific behaviour. If the link between the two is not direct, a poor correlation results. The strongest correlations are forthcoming when the attitude is directly related to the behaviour in question.

One form of knowledge, experience, was seen to be a better predictor of behaviour. For example, almost at the outset of research on natural hazards, Kates (1962) found that in places with frequent floods and a greater amount of experience adjustments were more likely to be adopted. In areas with less certainty and less experience, adjustments were also less certain. The important factor is not simply whether a person has experienced the hazard event but what is the nature and frequency of that experience. Limited experience can lead to a misperception of the risk and to less than optimal decisions. This has been noted in connection with Hurricane Camille, where experience with a smaller event contributed to the many fatal decisions to attempt to ride out the greater storm in place rather than to evacuate.

Part of the difficulty in relating perception of risk to behaviour in the case of natural hazards is their rarity. The infrequency of extreme natural events makes it unlikely that most people in most places will have had sufficient experience to accurately estimate the magnitude of such events.

In a recent paper Neil Weinstein (1987) related self-protective behaviour to experience in a review of the literature on the effects of automobile accidents on seatbelt use, of criminal victimization on crime prevention measures, of natural hazards experience on natural hazards preparedness, and of myocardial infarction on smoking. He concluded that personal experience may correspond more directly with behaviour for a number of reasons. Personal experience may be processed more thoroughly, and recalled more easily and more clearly. There is less uncertainty in information gained from personal experience than that gained in other ways. Victims may be more likely to seek out or attend to information about risk and precautions and thus have a greater amount of total information than non-victims. Furthermore, attitude change is more permanent and there is a greater correspondence between attitudes and behaviour when personal involvement is high. But the experience and protective behaviour are specific to the hazard experienced, rather than nonspecific, and the duration of the increased tendency to act may be short. People take the precautions they believe to be appropriate for the type of hazards they experienced.

For a wide range of risks, personal experience is associated with self-protective behaviour. Obviously all of us cannot have extensive experience of all hazards. Thus it is important to raise a key question: are humans capable of learning from the experience of others, and if so, under what circumstances? If we understand these circumstances we would have a better chance of fostering this kind of learning.

It is not only the lay person who has not had enough experience. Sometimes expert judgement is based on a limited record or on assumptions that may not be correct for the area in question. For example, the reactor accident at Chernobyl in the Soviet Ukraine will undoubtedly lead to readjustments of the probabilities of such an accident. A 1 in 100,000 to 1 in 10,000,000 probability per reactor year would normally be associated with such an accident in the United States. But the Chernobyl accident, coming as it did after only 3,000 reactor-years worldwide, may lead to adjustments of these probabilities (Hohenemser 1986). In the case of the Tucson floods, faulty assumptions based on models developed for humid-area streams provided poor predictions for local impermanent desert streams (Saarinen et al 1984).

The perception of risk involves a high degree of abstraction and generalisation of a complex reality. Although experts may be able to calculate with some precision the chances of recurrence of various hazards, they cannot predict exactly when they will occur in any one area. When considered from a global perspective, so-called rare and random events no longer appear infrequent or unusual. Hewitt (1969) noted that the 1 in 2,000 year event for a 10,000 square mile area in North America may turn out to have a global recurrence of several times per year.

Although many experts are familiar with these types of calculations, and have no trouble dealing with such probabilities and uncertainties, the public may find them difficult to comprehend and use. When lay people are asked to evaluate risks they seldom have statistical evidence on hand. They must rely on what they remember hearing or seeing about the risk. In such cases people tend to use a number of general judgemental rules to reduce difficult mental tasks to simple ones, known technically to psychologists as heuristics (Slovic et al 1979, 1987). Although helpful in some circumstances, in others they can lead to large and persistent biases with serious implications for risk assessment. Some of the heuristics which have been identified are the availability bias, overconfidence, desire for certainty, and unrealistic optimism.

Heuristics

The *availability bias* is the tendency for people to judge an event as likely or frequent if instances of it are easy to imagine or recall. There is a reasonable basis for this heuristic since, in general, frequently occurring events tend to be easier to recall than rare events. However, availability is also affected by factors not related to frequency or occurrence. As a result, such dramatic and sensational causes of death as motor vehicle accidents, tornadoes, floods, fires and homicide tend to be overestimated. The common undramatic events involving only one person at a time such as the diseases diabetes, asthma, stomach cancer, or emphysema tend to be underestimated.

Despite such problems as the availability bias people typically are very confident about their judgements. This *overconfidence* is dangerous and experts seem as prone to it as lay people. People often do not realise how little they know, which means that potential risks are overlooked such as those created by human error in violation of safety procedures; or there is a failure to anticipate human response to safety measures as in the levee effect, where the false sense of security provided by dams and levees promotes development of the floodplain. There is also overconfidence in current scientific knowledge and a failure to anticipate all the effects of technological systems such as the effect of power generation systems on acid rain.

People have a strong *desire for certainty*. Uncertainty provokes anxiety. Corporate managers or government officials may become annoyed with advisors who do not tell them exactly what to do. Senator Muskie, for example, has expressed the desirability of having one-armed scientists who do not respond, "on the one hand this, on the other hand that", but give a straight answer. In dealing with hazards this desire for certainty may lead to a denial of any hazard, or postulation of a regular cycle making the occurrence of events knowable.

People tend to be unrealistically optimistic about future life events (Weinstein, 1980). There is a tendency for people to perceive their chances to be above average for experiencing positive events and below average for negative events. This may be because they focus on factors that improve their own chances and fail to realize that others may have just as many factors in their favour. It is as if they compare themselves to a hypothetical person who does nothing.

Another major problem is that disagreements about risk are unlikely to disappear in the presence of "evidence". Definitive evidence is hard to find and weaker information is likely to be interpreted in a way that reinforces existing beliefs. Furthermore, acceptable risk varies according to whether it is voluntary or involuntary. People are more likely to accept high risks when they do it voluntarily, as in skiing, mountain climbing or other hazardous activities, than if it is imposed involuntarily without their control, as in nuclear power.

In spite of these limitations of human rationality I believe it is possible, though not simple, to improve the public's response to hazards by providing accurate risk information in the right way. I will illustrate this by drawing on personal case study experience in assessing the United States Geological Survey (USGS) hazard warning system.

Hazard warnings from the United States Geological Survey (USGS): The institutional context

In the 1974 *Disaster Relief Act* the President of the United States directed appropriate federal agencies to provide technical assistance to state and local governments to ensure that timely and effective disaster warnings were provided. The Director of the US Geological Survey was given the responsibility for doing so with respect to geological hazards such as earthquakes, volcanic eruptions, landslides, subsidence, and mudslides. In response to this directive the USGS developed procedures for providing warnings and began to issue hazard notifications in early 1977. The federal pressure supported a need felt by some geologists to provide better information to the public.

The USGS was not eager to get into the hazard warning business and did not have within the agency many people with the appropriate communication skills. Most USGS employees tend to be geologists, geological engineers and other types of physical scientists. They had limited experience in providing warnings, and there was limited talent within the agency to design an effective warning system. In spite of this the USGS was soon involved in the business of providing warnings and within two years had given eleven warnings about a wide variety of geological hazards. Some of the warnings were not well done and led to problems.

It was about this time that I became involved in a project to assess the USGS warning system. The USGS scientists have a reputation for doing high quality research and the key question of interest was how well this scientific information was communicated to the public. The project involved going to the communities to see how the warnings were given and how the community responded. Two major sub-projects were used to analyse the USGS hazard warning system. The first was a warning about a potential landslide in Kodiak, Alaska, where many mistakes were made resulting in an intense public uproar (Saarinen and McPherson 1981). The second was at Mount St Helens where warnings about the volcanic eruption were in part highly successful, and in part badly botched (Saarinen and Sell 1985).

Landslide warning in Kodiak, Alaska

The May 1978 warning to the community of Kodiak concerned a potential landslide. In the worst-case scenario 5-10 million cubic yards of material could slide into Kodiak harbour. If this occurred suddenly, triggered by an earthquake, it could generate a 10 foot tidal wave which could create havoc in the low-lying urban area surrounding parts of the harbour.

The people of Kodiak were not pleased to receive the warning about the potential landslide. Indeed they were outraged. They said they would have preferred the landslide to the warning. If the landslide had occurred they would have received public funds to help them overcome the disaster. But with only the warning, and no disaster, they claimed they suffered great economic damage without any compensation. The alleged economic damage was the chilling effect on loan applications for new harbour development resulting from the warning. The local population castigated the USGS and denied that there was any landslide problem. In addition, this Kodiak population is used to dealing with risks. They have earthquakes, volcanoes, and avalanches nearby. The community is a fishing port and the fisherman regularly go out in high seas with small boats. Faced with many risks on a daily basis they ask why should they worry about the remote possibility of a landslide.

The USGS made many mistakes in their warning to Kodiak which helped to create the public outcry and bitter resentment among the local people. Their warning appeared with dramatic suddenness as a major national announcement without careful preparation by the local officials (Appendix). Many people in Kodiak first learned of the risk when anxious relatives telephoned from interstate about the imminent disaster. Although the USGS officials might have understood the geological time frame within which the risk was located, this was not shared by the public who interpreted the warning as meaning a disaster was imminent.

No probabilities were given. People such as those in Kodiak, used to dealing with risks, would need to know how the potential landslide should fit within their list of priorities. They were further enraged when they learned that a great deal of research would be necessary to determine the probability and magnitude of the potential landslide. This research would cost $500,000 and the USGS was not prepared to provide the funding. This created strong feelings of anger and frustration because the community did not have full and accurate information, nor could they afford to carry out the necessary research.

Government officials and agencies did not make an organised effort to ensure that the public was accurately advised. Instead, information was filtered through the local newspapers. The lack of direct communication between public officials, government agencies and the public contributed to an atmosphere of disbelief and suspicion, and led to hostility, anger, rumours, and erroneous impressions of what was taking place. An additional error on the part of the USGS was to blunder into the midst of the local city-borough rivalry by allowing one party to arrange the first public appearance of the USGS team and their results. Some of the USGS's ideas were thus discredited by association with what the rival faction would consider an undesirable local group. As a result, the messages imparted were not always judged on their merits, but as political ploys.

The local people were aware of the slide area because it was dark and without vegetation in a very humid area where fresh green vegetation was normal even on steep slopes. In the past, rocks, wrecked cars and walls were placed at the

285

base to protect the road from falling rock. There had even been attempts to bring the slide down by planting explosives, shelling the mountain from a destroyer, and bombing it. Community awareness is present, but it is based on no real understanding of the evidence on which the warning was based, who was responsible for raising the alarm, what is being done by whom, or what it is costing or who is paying. The community remained unconvinced that scientists have the ability to predict landslides.

The warning in Kodiak generated an intensive local outcry. The USGS was accused of destroying the town's economy and were castigated by the public and local officials. There was vociferous denial of the problem and a residue of bad feelings. The lack of an information centre or presence of competent officials to explain, confirm facts, or deny wild rumours, allowed hostility, suspicion and disbelief to feed on itself and create an emotionally charged situation.

Volcanic eruption warning for Mount St Helens

At Mount St Helens the circumstances were quite different. The volcanic eruption was preceded by more warnings than any hazard event in American history. The warnings began years before the event and increased in number and intensity as the time of the eruption approached.

The introductory abstract in the slim, informative, "Blue Book" by Crandell and Mullineaux (1978) opens with the statement: "Mount St Helens has been more active and more explosive during the last 4,500 years than any other volcano in the conterminous United States". In the publication, the past behaviour and future probabilities of volcanic eruptions are succinctly outlined and the areas likely to be affected by lava, pyroclastic flows, mudflows, floods, and ash are clearly marked on maps. In addition, the bulletin includes step-by-step instructions for identifying the warning signs of an eruption, monitoring the premonitory events, and informing governmental agencies and private companies. This publication was a product of a research programme focussed on hazard appraisals for volcanoes in the Cascade Range. A report discussing the Mount St Helen hazard appraisal appeared in *Science* as early as 1975, and geologists and some United States Forest Service personnel were aware of the work one or two years earlier

As the 1978 report neared publication it was forwarded to the USGS hazards information coordinator. Mount St Helens thus became the eighth notice of the new USGS hazard warning system. When the volcano erupted on May 18, 1980, it followed very closely the pattern predicted years earlier, except for the initial blast which was larger than anticipated. Given such excellent information so far in advance of the event, the most interesting social science research question becomes how well did the USGS communicate the risk information to those who could use it. This became the object of a second study I was involved in which also aimed at determining the effects of the warnings on the responses to the hazard event.

The early warnings provided years before the eruption were followed by a very intensive and continuous series of warnings for close to two months preceding the cataclysmic eruption in May 1980. On March 20, 1980 the first of a series of moderate earthquakes was detected on seismographs operated by the University of Washington in cooperation with the USGS earthquake studies programme. At first it was not known whether the earthquakes were of volcanic origin, but this became apparent with the first steam eruption on March 27, 1980, and a hazard watch was initiated for the volcano. The United States Forest Service (USFS) became involved and took two important initiatives.

The Forest Service set up an information centre in their office in Vancouver, Washington, which is the headquarters for the Gifford Pinchet National Forest, where Mount St Helens is located. Here they provided space for the USGS scientists who were arriving to monitor the awakening of the mountain. They also provided frequent news conferences for the media where the latest information was obtainable as the situation developed and where clarification could be sought and inaccurate rumours squelched. Setting up the information centre was a very valuable step in the warning process and it made an important contribution to eliciting positive responses.

The second initiative of the USFS was to develop the Mount St Helens Contingency Plan (Osmund 1980). They called together "key actors" to discuss how they should respond individually and as a group to the impending eruption. By action they linked the country law enforcement offices, the major private industries, the State of Washington Department of Emergency Services and the USGS and USFS. The organisational ability and leadership capacity they demonstrated on this occasion made the Forest Service the logical choice for the leadership role in coordinating responses to the volcanic eruption. This had both positive and negative consequences for the warning process.

So far the warning had proceeded smoothly and efficiently. Most of the scientific personnel were alerted immediately and monitoring activities were soon set in motion. The early information about the volcanic hazard of Mount St Helens had been well distributed to scientists and they were well informed and ready to respond immediately.

The *positive* consequences of the USFS leadership role were the setting up of the information centre and the development of the contingency plan. The USGS was quite willing to relinquish the warning role and serve as technical advisors for they had far less experience in providing public information and in organising for emergencies. The USFS on the other hand, had considerable experience with both, because of their role in dealing with forest fires. Thus,

287

they had public information officers available, and immediately put them to work at their headquarters which became the information centre for the developing event.

The *negative* consequences of the Forest Service leadership role could be attributed to the differences between a forest fire emergency and that due to the eruption of Mount St Helens. The key actors the USFS called together to develop their contingency plan were those with whom the Forest Service was most familiar. This included people from private companies and government agencies close to the mountain, but very few from areas east of the mountain which were later affected by ash. It also included county sheriffs but not the directors of county emergency services. The USFS were most concerned about the areas west of the Cascade Mountains where the greatest potential for disaster was concentrated and did little to warn about the potential ashfall problem east of the Cascades.

During the period in which the contingency plan was developed the volcano showed increasing signs of activity and the warnings increased in number and intensity. Special warnings were sent out when harmonic tremors were detected, and when a bulge on the north side of the mountain developed and grew. Radio, television and newspaper reporters converged on the information centre and the Mount St Helens awakening became a media event. People all over the United States and the world became aware of the dramatic developments. In spite of all this information the warnings were not equally effective east and west of the Cascades.

West of the Cascades the warnings were effective. In addition to the general information and official warnings, there were many public meetings at which the USGS scientists presented their maps and showed why and where various problems might be expected. Their authoritative presentations convinced officials and members of the general public of the seriousness of the situation, and of the need for preparation, as well as providing opportunities for feedback to confirm ideas or raise additional questions. The information was interpreted in terms of specific places and particular people. The officials responsible for particular emergency responses were directly involved and decided what they should do in the event of an eruption.

East of the Cascades people were certainly aware of the awakening of Mount St Helens and watched developments with fascination. But their officials were not involved in the contingency planning process and never received warnings specifically relating potential ashfall problems to their areas. The USGS, who knew there would be problems with ash, relinquished the warning activities to the Forest Service, who concentrated their warnings near the forests on the west side of the mountains. The State of Washington Department of Emergency Services, who had the responsibility of warning the citizens of Washington, were underfunded, lacked resources and trained personnel, and were led by a political appointee rather than a hazards professional. They sent out general information about the impending eruption to all the county emergency management offices, but did not specify who should be concerned, nor what could be done.

The differences in the warning processes profoundly affected the responses. West of the Cascades people prepared plans, and the response was appropriate, timely, and handled efficiently. Roadblocks were set up to keep people out of the danger zones. Many people were evacuated, supplies and shelters were provided, and search and rescue operations undertaken. East of the Cascades everyone was surprised by the approaching huge black cloud of ash and the response was not appropriate, efficient, or timely. Roadblocks were not set up, people became stranded on the highways, emergency service vehicles were soon out of commission, and there was no information, no plans, and no emergency supplies or equipment to deal with the situation. Extra problems were created by the lack of preparation, and people had to improvise in dealing with the emergency.

Conclusions

The literature review and case study material discussed in this chapter provides some clear lessons in how to, and how not to, communicate hazard information to the public.

It is clearly not sufficient to make official announcements or give out general warnings. Neither the bold official warnings provided about Kodiak nor the general information disseminated east of the Cascades in the State of Washington led to appropriate planning and response. As the hazard literature has demonstrated, and as these case studies confirm, people have difficulty in grasping the significance of rare events and relating it to their own location and circumstances.

Therefore much interpretation is necessary to establish the credibility of the warning, and to communicate the message to those needing it in a form they can understand. Only when they understand how the hazard event can affect them will they become motivated to make plans to mitigate the impacts. Since most people lack direct experience with high-risk low-probability events the consequences of the potential hazard must be made concrete and tangible by those providing the warning. They should also provide information on what can be done to plan for the event.

West of the Cascades the warnings about the eruption of Mount St Helens generally led to appropriate planning and response measures. For other scientists the "Blue Book" sufficed. By distributing this well in advance of the event the USGS helped to ensure that the warning process got off to a good start.

For other officials and the general public more interpretation was necessary. This was provided through the media who received accurate and timely information from public information officers at the information centre established at the US Forest Service headquarters in Vancouver, Washington. Further interpretation and opportunities for confirmation and questions were provided through public meetings where the scientists displayed their maps and explained them to various communities who sought this information. Once convinced of the potential hazard and informed as to the likely impact on their area people were willing and able to develop plans.

The importance of planning cannot be exaggerated. In the aftermath of the Mount St Helens eruption it was the individuals, agencies and communities with plans that were the best able to cope with the disaster. In the absence of plans, people fell back on the closest comparable experience for clues as to action. Under these circumstances responses only work to the extent that the experiences are comparable. When the magnitude, or type of disruption differs, the response begins to fail.

Preparation for future volcanic eruptions in the United States was enhanced by the experience gained at Mount St Helens. As a landmark hazard event it provides a dramatic symbol of the power of nature and the need for planning to deal with disasters. The nation should capitalise on the experience of those who were involved to develop plans for all types of agencies and individuals. Those who experienced the event can attest to the need for planning, and make credible to their counterparts in other areas the likelihood and consequences of high-risk low-probability events.

It is important to maximise the benefit of experience. Hazards professionals with experience become believers and convey the importance of making emergency plans. One way to enhance the benefit of experience is to utilise the services of outside emergency service personnel in the aftermath of each major hazard event. This was done in the Mount St Helens eruption when state emergency personnel from Oregon and British Columbia helped to supply the emergency need for trained people and in turn gained valuable experience.

A major problem in dealing with rare events is that the perceived need for plans fades quickly. That is why hazards professionals must be prepared to act quickly in the aftermath of a disaster. Plans adopted then will provide a starting point for the next emergency. They can be taken down from the shelf, dusted off, and quickly adapted for the next disaster. But if emergency plans are never made, nor adopted, the community will respond less efficiently and fail to benefit from past experience.

References

Crandell, Dwight and Mullineaux, Donald (1978) *Potential Hazards from Future Eruptions of Mount St. Helen's*

Volcano, U.S. Geological Survey Bulletin 1383-C, US Government Printing Office: Washington DC.

Crandell, D.R., Mullineaux, D.R., Rubin, M. (1975) Mount St. Helen's volcano: recent and future behavior. *Science*. Vol 187, pp 438-451.

Crandell, D.R. and Mullineaux, D.R. (1978) *Potential Hazards from Future Eruptions of Mount St Helens Volcano, Washington*. US Geological Survey Bulletin. Government Printing Office: Washington DC.

Hewitt, K. (1969) *A Pilot Survey of Global Natural Disasters of the Past Twenty Years*. University of Toronto, Dept of Geography. (Natural Hazard Working Paper No. 11).

Hewitt, K. (1969) *A Pilot Survey of Global Natural Disasters of the Past Twenty Years*. Institute of Behavioral Science, Univ of Colorado: Boulder. (Natural Hazard Research Working Paper 18).

Hohenemser, Christoph (1986) Chernobyl: the first lessons. *Natural Hazards Observer*. Vol XI, No 1 (Sept), pp 1-2.

Kates, R.W. (1962) *Hazard and Choice Perception in Flood Plain Management*. University of Chicago, Department of Geography: Chicago. (Research Paper No. 78).

Kates, R.W. (1971) Natural hazards in human ecological perspective: hypotheses and models. *Economic Geography*. Vol 47, pp 438-451.

Osmund, E. (1980) *Mount St. Helen's Contingency Plan*. US Forest Service: Vancouver, Washington.

Saarinen, T.F. and H.J. McPherson (1981) *Notices, Watches and Warnings: an appraisal of the USGS's warning system with a case study from Kodiak, Alaska*. Institute of Behavioral Science, Univ of Colorado: Boulder. (Natural Hazards Working Paper 42).

Saarinen, T.F. (1982) The relation of hazard awareness to the adoption of approved mitigation measures. Chapter 1 in Saarinen, T.F. (ed) *Perspectives on Increasing Hazard Awareness*. University of Colorado: Boulder. pp 1-35. (Program on Environment and Behavior Monograph #35).

Saarinen, T.F. Baker, V.R., Durrenberger, R. and Maddock, T. Jr. (1984) *The Tucson, Arizona Flood of October 1983*. Committee on Natural Disasters, National Academy of Sciences Press: Washington DC.

Saarinen, T.F. and J.L. Sell (1985) *Warning and Response to the Mount St Helen's Eruption*. State University of New York Press: Albany.

Slovic, P., Fischhoff, B. and Lichtenstein, S. (1979) Rating the Risks. *Environment*. Vol 21, No 3 (April), pp 14-39. (See also Fischhoff,B., Svenson, O. and Slovic, P. Active Responses to Environmental Hazards: Perceptions and Decision Making. Chapter 29 in Stokols, D. and Altman, I. (eds) *Handbook of Environmental Psychology*. John Wiley & Sons: New York).

Weinstein, N. (1980) Unrealistic Optimism About Future Life Events. *Journal of Personality and Social Psychology*. Vol 39, pp 806-82.

Weinstein, N. (1987) Effects of Personal Experience on Self Protective Behaviour. Draft paper, Department of Human Ecology, Cook College, Rutgers University: New Brunswick.

APPENDIX

In Reply Refer To:
EGS-Mail Stop 720

Dr. Ross Schaff   10 MAY 1978
State Geologist
3001 Porcupine Drive
Anchorage, Alaska 99501

Dear Dr. Schaff:

As Governor Hammond's designee to work with the U.S. Geological Survey
to reduce geologic-related hazards, we are bringing to your attention
a possible hazard from landsliding near Kodiak, Alaska. The enclosed
U.S. Geological Survey Open-File Report 78-217, Pillar Mountain Landslide,
Kodiak, Alaska, by Rauben Kachadoorian and W.H. Slater, describes a
large landslide, portions of which appear to be active. If the entire
slide mass were to fail suddenly, it could generate a wave comparable
in height to the tsunani that damaged Kodiak and environs during the
Alaskan earthquake of 1964.

At the request of Mr. Harry Milligan, Planning Director of Kodiak
Island Borough, Mr. Kachadoorian attended a meeting with a number of
local, State, and Federal officials on April 11, 1978, to determine
additional steps needed to better define the nature and degree of
the hazard. The U.S. Geological Survey will continue to be available
to provide technical assistance within our manpower and budget constraints. Because of the possible impact this landslide could have
in the Kodiak area, we are sending copies of this letter to the persons
listed on the enclosed pages.

Sincerely yours,

H. W. MENARD

Director

Enclosures 2

cc: Honorable Jay S. Hammond, Governor of Alaska

17 Hazard and Risk in the Modern World: Political Models for Programme Design

Tim O'Riordan

Abstract

Natural and technological hazards have more in common than in opposition; the common themes are the power of risk creators and the vulnerability of risk receivers. Hazards and risks are thus at least as much a product of power relationships between competing groups as a function of the technologies or the natural phenomena concerned. Risk communication is not seen as a matter of language or even symbolic concepts, but as a political process. A number of models are presented for risk communication and mediation, including the concept of a community risk communication office. Only with such an approach to empowering people to make their own risk and hazard assessments might a more caring and equitable - and less vulnerable - world emerge.

Introduction: hazard and risk

Hazard and risk are part of the same phenomenon that pervades all the chapters in this volume. Hazards may be a "normal" or "natural" event that afflicts vulnerable people because they choose - or are effectively forced - to live in areas where damaging events occur with noticeable frequency. In either case the "hazard" is the interaction between a "natural" event and the character of human settlements and economics beyond the point where adaptive capacity to cope can avoid serious damage or death (see Burton et al 1978). But natural hazards are not necessarily "natural" in provenance, and few natural hazards are beyond the realm of the capability of humankind to cope: the damage they inflict is as much a reflection of corruption, bullying, elitism, stupidity, ignorance and desperation. This perspective is analysed in general by Hewitt (1983) and in detail by Blaikie and Brookfield (1989).

There is another kind of hazard. This is the so called "man-made" or "technological" hazard, equally linking human deed to natural circumstances but associated with chemical plants, radioactive materials and the manipulation of organisms and ecosystems by methods that are non-natural. Just as the "natural" hazard interacts with human folly and intent, so the "man-made" hazard interconnects with geology, hydrology, ecology and fluid mechanics.

"Risk" on the other hand is a more slippery concept to define. The term applies to the individual, group and societal judgements about the factors causing, managing, regulating and compensating for hazard before, during and after it occurs. Risk is a socially derived phenomenon within which the technical interpretation of risk as hazard multiplied by probability plays some kind of role, but only as a basis for judgement and responsiveness. Risk is essentially the cultural interpretation of hazardousness (Douglas and Wildavsky 1982, Slovic 1986, Kasperson et al 1988).

In this respect ideas have changed. There is now a general recognition that "risk" combines natural science with social science. Four reasons have intertwined to cause this change of perspective. First, demands have grown for the public to be better informed and for people to assess their own risks or hazards that they face. Then there are demands to have more effective personal influence over events that could endanger health and from which there is no ready means of escape. Secondly, there is a distrust of "official" expertise. When probabilities are unquantifiable and potentially catastrophic events can only be imagined, expertise no longer carries any special status. This reinforces people's desire to be their own risk assessors: they do not automatically trust the supposed superior judgements of others.

The third reason for these changes in perspective relates to putting the "blame" on disliked or misunderstood management and regulation. When a risk creator increases risk levels or considers any new investment - such as a chemical corporation or nuclear establishment - or experiences a serious accident, then the public's frustration and powerlessness becomes translated into social criticism of corporate power. Fourthly, and finally, failure of risk communication (where success is defined as meaningfully and effectively drawing the public into the hazard management process), itself creates a sense of alienation and distrust even when safety measures may be more than adequate.

Risk communication is thus not a matter of language or even symbolic concepts. It is about extending hazard management into the vernacular of all those who have to live beside, or are faced with the prospect of, a perilous installation, or those who are expected to consume a risky product. The problem is that identifying and predicting the "true risk" is a holy grail. This adds to the sense of alienation and widens the gulf of mistrust between the risk creators and risk receivers. The latter begin to concentrate on the dangers without fully contemplating the associated benefits of risky activities. It is worth re-quoting William Waldegrave:

> One of the most important tasks facing government is to inspire a development process which takes into account not only the nature of any environmental risk, but also the perception of that risk by the public who must suffer its consequences. We cannot always agree but we must at least create the circumstances and the means to discuss the risk in terms that both risk assessors and the public understands before irrevocable decisions are taken (Waldegrave 1987).

Here there are fears that government cannot handle the difficulties of siting risky installations without running into enormous political trouble. The result is a further tightening of the regulatory screws, adding further costs and delays to industrial production. The fear is also that the economic future of the emerging biotechnology industry, with its propensity for creating new genetic formulations, could be jeopardised.

Responding to hazard and coping with risk

Research reported in this volume suggests that there is more in common than in opposition between natural and technological hazards. The common themes are power and vulnerability.

Power is exercised when one person or group is so dominant over others that the latter are forced to obey, or to live and work in perhaps hazardous areas because those with power have effectively closed off any alternative locations or occupations. This is *overt* power, or first dimension power in the terminology of Stephen Lukes (1974). Power can also be exercised when those with power exert such a comprehensive influence over the way in which others see the world and their life chances, that the powerless actually believe that they are acting through choice and self will, even when they are being manipulated. This is the exercise of *covert* power. *Vulnerability* is the state of powerlessness in the face of a known or unknown hazard.

The concepts of power and vulnerability also apply to the so-called human provenance or technological hazards. The landless of Bophal lived near the chemical plant because they had nowhere else to go. Nobody in the plant had increased the safety management standards for the factory - which was deliberately sited away from the city for safety reasons - when it subsequently became surrounded by those needing or forced to live nearby. Plant mismanagement was always deemed a possibility and the Bophal accident was all the more tragic because the hazard was worsened by uncontrolled settlement, itself driven by powerlessness and poverty. Planners, managers and migrants combined through miscommunication, incompetence and other factors to produce a particularly hazardous situation and an event with desperate human suffering. The long delay in paying compensation to victims shows all too clearly how vulnerability, poverty and misery intertwine, well beyond the margins of the individual's adaptive ability.

An example of covert power in the risk area is the current fettish with sun tanning among white populations, owing to seemingly irresistible social and commercial pressures. Yet the incidence of melanoma or skin cancer has increased ten fold over the last five years, from 20 per 100,000 to 200 per 100,000, while in Australia it is over 400 per 100,000 (UN Environment Programme 1987, pp 27-29). All are needless victims of a failure to communicate the hazard: the risk is the lack of perception of danger and in that respect it is the inverse of the risk perceived to be associated with well managed nuclear power plants.

There is no easy solution to the management of risks (as opposed to hazard) in the modern world. Figure 17.1 suggests one possibility for natural hazards and Figure 17.2 outlines a way forward for technological hazards. For the natural hazards, coping means providing a mix of responses coupled to devices for reducing poverty, powerlessness and vulnerability (O'Riordan 1986, see also Chapter 6). Since these malaises cannot be removed in the foreseeable future it is tempting to be pessimistic and equate misery with continuing vulnerability on a mass scale.

Such need not be the case. The work of the non-governmental charities, the "greening" of aid schemes, the slow but sure shift towards more sustainable patterns of rural development via self-help schemes; all offer hope of lower vulnerability. An extension of disaster relief schemes with sustainable development is another way forward, and small successes here could put pressure on the international community to reduce militarism and to promote the cause of sustainable development.

For technological hazards, Figure 17.2 shows that ignorance needs to be countered. Ignorance in this context applies to any condition where relevant and legitimate viewpoints are not fully understood and appreciated. This suggests that communities and "experts" need to establish cultural risk translators or mediators to provide an intelligible bridge between the different parties. This will not be easy, however, since the risk translators, or communicators, are not themselves acting either with perfect knowledge and understanding or in a world of equal power relationships.

Empowering communities to be their own risk appraisers and mediators

What follows is a proposal designed for a community faced with a decision to have a "stigma-linked" risk-laden facility in its locality, such as a nuclear installation or hazardous chemical dump. The concept could, however, also apply in a regional context to toxification of groundwater, the use of chemical pesticides or genetically engineered organisms over a large area whose perilous characteristics are almost unknowable and where the consequences of

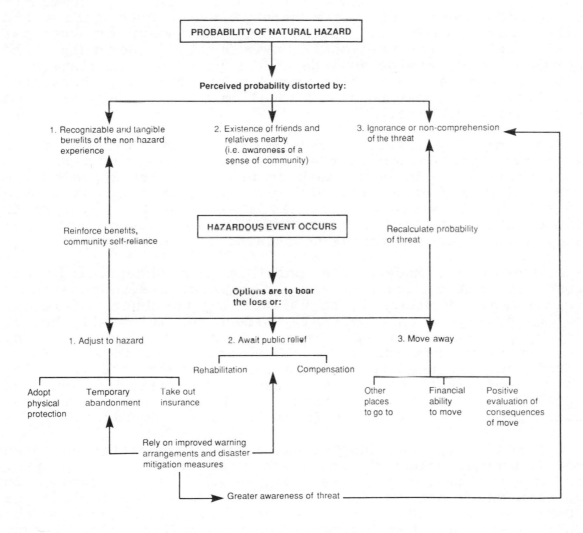

Figure 17.1: Behavioural response to the threat of natural hazard. The diagram indicates some of the possible options open to an inhabitant of a hazard prone area, and some of the interactive consequences of an actual disaster.

uncontrolled exposure to toxic substances could be lethal and widespread, with huge implications for medical insurance and house prices.

In such cases there is a need to establish some kind of community control over the manner in which risks are understood and communicated, bearing in mind the conceptual framework of Figure 17.1. The generic concept is of a *community safety service* that gives people access to equivalent levels of understanding over the technical assessment of safety, under both accidental and normal conditions.

This type of service would have three roles to play. First, it would provide the community with its own assessment of possible dangers and safety requirements, rather than it having to accept the assessments of others. The service would become the focal point of community bargaining over appropriate safety levels both before and after the siting, or during the management of chemical residuals in the regional environment. Secondly, the service would provide an independent point of translation of risk principles and risk management for the hazardous facility or phenomenon in an intelligible language set in a comparative context.

The community safety service's third role would be to act as a trouble shooter in the event of a near accident or a real disaster. It would help to provide information on the scale of the damage, and advice on what precautions should be taken. It would also act as a mediator for appropriate compensation claims so that local people could feel that they have an authoritative negotiator on their side.

A number of models are possible for undertaking this community safety service task. The *local liaison committee* is the most popular, least threatening to other interests, but generally is only partially effective. It usually has no power, is mostly a talkshop, and it rarely carries any influence on post-disaster compensation dealings. These committees can nevertheless play an important role in acting as a communications bridge between the risk creators and receivers. In the right hands the local liaison committee could provide a low budget forum for risk communication.

Alternatively, the *independent advisory committee* composed of academics, industrialists, and knowledgeable lay people, is another well-established mechanism. For example, in Britain there are numerous such bodies (examples include the Committee on the Medical Aspects of Radiation on the Environment, and the Advisory Committee on Pesticides), many of which are highly respected. These committees are generally established to advise, not to mediate, and as such they have no power although they may carry authority.

Some of these committees, however, have power under statutes to license products or processes, and their

298

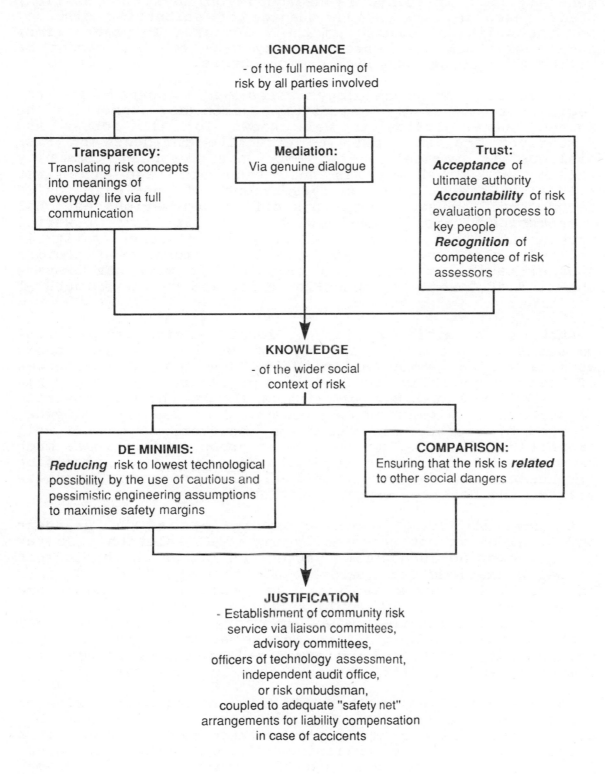

Figure 17.2: Principles of tolerability for
technological hazards.

composition reflects their expertise and independence. In general their influence is dependent on their composition, their research back-up, the degree of scientific dispute, and the political context of their advice. In power terms, such committees are currently very weak so they cannot be relied upon to be good risk communicators.

An *office of technology assessment* located at the legislature is also a relatively common development. The United States office is well known for its robust and forthright analysis, but its effective influence on risk dialogue is variable. An embryonic European Community version at Strasbourg has just begun to take its first faltering steps over an assessment of nuclear fusion technology. However, both this office and various national institutions are viewed with suspicion by powerful governments that dislike meddling legislatures. It is unlikely that such an office will do more than provide another basis for judgement; certainly it will not provide the kind of "people's empowerment" implied by its structural position.

Another possibility is a *local environmental risk ombudsman*. This would be a nascent version of a full-blown community risk communication office, but has the advantages of being potentially nimble-footed procedurally, and capable of tackling a variety of risk analyses through contract consultants. Ombudsmen's powers are usually somewhat limited by statute and convention, however, so even a well organised office may not be able to probe or mediate as much as might be desired or needed. Yet this is a promising arrangement as a non-threatening precursor to a community office, and deserves experimentation.

A *community risk communication office* is the grandest model, although not necessarily the ideal solution. So far as is known, no such office yet exists, although the concept is being examined for the disposal of radioactive and other chemically hazardous wastes. It could be a tailor-made office, but its powers would still be fettered by the lack of a general right-to-know as statutorily defined, by legal restrictions on class action in the event of initiating a compensatory claim, and by power relationships between the community and the risk-creators as discussed above.

The logic implied in Figure 17.2 regarding a free flow of information and the case for some sort of independent but authoritative risk communication service may not result in a better approach to establishing tolerable risk strategies. The little empirical analysis that exists of such schemes suggests that subtle and not so subtle power relationships define what information is made available and how it is "packaged" or "framed", received and responded to. The effectiveness of any such community safety service cannot be separated from the legal status of rights-to-know, the willingness of risk creators and official regulators to expose their dealings and judgements honestly and openly, and the recognition by community groups that such a forum is designed to be used, rather than abused in promoting sectional or self-serving interests.

Conclusions

Hazards and risks tell us much about ourselves, our attitudes to forms of governance and our relationships with others and with the natural world. The more stressed are these relationships the more hazardous will be the world and the more polarising and antagonistic will be the reaction to risks. Only when we come to recognize that caring, sharing, providing basic needs and compensatory safety nets through promoting self reliance, community networks and international endeavour to reduce hazardousness will we begin to turn the tide of the remorseless and pernicious rise of risky and hazardous phenomena in the modern world (see Brundtland 1987). A more equitable, less vulnerable and more harmonious world is not just a dream; it has become a necessity for civilised survival.

References

Brundtland, H.G. (1987) *Our Common Future*. Oxford University Press: Oxford.

Blaikie, P. and Brookfield, H. (1987) *Land Degradation and Society*. Longmans: London.

Burton, I., Kates, R.W., and White, G.F. (1978) *The Environment as Hazard*. Oxford University Press: Oxford.

Douglas, M. and Wildavsky, A. (1982) *Risk and Culture*. University of California Press: Berkeley.

Hewitt, K. (ed) (1983) *Interpretations of Calamity*. Allen and Unwin: London.

Kasperson, R.E. et al (1988) The social amplification of risk. *Risk Analysis* Vol 8, No 2, pp 177-188.

Lukes, S. (1974) *Power: A Radical View*. Macmillan: London.

O'Riordan, T. (1986) Coping with environmental hazards. In: Kates, R.W. and Burton, I. (eds) *Geography, Resources and Environment*. Vol II. University of Chicago Press: Chicago. pp 272-309.

Slovic, P. (1986) Perception of risk. *Science*. Vol 236, pp 280-290.

UN Environmental Programme (1987) *The Ozone Layer*. UNEP: Nairobi.

Waldegrave, W. (1987) Introduction to special issue on environmental research. *Newsletter of the Economic and Social Research Council*. Vol XX, p 9.

Section Summary V
Design and Implementation of
Risk Communication

Designing and implementing a risk communication system is somewhat of a fool's errand: it is prone to failures, which will be seen by all, and any success - if it can be discerned - is likely to be dismissed as either accidental or liable to have happened in any case. Those attempting to communicate risks to the public are likely to be humbled by the task and ill-rewarded by those whose attention is sought and whose well-being is being promoted.

In this context, what are the lessons that emerge from the preceding five chapters, and the other parts of this volume that deal with this topic? It is important to design effective risk communication systems for two main reasons. First, these systems tend to be expensive and, secondly, the agency concerned may implicitly be accepting some obligations and responsibility vis-a-vis the hazard or risk with regard to its audience and/or customers. Among other possibilities, poor discharge of responsibility may lead to legal liability.

Some lessons are discussed below, using the framework provided by Chapter 1 of this volume and especially by Figure 1.2. This summary also draws on a typology of design elements from an analysis by Lee (1988) of the public presentation of issues concerning risk management.

Four groups of variables can be seen to influence the effectiveness of risk communication. These are *source* variables, *message* factors, the *target* audience(s) and the *channel* used for the risk communications. Each needs the close attention of those attempting to design or improve a risk communication system.

The source

Figure 1.2 stresses that risk message delivery will be seen by the audience to be related to the role, nature and credibility of the message source: such messages are both delivered from, and received in, a context that affects their meaning and acceptability.

This leads O'Riordan to suggest that the source of risk communication should be located within the community to be effective or at least it should be seen to be "on their side". Lee (1988) suggests that the risk communication source needs to be prestigious, expert, honest and objective. O'Riordan stresses the importance of independence, above all else, despite this being inherently ethereal. Source attractiveness is also important, as is developing "common ground" between that source and its audience. Power can also be significant in overcoming opposition, even to the extent of the source "bribing" its target, either overtly or covertly, to respond in a desired way.

In the preceding chapters Gardiner in particular recognises the importance of message source: the credibility of Thames Water as a whole is crucial to the success of his flood risk communication exercise. The lack of neutrality of his flood risk video - too "promotional" rather than "consultative" - reduced its impact. Tyrrell sees the neutrality and non-moralising aspect of the AIDS message as important to its success: the deliberate policy was to be factual, non alarmist, and to de-moralise the issue. Without such a stance there was a danger of alienating important supporting message sources - such as the established churches - without whose tacit support the government would have been vulnerable to widespread opposition to its frank approach.

Saarinen provides a "controlled experiment": one source, two channels. The United States Geological Survey's approach to risk communication in Kodiak, Alaska, showed that the lack of credibility of the USGS scientists - with deficient skills in risk communication - created the observed alienation between the agency and the inhabitants. The acknowledged objectivity and neutrality of the scientists concerned was an important, but not a sufficient condition for risk communication success. In contrast, when the USGS used - at Mount St Helens - scientists from another agency, who were familiar with a risk communication role, then success was more assured. This "paired" comparison developed by Saarinen - of the USGS in different roles and with different partners - is a classic two-way comparison of success at Mount St Helens following careful preparedness exercises, and risk communication geared to that design, whereas the Kodiak failure is attributable to lack of design and thoughtless risk communication.

Source agencies need to collaborate closely with other "actors" within the communication chain, hence the feedback loops stressed in Figure 1.2. Filderman's diagnosis emphasises the significance of researchers, producers and educators working together in the extensive checking process in developing a risk communication "product". Her analysis of the development of the Red Cross *Resource Guide* shows the same features; success came from the agencies working with the professional associations to prepare the Guide, rather than independently.

Any source agency or individual involved in risk communication cannot ignore the influence that their own characteristics will have on the receipt of their message by their target audience. That message comes with associations, intimately connected with the source's "image" credibility and history. The most careful attention to message character, timing, channel and feedback mechanisms will be of no avail if the audience is antipathetic to that message owing to hostility towards the source. The design of risk communication systems cannot ignore this and must start by tailoring the source's character and approach to its task.

The message

Few examples exist of controlled experiments of real risks being communicated with different messages to determine the effect of message characteristics on response. What is clear, however, is that more detail in the message does not necessarily help; Lee (1988) also concludes that the scientific "depth" of a risk message does not affect its influence. In this respect we saw from Brown's analysis of the Sizewell scientists that their approach was to attempt to persuade the public of the *scientific* merits of their proposal, and that this was not altogether successful.

Tyrrell's work on the AIDS campaign stresses that "fear appeals" can be counter-productive, but that attitude changes by the public will be stronger if the conclusions derived from risk analysis can be shared between message giver and message receiver. Lee (1988, p8) agrees:

> it will be more effective in changing attitudes if (the message's) conclusions are explicitly shared as distinct from being left in a form from which the receiver can "draw his own conclusions".

O'Riordan also suggests that risk communication must be based on mutual understanding of the message by the communicator and the receiver, hence the importance of mediation by "translators" of the risk message. Failure in risk communication is likely when a "take it or leave it" attitude pervades; thus a failure of the Kodiak risk communication, as described by Saarinen, was not just that the conclusions were left by the United States Geological Survey to be drawn by the public, but that they also left the public to do the necessary research.

Another key element in message design is that the communicator should build on the existing knowledge of the receiver, but not provide so much information that "overload" is the result. (See Stallon and Coppock 1987, and Perrow 1984, on the question of overload.) Filderman's approach was to do this, to provide just sufficient but not too much information, and "package" it in such a way as to be attractive and enduring. Careful attention was given to standardising terminology, commensurate with the child audience being addressed. The communication process did not assume prior knowledge; it proceeded from simple to more complex aspects of the subject to build the audience's understanding.

In contrast, O'Riordan's example of skin cancer (UN Environment Programme 1987) reminds us that risks such as those from sun tanning may well not be comprehended at all, and that at the start of a risk communication campaign there may be no knowledge base on which to build. It also reminds us of our emphasis in Figure 1.2 that risk messages have to compete with other societal pressures, encapsulated in the skin cancer case by mass-media holiday advertisements stressing the apparent healthiness of sun-soaked beaches.

Message target and channel

Our framework in Figure 1.2, and virtually all the empirical evidence in this volume, points to the need to design risk communication systems so that the message is targeted as accurately as possible to the relevant audience or audiences.

Much evidence also confirms the need to personalise the messages as much as possible, to catch attention and thereby enhance comprehension and response. Evidence from research into propaganda, mentioned in Section II, indicates that face-to-face communication is more effective than distance communication (Brown 1963), although face-to-face contact can reach a far smaller population than can the mass media.

The USGS Kodiak experience shows that casual message dissemination, via local newspapers, was damaging, and Brown's research on different media in risk communication at Sizewell shows that the more personalised media were the more efficient at gaining understanding and successful persuasion. However, to target messages in this way requires that the attitudes of the audience be understood, so that the target has to be researched to reveal the attitudes and perceptions that the communicator hopes to influence (a theme also stressed in this volume by Marks and Green). O'Riordan's prescriptions favouring community risk communication offices are based on notions of the need for two-way communication and a close understanding of community attitudes to risk and power.

Thus risk communication without adequate "market research" is likely to be poor. Comparing the video discussed by Gardiner with the material more carefully compiled by Filderman shows the difference in impact that market research can have. Again, the differences between the effectiveness of risk communication on the east and the west sides of Mount St Helens, where messages were appropriately tailored for different audiences, shows the power of message targeting.

The British AIDS risk communication programme also sought to understand the attitudes of the target audience before addressing them. However, until recently the campaign has treated the public as a homogeneous audience, rather than identifying the different constituencies and then developing appropriate messages. Overall awareness-raising was seen as the immediate goal, without perhaps sufficient attention to the mechanism by which this can or cannot influence behaviour. It appears that the programme is not being monitored sufficiently rigorously to determine precisely the effect of the risk communication on behaviour, and thus the need to retarget messages once their impacts are understood.

Moreover, there is doubt over the impact of mass-media campaigns. McGuire (1985) could find no conclusive evidence that such campaigns had led to substantial (measurable) attitudinal or behavioural change. From the discussion in Section II we would conclude that personal contact would have much greater effect.

A key conclusion is that risk communicators need to take advantage of "teachable moments": those instances when the audience is likely to be most receptive to being taught - as suggested by arousal theory (see Section II). These moments may arise owing to the occurrence of a hazard event in the vicinity or elsewhere - such that awareness is heightened and there is a recognition by the relevant audience that they too might be affected. Such instances penetrate the psychological defences examined in Section II such as "denial", and may raise the salience of the hazard dramatically. Risk communication at these times may have an impact disproportionate to the resources then committed. This points to the need to recognise that risk communication is a long term process, and to have risk communication material ready and available for these "teachable moments".

Assessment

The constituents for successful risk communication, discussed above, will provide some general insight on the better design of risk communication programmes. Greater attention to the message, the channels, the source and the target should yield better results. This should be based on serious research on the nature of the audience being addressed, and a measure of independence of the risk communicators from the risk creators.

However, it is clear elsewhere in this volume that we cannot always - or even often - definitively assess the success of risk communication initiatives in terms of altered responses. But, on the other hand, we can also see that many failures occur when insufficient attention is given to communication design because it is assumed - incorrectly - that the communication of risks can be handled adequately by those who analyse them.

Therefore, an important conclusion must be that risk communication system design needs care and specialists, not hasty amateurism. It also needs resources. However, this is generally not the attitude of agencies with risks to communicate. Many tend to rely on their own staff to design their own communication systems, with insufficient research, expertise and resources. Thereby they often create some startling failures.

References

Brown, J.A.C. (1963) *Techniques of Persuasion*. Pelican.

Lee, T.R. (1988) The public presentation of issues involving risk management. Paper 14 in: *Risk Management in Water and Environmental Services*. Institute of Water and Environmental Management: London.

McGuire, W.J. (1985) The myth of massive media effect: savagings and salvagings. *Public Communication and Behaviour*. Vol 1, pp 173-257.

Perrow, C. (1984) *Normal Accidents*. Basic Books: New York.

Stallon, P.S. and Coppock, R. (1987) About risk communication and risky communication. *Risk Analysis*. Vol 7, pp 413-414.

UN Environment Programme (1987) *The Ozone Layer*. UNEP: Nairobi.

SECTION VI
CONCLUSIONS

18 Is Success Achievable?
John Handmer and Edmund Penning-Rowsell

Introduction

This concluding section draws on the major themes of
individual contributions, section summaries and the results
of Workshop discussion, to produce a summary of the main
issues and recommendations for policy and research. We
recognise that there is substantial overlap between policy
and research, but separate the recommendations below for
convenience and to emphasise the priorities in each area.

We should restate an important limitation to the scope of
the volume. As mentioned in Chapter 1, most of our
contributors, though not all, have confined themselves to
two of the three distinct purposes served by risk
communication. The two purposes are: first, to raise
awareness of, and preparedness for, an identified threat;
and second, to provide warnings of an imminent event which
requires some protective act, physical and/or psychological,
on the part of those being warned. This is in contrast to
the bulk of the current risk communication literature which
addresses a third purpose: to initiate or facilitate
discussion between those imposing and those bearing the
risk. Usually this concerns technical risk, and is
frequently directed at persuading a reluctant public to
accept industrial, energy, military or other facilities that
they would prefer were located elsewhere, or were dispensed
with altogether.

The importance of context: the political nature of risk communication

One of the main points to emerge from the preceding chapters is the importance of context in risk communication and response. Much risk-communication research has ignored this dimension, and has focussed instead on the psychology of individual information processing and decision making. This may be seen as the "micro" level. However, all individual and group decisions on risk take place within a social, political and economic context: the "macro" level (see Figure 1.2). The context strongly influences such fundamental issues as risk acceptability, commitment of resources for public information programmes and warning systems, and attitudes to the ethics of programmes designed to persuade people to accept higher risks. Thus, failure to take account of context may undermine or invalidate research results. Results of risk perception research frequently have poor predictive power even though the research may have offered plausible explanations for particular behaviour. This is partly because the explanations are based on false cause and effect linkages.

Context has many levels, for example: the dominant political-economy and ideology of the society; culture, attitudes to gender, group cohesion, building styles; religious factors; and socio-economic status. In considering the influence of these factors it is most important to realise that even very small communities are not homogeneous. Among other factors, different economic status, social networks, levels of social participation, personality traits such as risk taking propensity, ambitions and perceptions of expected behaviour divide the smallest group, and affect risk communication.

Risk is frequently seen as a technical or scientific issue. It has, of course, a technical dimension, but it is essentially about the allocation and distribution of tangible and intangible costs and benefits, and power. Some writers see the issue of power or control as the essence of risk. The important point here is that issues of power and the distribution of costs and benefits are political, and not technical, issues. We return to these questions below.

The enormous difference to risk communication made by high level political commitment is demonstrated by the British AIDS campaign. Cabinet approval, the personal endorsement of the Prime Minister, and the absence of party politics ensured that the responsible agency had ample funding and freedom to experiment. Despite criticisms of this campaign, and doubts over its real effectiveness, it stands in contrast to risk communication efforts by technocratic organisations operating without direct political endorsement or public accountability. For example, the UK Meteorological Office prepares and issues predictions of severe weather, but at the time of writing does not concern itself with the consumers of the information. Similarly, those responsible for flood warnings in Britain - the water authorities - show little or no interest in warning dissemination and response. A catastrophic flood would almost certainly put flood warnings on to the political agenda, resulting in funds and the political will to effect change. Funding alone, however, does little to ensure successful communication as shown by the CEGB efforts to persuade people about the desirability of nuclear power, and some spectacular commercial and political advertising failures.

The political economy is important in other ways. In particular, the attitude of the machinery of government - the bureaucracy - is central to much risk communication (see Chapter 1). In Britain the bureaucracy is relatively closed. Administrative practice is to make the minimum amount of information public on most matters, to protect officials and politicians from criticism. This applies also to many areas of risk. Where information is made available on technical matters the messages are likely to reflect the professional bias of the organisation's personnel, which in turn will reflect the agency's perceived "mission". For the Meteorological Office in the UK, for example, this is most likely to be technical accuracy in weather forecasts. Some other meteorological agencies are more subject to public scrutiny and have a less single-minded technocratic orientation. Thus the Australian agency pays a great deal of attention to the end user of its "products".

The human factor

The general dominance of context does not mean that the micro level of individual decision-making is unimportant. Some authors regard individual decision making as the critical issue. And there is a presumption in most official risk communications that people can make choices, however constrained those people may be by the factors discussed above. Most risk communication programmes assume that a series of simple steps exists between providing information and changing behaviour by influencing decision making. These assumptions, that knowledge is linked to attitudes which are linked to behaviour in a predictable fashion, have been thoroughly examined elsewhere in this volume. Unfortunately for those dealing with risk communication there is little evidence for such a simple set of linkages.

Apart from the influence of contextual factors, people's ability to initiate or respond to risk communications will be limited by their attitudes and values, which in total make up their world views. To illustrate the importance of "world views" consider the approach to risk by technocrats, and contrast it with that usually adopted by lay people. As discussed in Chapter 1, specialists tend to view risk as some function of likelihood of occurrence and resulting damage: generally this is expressed as a probability. The world of risk is seen as capable of objective quantification. Non-specialists often find the preoccupation with probability irrelevant, and instead concentrate on the possible harms, and issues of fairness, equity and control. Note that "harms" is used deliberately. Non-specialists will frequently be concerned about aspects of risk completely ignored by specialists who will generally concentrate on mortality rates and other factors which are relatively easy to quantify. To the technocrats and those imposing risks such emphases are often seen as emotive and unreasonable.

The difference in views is most obvious where risk commensurability is concerned. The view will be expressed that the annual risk from a particular technology is equivalent to smoking 20 cigarettes, or driving to work, but for a range of well documented reasons people do not see the risks from driving, flying, smoking, football, nuclear power, toxic waste, AIDS, etc as comparable. Choices between such activities are not made in real life, nor are the risks from the different activities thought of as equivalent. The evidence suggests that they are not equivalent in terms of the wide ranging criteria employed by non-specialists. For these and other reasons, comparisons between them are frequently seen as contrived and irrelevant. Arguments that the public are failing to appreciate the real likelihood of harm, simply indicate ignorance of the social construction of risk.

One issue, which emerges throughout this analysis of risk communication is the role of experience. Despite considerable research effort it emerges that its role is unclear. The concept of a "disaster sub-culture" aroused much interest. When and where does it exist? How do we know it is there? Is it an advantage in dealing with hazards? How can it best be harnessed, and can the concept be transferred operationally to other places?

The role of the media

In industrialised countries the broadcast and print media are major sources of information for most people. The media play a substantial role in the "social construction of reality" and in attitude formation (Berger and Luckmann 1975). However, its real influence may be more in terms of agenda setting than attitude change. Nevertheless, media cooperation is vital for the maintenance of organisational credibility and for effective warning dissemination.

It was also noted that technocratic organisations, which have been relatively sheltered from public scrutiny, do not find the mass media easy to deal with and prefer to have nothing to do with it. This is the case even where the broadcast media may be the best way of disseminating warning messages. Table 18.1 sets out suggestions for improving the liaison between emergency planning and management organisations and the mass media; it is for the risk communication agency to initiate improvement, not the media.

Table 18.1

Suggestions for improving liaison between the
media and emergency service organisations
involved in warnings and response.

Clearly specify official sources for emergency related
  information. Apart from making information easier to
  obtain, this should reduce the problem of conflicting
  official reports. These sources could take the form of a
  widely publicised telephone number, or establishment of a
  media centre or briefing room at the relevant
  organisation.
Provide phone line(s) exclusively for media usage direct to
  the designated information source. Media representatives
  have reported having great difficulty obtaining and
  confirming information during emergencies.
Provide and regularly update lists of key contacts and phone
  numbers.
Organise media pooling. For example TV stations might agree
  to share film of the operations room or of rescue scenes.
News of the emergency should be monitored by the official
  information centre, which should act quickly to correct
  any erroneous information.
*Develop contracts between the forecasting and emergency
  management groups and individual radio and TV stations*
  concerning the broadcasting of warnings. These could be
  negotiated to satisfy the requirements of individual
  stations and would be legally binding. This cooperative
  arrangement is superior to the use of legislative
  coercion.
Invite media representatives to participate in planning
  meetings, for example to identify special capabilities and
  resources and how they might assist with warnings.
Organise field days where media and emergency management
  personnel get to know each other informally; for example
  in a simulation exercise media and emergency service staff
  could swap roles.
Hold a debrief after each major emergency which includes
  media representatives. A special effort should be made to
  include media organisations felt to have been unhelpful or
  obstructive during the emergency.
Investigate ways of overcoming the difficulties posed by
  media networking commitments. These are likely to
  increase.
Plans and procedures should be rehearsed regularly to
  identify and resolve problems. It is important that all
  the organisations involved in the warning system take
  part.

The emerging problem of legal liability

Expanding concepts of liability for professional activities, including the provision of information, are of growing concern to those providing these services (Bakos and Hake 1987, Partlett 1985). In the past, government bodies were protected from liability by the doctrine of "sovereign immunity". However, this protection has gradually eroded as the courts and legislatures extend to government the liability concepts traditionally applied to individuals. This is occurring in an environment where the legal system appears increasingly ready to find that liability exists. Thus, government, commercial and non-profit organisations, their agencies and employees, and private individuals are facing a growing threat of liability for incorrect or inadequate risk related information.

In this legal environment the focus of the law on individual cases, rather than the level of risk found acceptable by society, means that there is a tendency for courts to demand impossibly high standards of safety. These are impossible because we simply do not have the resources to guarantee complete safety, and even if the resources existed we lack the knowledge to eliminate risk completely. In some United States product liability cases courts have awarded huge damages against manufacturers, in effect overturning the intent of legislatures by insisting on much higher safety standards (Partlett 1987). Examples include automobile safety and vaccination programmes, where damage awards have gone beyond compensation for injuries and have included a "punitive" element. Gillette (1987) argues that victims are compensated for risks "that, while real, were offset by the social benefits of the underlying activity".

Risk communication may have to satisfy a number of legal requirements. It may be required by legislation. Typical examples are disclosure of the contents of packaged food, of the side effects of medicines, and the potential risks in using household and agricultural chemicals. In addition, failure to clearly indicate hazards may expose manufacturers and those providing services to substantial common law liability (Clement 1987, Conrads 1987). Modern legal trends may render some well established boundaries to common law obsolete. For example, the burden of potential liability is increasing greatly with the expanded application of the "strict liability" concept. Under this approach no evidence of negligence is required to find liability. Courts have been reluctant to apply such concepts to information but there is pressure for change (Walter and Marsteller 1987).

The possibility that risk communication could be subject to the rules of strict liability has enormous implications. Authorities providing the risk information would probably demand and obtain statutory protection from liability - a typical response which costs little and solves the liability problem, but may create other difficulties by removing incentives to perform risk communication tasks carefully.

Concern over liability for risk communication is not new and has deterred some authorities from providing information on risks. The concern may extend to the issuing of warnings, where it is sometimes felt that it is better to have no warning system at all than to have one and risk being sued if the system fails. This attitude is related to legal concepts of dependence and reliance by one party on the services of another (Partlett 1987, Handmer and Partlett 1988). However, some US legal scholars argue that doing nothing does not avoid liability (Kusler 1986).

Assessing success: methodological and ethical problems

The methodological problems raised elsewhere in this volume suggest that it is almost futile to attempt risk-communication programme assessment.

The first step is to define "success", the definition of which in turn depends on programme objectives. The objectives will often, implicitly at least, raise ethical issues. For many risk communication programmes, especially those concerned with flooding, the stated objectives are to improve safety and to reduce tangible and other intangible losses. Alternatively, the aim may be to convince people that the risk they are concerned about is not a problem. To achieve this the programme would generally need to change people's behaviour and attitudes.

Programme objectives may include the need to; satisfy legal requirements; conform to some technical specifications; and to have a cost-effective programme. Success may be seen in other ways as well. Those responsible for programmes may have objectives which are not stated in public; for example, the main objective may be to enhance the profile of the agency conducting the programme, or for political gain by a government wanting to be seen to be dealing with a problem. This is not an entirely cynical point: many politicians and bureaucrats may believe that they have a moral duty to provide information on hazards, even if the evidence is overwhelming that the action will be ineffective. Such objectives frequently result from pressure applied by groups including the environmental lobby or consumer protection organisations.

At another level professional or personal "world views" may provide objectives, which may be held largely subconsciously: for example, an advertising company is unlikely to find that an advertising programme has been unsuccessful. Objectives such as organisational survival are likely to be much more important when the organisation is under threat. With the current close scrutiny in many countries of the role of government vis-a-vis the private sector, we can expect to see an increasing amount of this survival behaviour.

The methodological problems of assessment, discussed in detail in Section III, are formidable, such that a proper evaluation controlling for general social trends and other influences may not be possible. It may be that the risk communication programme changed the behaviour of a group of people not part of the evaluation, or that an apparently successful warning response had nothing to do with the official warning, but was a result of environmental indicators and a local telephone network.

Two other confounding factors are usually overlooked. One concerns the processing of information below conscious awareness. This is common, for example, with learning associated with role modelling and language, but may occur with most information sources. Information processed in this way may still exert considerable influence on attitudes and behaviour (Bargh 1984, Lewicki 1986). The other factor relates to the way risk communication messages may actually *increase* risk taking behaviour among some members of their target audiences. Goldhaber and deTurck (1988) suggest that a sign warning of the hazards of diving into shallow water "seemed to encourage risk-taking among [high school] males", although it "produced the desired outcome among females". Both factors raise methodological difficulties, and the second factor ethical problems.

Nevertheless, efforts to develop improved criteria and to avoid the trap of using only what is easy to measure should continue. Evaluations should specify the boundaries of the analysis, both in terms of the time period involved and the extent of societal and other influences included.

Is success in risk communication achievable?

Given the assessment difficulties raised throughout the volume a definitive answer to this question is not possible. Nevertheless, there is intense debate on the question, at least as far as success to date is concerned. The different answers reflect the variety of criteria, definitions and objectives employed. They may also reflect the expectations and professional ideology of those involved in assessment of risk communication. Definite success is frequently claimed in the political and commercial advertising worlds. However, in these fields a change in a very small proportion of the target audience, of only a few per cent, may mean an enormous increase in sales or a seat won or lost in an election. Such small changes are of little practical significance to risk communicators.

The first step in responding to this question is to define "success" in terms of programme objectives, as discussed in the previous section.

Certainly, in terms of changing behaviour many public education programmes appear to have been complete failures (IDT 1980). Even if the criterion is simply to improve knowledge there are few definite successes. It is stressed that the ability to impart knowledge is not by itself an ability to change behaviour: linkages between knowledge, awareness and behaviour are at present poorly understood.

Currently successes are few, but most workshop participants felt that the future would bring improvements. However, improvements may be more apparent than real, in that they may result from changes in assessment criteria, a recognition of the importance of political objectives and other contextual factors.

Are we moving towards success?

It appears that we may be getting better at communicating the message, but probably not at persuading people to take action or change their behaviour. The optimistic view is that risk communication is slowly becoming more effective. We also need to ask to what extent apparent improvements are a result of issues canvassed above: such as changing professional ideology and expectations, and changes in assessment methodologies.

Communication is improving partly because of technological advances, but more due to improved understanding of the processes involved. There is greater recognition that even relatively small communities are far from homogeneous, and that precise identification of target groups is essential if the message is to arrive, be noticed, processed, understood and acted on. The concept of the "teachable moment", predicted by arousal theory, suggests that programmes will be much more effective if they are concentrated at particular times. Progress is being made, albeit slowly, in understanding the psychology and the sociology of information processing, attitude formation and behaviour. Specifically in terms of risk communication, appreciation of the importance of issues of equity, fairness and controlability are helping to ensure that the right questions are addressed.

One could argue that part of the problem is the preoccupation with use of mass media, when the literature on education, propaganda, etc, indicate that personal contact and role modelling provide more powerful avenues for effecting attitude and behavioural change (Brown 1963, Goldhaber and deTurck 1988).

The poor predictability of much risk research in terms of people's attitudes, but especially in terms of likely behaviour, may be due to over-concentration on individual psychology, the "micro" level, and a lack of appreciation of the importance of context, the "macro" level. This is particularly apparent when seeking to explain response to risk communication. An understanding of the context is a prerequisite to improving persuasion, which implies changes in attitude and ultimately in behaviour. Improvements here will come from further study of the sociology, political economy, philosophical basis, and ethical and legal dimensions of risk identification, acceptability, communication and response. Of course, major gaps remain in our understanding of individual psychology. Two areas of particular interest for risk communication are the role of "subconscious" information processing, and the potential for risk communication to backfire and increase risk taking.

Is risk communication worth it?

In view of all this pessimism we need to ask whether it is worth continuing with risk communication programmes.

As stated in the volume's introductory section, and by other contributors, governments have a moral responsibility to protect the population and to ensure that people are able to make informed choices where this is necessary. Part of this responsibility concerns the need to communicate information on hazards to the non-specialists at risk and others. The real ethical difficulties come in deciding the level of government intervention, for example in regulating risk, in requiring disclosure of the side-effects and potential for disaster from industrial and transportation activities, medical treatments and so on, and in deciding just how large the resource commitment should be; this takes us straight into the political arena.

The importance of the ethical dimension should not be underestimated. Cynicism aside, the concepts of social justice and equity are very important in western industrialised societies. Decisions about communicating information on risks, and decisions based on such communications, play a major part in shaping the sort of society we live in. The burden of risk in society is far from evenly distributed. Risk communication can reduce or exacerbate such inequities; for example, the information may be incomprehensible to segments of the population or may be conveyed by media which do not reach many of those at risk.

The first response to the question therefore, is ethical, and is not concerned with the practicalities or economics of "doing something". The practical aspects have been discussed above - taking into account that it is difficult not to be ambivalent about the effectiveness of risk communication programmes.

Economics are important too; programmes should be cost-effective. Often the issue is not so much the cost of doing something, but the cost of failing to take action. AIDS, for instance, is expected to cost the UK billions over the next decade unless the course of the pandemic is altered by an effective risk communication programme.

But people without official warnings in many cases may do just as well as those with warnings, and therefore government involvement may be a waste of resources. However - putting aside ethical issues - there are many instances across a wide range of hazards where warnings appear to have been reasonably effective, although we do not know precisely

why this is the case. Furthermore, in some cases effective
response depended on knowledge of appropriate action,
emphasising the important linkage between long-term
preparedness and warnings requiring immediate response.
Examples include the natural hazards of tornadoes and hail
storms. Success here is generally restricted to areas where
the hazard is of high salience or to rural areas.
Technological hazards where warnings have been effective
include dam bursts and contaminated food, and biological
hazards such as AIDS. Widely publicised spectacular events
which become part of the institutional and public memory may
have helped response in these cases. Unfortunately, even in
these examples we are not sure that the official warnings
had much impact. Other factors may have been more
important. Perhaps the development of a disaster
subculture, the media publicity surrounding the events, or
the involvement of well known politicians or other
personalities may have ensured appropriate response.

Whatever the cause and effect linkages, there is no
question that persuading people to change their behaviour is
an enormously difficult task. In devising a risk
communication programme we need to consider whether people
want the information, and whether they would be likely or
indeed able to act on it. The context will generally act to
limit choice of action. Furthermore, once informed about
the dangers of one activity or product, is the target
audience likely to take up another equally dangerous
activity or product, as the risk compensation or homeostatis
theory suggests? Even worse, is the message likely to
encourage the very risk taking it is designed to prevent?
These difficulties should not be seen as excuses for
avoiding the moral responsibility to provide information on
risks. Rather, those charged with the responsibility need
to continue to search for ways of achieving their
objectives.

Recommendations

Recommendations are listed in Table 18.2. The main points
are discussed below under headings of research and policy,
categories that are indicative rather than exclusive.

Research

In considering recommendations for research we are well
aware that a major problem is the *implementation of the
results of existing work*. Many major and well documented
research results continue to be ignored. Decision-makers,
their advisers, and researchers are guilty of this. The
reasons why these results are ignored go well beyond
individual obstruction and ignorance, and relate to the
structure of the organisations which fund, conduct and
implement the research. Research devoted to finding ways of
overcoming these impediments is urgently needed.

321

Results that appear to be largely ignored include those as basic and inconvenient as the limited evidence for successful programmes, the weak linkage between knowledge, attitudes and behaviour, the importance of poverty in preventing adaptive behaviour, and the rather low salience of most hazards to most people most of the time. To take this last point, not surprisingly people are overwhelmingly pre-occupied with the social and economic hazards of daily life. Yet, they may be expected to study and learn the contents of uninspiring pamphlets, or to give considered responses to questions, on apparently obscure or, to them, irrelevant hazards, such as floods, earthquakes or CFCs.

One partial counter to these points concerns the degree to which research results may be transferred between countries. Much of the published research is from the United States, yet major differences exist between the U.S. and Western Europe, for example, in their approaches to risk (Wassersug 1989), and to the mass media.

In view of the low salience of many hazards, and of the need to have the information available at the time of impact, effort should be devoted to finding *low-cost alternatives* to conventional risk awareness campaigns. In many cases these alternatives would need to be fully functional in the absence of normal communications and infrastructure.

A weakness in many risk communication programmes, and in much associated research, is the lack of attention to *methodology*. This problem may involve the use of certain research methods, as when people are expected to give, at a moments notice, considered responses to questions concerning hazards they rarely think of. Just as it is important to avoid measuring only what is convenient, so it is also important to be led by the research issue rather than the research instrument. Another frequent weakness is the failure to specify clearly the definition and boundaries of the analysis; so that for example, no mention or assessment is made of contextual factors which may be the most important explanatory variable, or that programme assessment might ignore possible longer term effects. Recommendations here apply particularly to programme evaluations. Much more evaluation work is needed, but few assessments demonstrate cause and effect. Research should be directed to improving the quality of this work, otherwise progress in developing effective risk communication programmes will be haphazard.

Finally, the emerging issue of *legal liability* must not be ignored, it will not go away. Legal research can identify the most likely problems before they are experienced and can suggest ways of dealing with them, given economic, political and other constraints.

Policy

On ethical and economic grounds it is entirely appropriate, and necessary, for governments to be actively involved in risk communication. However, given this, programmes may aim to satisfy many different objectives. Some of these objectives such as persuading sections of the population to bear particular risks, themselves raise difficult ethical questions. This greatly complicates programme design and evaluation.

Specification of objectives and clear definitions of the terminology used are prerequisites for success, and should help ensure that the messages are properly targeted. Risk communications frequently assume that the target audience is homogeneous. As we have seen this is not the case and is an assumption which has contributed to many failures.

There is a need for training and rehearsal at all levels, especially for very rare events. Training is complicated by the wide variety of potential disasters and different appropriate responses. The solution may be to train for the frequent events on the grounds that these are more likely to be seen as relevant and the risk communication may therefore be effective, and to prepare a few key disaster managers for the unexpected and the possible but low probability events. Many of the necessary measures can be implemented for virtually no cost.

This highlights the desirability of designing as a whole the risk communication programme for a particular hazard. The approach would help to ensure that the long term preparedness was closely linked to the system providing warnings of imminent events. Many points concerning design have been raised in this volume. One important general observation is that "passive" coping measures tend to be ignored, yet it appears that to many people these are more important than "active" measures. Thus attention should be given to the affective and emotional aspects of messages.

Another important observation concerns language. People express uncertainty in many different ways. Probabilistic statements may be favoured among specialists, but may be misleading or confusing to non-specialists, especially where rare events are concerned. A related problem is the use of probabilities as the sole means of comparing different risks. Often such comparisons will be seen as spurious, because people compare risks using other criteria as discussed above. In fact, in many instances occurrence probability is simply not seen as relevant compared to issues such as who imposes, who profits and who bears the risk.

We need to remember that we seek people's attention. Our role is not simply to provide data or information to be lost among the nearly infinite number of competing messages, rather it is to *communicate* material on risks. Our responsibility extends beyond technical accuracy and professional ethics to those bearing the risk. This means that risk communication may be more than a message - to be really effective it may require complementary policies to alter the distribution of risk in society.

Table 18.2

Recommendations

Research

Major issues
Well documented research results should not be ignored.
This applies to policy makers as well as to researchers.
These results include:
- the weak linkage between knowledge, attitudes and
  behaviour;
- the importance of context, political, economic, social,
  cultural etc;
- the lack of evidence for successful campaigns;
- the lack of homogeneity in a community, even a very small
  one, and the consequent need to target sub-groups very
  carefully;
- the low salience of many hazards for most people most of
  the time;
- certain misconceptions about public behaviour such as the
  expectation of widespread panic and looting.

Much more evaluative research is needed, with greater
attention to methodology, including:
- development of performance indicators;
- not simply concentrating on standard or easy criteria and
  techniques;
- specification of the boundaries of the analysis, in terms
  of time frame and contextual factors considered;
- clear definitions and objectives;
- adequate controls;
- awareness of limitations in the data;
- possible use of an anthropological approach.

Effort should be devoted to finding low-cost alternatives to
the conventional risk preparedness campaign.

Proactive research into the legal liability
aspects of risk communication.

Research specifically directed at developing the third
definition of risk listed in Chapter 1, which starts from a
social, rather than a technical, perspective.

Other issues requiring research effort
- the various contextual factors of risk communication
- the role and limitations of experience, including
  "disaster sub-cultures";
- the importance of human error compared to other factors,
  such as those of social organisations;
- "passive" as opposed to "active" coping measures;
- how to utilise the powerful persuaders of role modelling
  and face-to-face contact.

Policy

Major issues

It is appropriate for governments to be actively involved in risk communication. But there are many reasons for involvement and many objectives may be served.

Objectives should be specified clearly.

Risk should not be defined strictly in technical terms. This would ignore critical dimensions of risk and invite policy failure. Issues concerning the distribution of risk in society are often seen as more important by non-specialists.

Terminology should be defined and care taken to express uncertainty in language familiar to the target audience.

Programmes should assume a diverse target audience and plan accordingly.

Risk communication programmes should be designed as a whole. Long term awareness efforts need to be linked to the warning system.

Training and rehearsal are needed at all levels. For rare events it may be better to concentrate on key emergency management staff rather than the public.

Other issues

Risk communication messages should not ignore passive coping strategies, and should deal with affective and emotional aspects.

Message context is critical. In the absence of appropriate context, messages will be incomprehensible or seem irrelevant.

In many cases material should be prepared in advance so that it is ready for immediate distribution when the time is appropriate, i.e. at the "teachable moment".

Risk communication programmes require strict quality control.

References

Bakos, J.D. Jr. and Hake, R.J. (1987) Professional liability exposure of casual consultants. *Journal of Professional Issues in Engineering.* Vol 113, No 4, pp 321-339.

Bargh, J.A. (1984) Automatic and conscious processing of social information. In Wyer, R.S. and Srull, T.K. (eds) *Handbook of Social Cognition.* (Vol 3). Erlbaum: Hillsdale.

Berger, P.L. and Luckmann, T. (1975) *The Social Construction of Reality.* Penguin: Hamondsworth.

Brown, J.A.C. (1963) *Techniques of Persuasion.* Pelican.

Clement, D.E. (1987) Human factors, instructions and warnings, and products liability. *IEEE Transactions on Professional Communication.* Vol PC30, No 3, pp 149-156.

Conrads, J.A. (1987) "Illustruction": increasing safety and reducing liability exposure. *IEEE Transaction on Professional Communication.* Vol PC30, No 3, pp 133-135.

Gillette, C.P. (1987) Institutional biases in the legal system's risk assessments. *Conference on Hazards and Society.* University of Colorado: Boulder.

Goldhaber, G.M. and deTurck, M.A. (1988) Effectiveness of warning signs: gender and familiarity effects. *Journal of Product Liability.* Vol 11, pp 271-284.

Handmer, J.W. and Partlett, D.F. (1988) *Flood Warnings and Legal Liability: the Georges River Floods, August 1986.* (Working Paper 1988/8) Centre for Resource and Environmental Studies, Australian National University: Canberra.

IDT (Illinois Department of Transportation) (1980) *Notifying Floodplain Residents: an Assessment of the Literature.* Division of Water Resources: Chicago.

Kusler, J. (1986) Liability and flood warnings. Presented at *What have we learned since the Big Thompson flood?* University of Colorado: Boulder.

Lewicki, P. (1986) *Nonconscious Social Information Processing.* Academic Press: New York.

Partlett, D.F. (1985) *Professional Negligence.* The Law Book Co.; Sydney.

Partlett, D.F. (1987) *Forecasts, Warnings and Legal Liability: High Pressure and Gale Warnings for Weather Forecasting.* (Working Paper 1987/7). Centre for Resource and Environmental Studies, Australian National University: Canberra.

Walter, C. and Marsteller, T.F. (1987) Liability for the dissemination of defective information. *IEEE Transactions on Professional Communication.* Vol PC30, No 3, pp 164-167.

Wassersug, S.R. (1989) The role of risk assessment in developing environmental policy. *International Environment Reporter.* (January), pp 33-43.

Index

Goldhaber, G.M. and deTurck, M.A., 133, 318, 319, 326
Gough, N., 70, 74
Graber, D.A., 89, 93
Gramsci, A., 66, 67
Greater London Council, 141, 155
Green, C.H. *31-52*, 50, 51, 69, 70
Green, C.H. and Brown, R.A., 34, 42, 51
Green, C.H. *et al.*, 35, 40, 42, 51, 140, 155
Gruntfest, E., 32, 51, *195-205*, 241, 244
Gurpinar, A., 119, 124
Habermas, J. 33, 51
Haight, F.A., 175, 192
Handmer, J.W., *3-15*, 51, 66, 67, 132, 133, 138, 139, 155, *311-26*
Handmer, J.W. and Ord, K.D., 40, 51, 127, 134, 143, 155
Handmer, J.W. and Partlett, D.F., 317, 326
Harding, D.M., and Parker, D.J., 35, 40, 51, 146, 155
Harvey, A.C. and Durbin, J., 192
Hauer, E., 175, 192
Hauer, E. and Persaud, B., 181, 192
hazard communication/warnings, (also see individual hazards)
    passim, see especially 8-11, 127-34, 157-8, 208, 234-5;
    evaluation of message, 211, 275, 295; public reactions,
    19-29, 140-1, 165-71, 209, 212-5, 240-2, 279-80, 306-7,
    313-4; unsatisfactory response, 23-4, 113-4, 129-30,
    138-9, 141-2, 145-51, 233-45, 284-6, 288-9, 313-4;
    social/political considerations, 12-14, 79-94, 94, 95,
    96, 105-6, 127-31, 276, 286-90, 312-4, 322-6; gender
    differences in reaction to warnings, 116-7, 124, 133-4,
    170; "learned helplessness", 55-6, 72, 133; role
    modelling, 55, 72-4
    criteria for success, 211, 311-26; for example
            (i)   credibility of the sender, in both knowledge
                  and good faith, 45-6, 72-4, 213-4, 273-4,
                  303-8
            (ii) message fully comprehensible by the
                  recipients, if possible in harmony with their
                  own context and experience, *see for example*
                  Children's Television Workshops, 219-31, and
                  see also Mount St Helens warnings, 286-90
            (iii) recipients precluded from action by their
                  condition of life (eg poverty, political
                  powerlessness or mistrust, fear of loss,
                  fatalism), *see for example* the victims of the
                  Andhra Pradesh cyclone 95-109
hazard/risk experience, influence of, 40, 53-4, 100-8, 128,
            138, 143, 144, 170-71, 212-5, 234, 241-2; memory
            and forgetting, 59-60; "learned helplessness", 55,
            72, 133; traditional coping methods, 105, 113
hazards, geo-physical, 293-4; *see*
            cyclones/tornadoes/hurricanes; earthquakes;
            floods; landslides; volcanic eruptions
hazards, life-style, 294, *see* AIDS; alcohol/drugs; road
            traffic accidents; smoking; sports, dangerous
hazards, technological, 293-301, *see* aircraft disasters;
            chemical spillages; explosions; nuclear power;
            toxic waste disposal

Persaud, B., 188, 192
Platt, R., 200, 203
Polanyi, M., 42, 52
police (UK) 177, 192
politics and risk, 9-13, 66, 79-94, 106-8, 111, 293-301,
    312, 319-20, 324; the "political amplification of
    risk", 80-3; politics and poverty, see status, socio-
    economic
probability, mathematical, 7, 143, 282, 294, 323
Proctor, S. et al., 188, 192
psychology of risk communication (see Hazard communication),
    19-29, 69-75
Quarentelli, E.L., 85, 94
Quinnell, A.L., 71, 73, 75
Raghavulu, C.V. and Cohen, S., 98, 102, 109
Rangachari, R., 137, 156
Rayner, S., 42, 47, 52
reconstruction, post-disaster, in India, 106; in Turkey,
    116, 118, 121-4
Red Cross (USA), 219, 222, 226-8, 305
research suggestions, 201, 209-10, 324; methods (Sizewell),
    164
risk reduction measures, 103, 121-4, 138, 181-92, 234, 261-
    77; benefit/cost appraisal, 271; opposing factors, 121,
    132-3, 264, 272-3
Rivers, J.P.W., 132, 134
road traffic accidents (UK), 54, 84, 173-93, 281;
    statistics, 173, 177-80, 186, 191; safety measures,
    175, 209; danger/safety relationship, 183-6, 209;
    injuries/fatalities, 176-83; seat belts, 180, 183, 281;
    US/UK comparisons, 185; IIHS (Insurance Institute for
    Highway Safety, USA), 188, 192; RAGB, Urban Road
    Appraisal, see Transport, Department of., 176, 178,
    182, 183, 189, 193; RoSPA, 189, 193; Transport and Road
    Research Laboratory, safety suggestions, 176, 192
Rogers, C.R., 57-9, 61, 67, 70, 75
Romiskowski, A.J., 57, 67
Rossi Report, 159, 171
Royal Society, the, 6, 14, 160, 172
Royal Society for the Prevention of Accidents (RoSPA), 189,
    193
Rummelhart, D., 73, 75
Ryder, N., 162, 172
Saarinen, T., 80, 94, 279-91
Saarinen, T. and McPherson, H.J., 284, 291
Saarinen, T. and Sell, J., 284, 291
Saarinen, T. et al., 282, 291
Sandman, P., 84, 94, 240, 244
Sandman, P. et al., 7, 9, 14
Scanlon, J., 233-45
Scanlon, J. and Jefferson, J., 238, 244
Scanlon, J. and Padgham, M., 241, 244
Scanlon, J. and Prawzick, A., 238-9, 244
Scanlon, J. and Taylor, B., 237, 244
Scanlon, J. et al., 237, 244-5
Schlesinger, P., 81, 94
Sears, R.R. et al., 55, 67

United States of America, hazard warnings, 195-205,
        279-91; systems, 202, 204-5; costs, 198, 200
        shortcomings in response, 198-9, 233-9, 285-9
        American Association for the Advancement of Science,
        93;
        American Red Cross, 219, 220, 222, 226-8, 230
                A Resource Guide (Red Cross), 227, 305
        Bureau of Reclamation, 196, 199, 202-3
        Children's Television Workshop, 219-31
        Community Education Services, 222
        Disaster Relief Act (1974), 284
        Environment Protection Agency, 6, 88
        Federal Emergency Management Agency, 201, 222
        Forest Service, 287-91
        Geological Survey, 284-91, 306
        National Weather Service, 5, 201, 222
        Natural Hazards Workshop, 197, 222
        Organisation of American States, 219, 228-9, 231
        Technology Assessment, Office of, 300
        US Army Corps of Engineers, 196, 198, 201, 203
        Water Data, Advisory Committee on, 196, 201, 203
Valussi, G., 64, 68
volcanic eruption (Mount St Helens), 279-91
        warnings, 280, 284, 286-90, 307
Waldegrave, W., 295, 301
Walter, C. and Marsteller, T.F., 316, 326
Wassersug, S.R., 12, 15, 129, 134, 322, 326
Watson, J.B., 46, 52
water authorities (UK), 138, 312-3, *and see* Severn-Trent,
            Thames, Wessex
Water Data, (USA Advisory Committee on), 196, 203
weather forecasting (UK), 5, 23-4, 312
Wessex Water Authority, 138-9
Weinstein, N., 281, 291
Westgate, K., 114, 125
Wettenhall, R., 236, 245
Wilkins, L., 73, 79-94
Wilkins, L. and Patterson, P., 79-94
Williams, H.B., 240, 241, 245
Wilson, C., 53-68, 69
Winchester, P., 95-109
Woodson, T., 60, 68
Wyer, R.S., 42, 52
York, floods in, 138